The International Gold Standard

Studies in International Political Economy will present new work, from a multinational stable of authors, on major issues, theoretical and practical, in the international political economy.

General Editor

Susan Strange, Professor of International Relations, London School of Economics and Political Science, England

Consulting Editors

Ladd Hollist, Visiting Associate Professor, Brigham Young University, USA

Karl Kaiser, Director, Research Institute of the German Society for Foreign Affairs, Bonn, and Professor of Political Science, University of Cologne, West Germany

William Leohr, Graduate School of International Studies, University of Denver, USA

Joseph Nye, Professor of Government, Harvard University, USA

Already Published

The Political Economy of New and Old Industrial Countries
The East European Economies in the 1970s
Defence, Technology and International Integration
Japan and Western Europe
Tax Havens and Offshore Finance

Forthcoming Titles

International Political Economy—A Text
Dependency Transformed
International Regimes for the Control of Nuclear Technology

The International Gold Standard

Money and Empire

Marcello de Cecco

 Frances Pinter (Publishers) London

Second edition first published in Great Britain in 1984
by Frances Pinter (Publishers)
5 Dryden Street, London WC2E 9NW

ISBN 0 86187 333 5

Printed by SRP, Exeter

CONTENTS

*Non solum aurum barbaris
minime praebeatur, sed etiam, si
apud eos inventum fuerit, subtili
auferatur ingenio*

COD. IUST. 2, 63

PREFACE

The first edition of this book appeared, in Italian, a few months before the fateful August 15, 1971. The first English edition was published in the equally fateful 1974. As this new English edition goes to press, I wonder what 1984 may have in store...

This book's main purpose is to show how the pre-1914 international gold standard worked, but also to emphasise the elements of the crisis that was brewing within the system during the 25 years before the outbreak of the Great War, and which brought it, via a series of increasingly damaging collapses, to its final destruction, in August 1914.

The International Gold Standard was an attempt to remedy the instability of prices which characterised the world economy between 1870 and 1890. Countries switched from silver to gold when the price of silver became too unstable to serve as a standard. The instability of silver, and the short-run unpredictability of its gyrations, convinced both creditors and debtors to adopt a more stable standard.

But the stability of the Gold Standard was eminently due to Britain's preparedness to serve as the centre of the system. The International Gold Standard, therefore, was a product of the British Empire, as Britain's adherence to it through thick and thin, until July 1914, was made possible by the pattern of imperial relations, both economic and political, which allowed Britain to look with equanimity at her loss of competitiveness on the world's free markets for industrial goods, as she kept control over the world's raw material markets and the Empire generated enough financial flows to serve as raw material for the City's intermediation capacity; and as long as the United States, the emerging giant of the world economy, remained without a financial head, as it did until 1913.

The book's message is thus that the pre-1914 international money system was stable while it remained a Sterling Standard, and that it began to oscillate more and more dangerously, till its final collapse in July 1914, as Britain declined and other large industrial countries rose to greater eminence, and adopted the Gold Standard as a form of monetary nationalism, in order to gradually deprive Britain of her last power, that of control over international financial flows. Thus an important part of the message this book wants to convey is that the countries which adopted the Gold Standard did so in order to *increase,* rather than *decrease,* centralised control over monetary affairs. Adopting the Gold Standard everywhere meant creating a Central Gold Reserve and a Monetary Agency to manage it. This was in most cases a giant step towards *dirigisme,* and it is highly ironical that the Gold Standard, after its demise, has been the centre-piece of the laisser-faire school of economists.

But then a whole book ought to be written to analyse the *Myth* of the Gold Standard. After the apocalypse of the Great World War, an international monetary system which had been extensively studied by level-headed scholars became the banner of all those who, like Talleyrand after the French Revolution, tried to bring the world back to what it ought to have been. Thus the Gold Standard became a synonym of order, of equity, of the "douceur de vivre" — the splendid frame which surrounded the benevolent images of Victoria and Franz Joseph.

This powerful myth has been recently revamped, after the transformation of the post-1945 Dollar Standard into something which should remind us of the decade immediately preceding 1914.

As the relative status of the U.S. economy declined and that of its main western allies grew, and it became more and more difficult for the United States to keep her currency stable; as the world economy, like in the pre-1914 decade, became more and more integrated and generated greater and greater international financial flows, national authorities tried with increasing despair to keep control over economic policy, which was increasingly being dictated by the fluctuations of international capital.

In these years of growing uncertainty the Gold Standard began to appear as the philosopher's stone, which would solve all problems. This mood was particularly strong in the United States, a natural place since it had housed the XIX century battles of the "Silver Party" and the 1930s quackery of the Warren & Pearson Doctrine.

A President was elected on a platform whose core was a pledge to bring the country back to gold. A campaign was launched, after he had been elected, to force him to stick to his promises. Congress created a 17 member Gold Commission to study the role of gold in the domestic and international monetary system. And in the course of the campaign, the advocates of gold have resurrected all the mythical features of the International Gold Standard. It is the humble purpose of this new Edition to make again available to the reader a more historically balanced view of a system which, like all human creations, was limited in life and full of warts.

I think that, as in the previous Editions, I ought to express again my gratitude to Robert A. Mundell who, in 1968, included my research project on the Gold Standard in his National Science Foundation Project on Crises and gave me the chance of writing this book. And I should also thank Alan Milward and Roy Hay for their advice, and Sir Alec Cairncross, Sir John Hicks and Franco Romani who read the book at various stages of its completion and made comments, but should in no way be held responsible for my mistakes. Some of which, cleverly spotted by the kind reviewers of the first English edition, I have managed to correct in this one. For those which remain, I invoke the reader's generosity.

Finally, I must again thank my wife who copied all the Public Record Office documents on which the last chapter is based.

ONE

The International Gold Standard
in Economic Literature

It is generally said that a country is on a gold standard when gold is used as the ultimate *numeraire* of that country's monetary system, and/or when other means of payments in use there, Government IOUs or banks' notes, are readily redeemable in gold at their bearers' request.

An international gold standard is said to exist when gold is the effective *numeraire* in most countries, and/or when the other means of payment used as monetary *numeraire* in those countries are readily redeemable in gold at their bearers' request.

These are, in my view, the most comprehensive definitions of the gold standard that can be given, if one wants to be fair to the opinions of the scholars who, since the eighteenth century, have studied that system.

It is well known that, since the Bank of England's return to convertibility at the end of the Napoleonic Wars, only Great Britain remained uninterruptedly faithful to the gold standard until the outbreak of the First World War. Some other countries—France, for instance, Germany, the United States—experienced long spells of (more or less) full convertibility. For others, such as Italy or Japan, the experience was a short-lived one and, in the case of Italy, it suffered several interruptions.

If different countries encountered varying success in their attempts to establish gold convertibility for their currencies, it can be said with absolute certainty that almost all countries, in the years from the early nineteenth century to the outbreak of the First

World War, made serious and often repeated attempts to get on the gold standard. Most of these experiments took place in the 25 years between 1890 and 1914.

If one sets out to study the International Gold Standard, therefore, the first thing one might try to discover is the motives behind those insistent and widespread attempts, on the part of monetary authorities all over the world, to link their currencies to gold, or to adopt gold as their currency. We must try at least to discover what advantages were expected from the gold standard.

We could begin that inquiry by examining the vast bulk of literature on the subject that has piled up in the course of two centuries. But, as Frank W. Fetter noted in his *Development of British Monetary Orthodoxy*,[1] when one gets to the bottom of the pile, one is left with a feeling of disillusionment. The adoption of a gold standard system is, in fact, recommended by most of those economists who wrote on the subject in the last two centuries, on the basis of more or less brilliant elaborations of the logical scheme of the causes of international economic relations as developed by Smith and Ricardo. It is therefore natural to begin the enquiry by examining the monetary implications of that logical scheme. We will not bother here with attributing the merits of its first discovery. That has been done by Jacob Viner, and his masterly piece of research cannot be easily improved upon. What we know today as the basic model of international economic relations, we know because of the very successful efforts to propagandise it made by Smith and Ricardo in their works. We shall therefore begin by examining their version of the model.

Exchange, in a contractual society of the type postulated by Smith, results from the discovery that men soon make of the principle of comparative advantage.

It is the maxim of every prudent master of a family, never to attempt to make at home what it will cost him more to make than to buy. The tailor does not attempt to make his own shoes, but buys them of the shoemaker. The shoemaker does not attempt to make his own clothes, but employs a tailor. . . . What is prudence in the conduct of every private family, can scarce be folly in that of a great kingdom. If a foreign country can

[1] Cambridge, Mass., 1965, especially p. 226 ff.

supply us with a commodity cheaper than we ourselves can make it, better buy it of them with some part of the produce of our own industry, employed in a way in which we have some advantage.[2]

The principle is further elaborated by Ricardo.

Under a system of perfectly free commerce each country naturally devotes its capital and labour to such employments as are most beneficial to each. This pursuit of individual advantage is admirably connected with the universal good of the whole. By stimulating industry, by rewarding ingenuity, and by using most efficaciously the peculiar powers bestowed by nature, it distributes labour most effectively and most economically; while, by increasing the general mass of productions, it diffuses general benefit, and binds together, by one common tie of interest and intercourse, the universal society of nations throughout the civilised world. It is this principle which determines that wine shall be made in France and Portugal, that corn shall be grown in America and Poland, and that hardware and other goods shall be manufactured in England.

In one and the same country, profits are, generally speaking, always on the same level; or differ only as the employment of capital may be more or less secure and agreeable. It is not so between different countries. If the profits of capital employed in Yorkshire, should exceed those of capital employed in London, capital would speedily move from London to Yorkshire, and an equality of profits would be effected; but if in consequence of the diminished rate of production in the lands of England, from the increase of capital and population, wages should rise, and profits fall, it would not follow that capital and population would necessarily move from England to Holland, or Spain, or Russia, where profits might be higher.

Experience, however, shews that the fancied or real insecurity of capital, when not under the immediate control of its owner, together with the natural disinclination which every man has to quit the country of his birth and connexions, and intrust himself with all his habits fixed, to a strange government and

[2] A. Smith, *An Inquiry into the Nature and Causes of the Wealth of Nations* ed. McCulloch, Book IV. ch. 2., pp. 354-5, London 1869.

new laws, check the emigration of capital. These feelings, which I should be sorry to see weakened, induce most men of property to be satisfied with a low rate of profits in their own country, rather than seek a more advantageous employment for their wealth in foreign nations.

Gold and silver having been chosen for the general medium of circulation, they are, by the competition of commerce, distributed in such proportions amongst the different countries of the world, as to accommodate themselves to the natural traffic which would take place if no such metals existed, and the trade between countries were purely a trade of barter.

Thus, cloth cannot be imported into Portugal, unless it sell there for more gold than it cost in the country from which it was imported; and wine cannot be imported into England, unless it will sell for more there than it cost in Portugal. If the trade were purely a trade of barter, it could only continue whilst England could make cloth so cheap as to obtain a greater quantity of wine with a given quantity of labour, by manufacturing cloth than by growing vines; and also whilst the industry of Portugal were attended by the reverse effects. Now suppose England were to discover a process for making wine, so that it should become her interest rather to grow it than import it; she would naturally divert a portion of her capital from the foreign trade to the home trade; she would cease to manufacture cloth for exportation, and would grow wine for herself. The money price of these commodities would be regulated accordingly; wine would fall here while cloth continued at its former price, and in Portugal no alteration would take place in the price of either commodity. Cloth would continue for some time to be exported from this country, because its price would continue to be higher in Portugal than here; but money instead of wine would be given in exchange for it, till the accumulation of money here, and its diminution abroad, should so operate on the relative value of cloth in the two countries, that it would cease to be profitable to export it. If the improvement in making wine were of a very important description, it might become profitable for the two countries to exchange employments; for England to make all the wine, and Portugal all the cloth consumed by them; but this could be effected only by a new distribution of the precious metals, which should raise the price of cloth in England, and lower it in Portugal. The relative price of wine would fall in England in consequence of the real advantage from the improvement of its manufacture; that is to say, its natural price would fall; the relative price of cloth would rise there from the accumulation of money.[3]

Those two quotations are long but essential to our purposes. They contain the basic elements of the model that Smith and Ricardo built to describe how economic relations among nations should be, in order to get a maximum of world economic welfare.

Let us try to establish what those elements are. What our two authors had clearly in mind was a society of entirely homogeneous nations. This is shown by Ricardo's reference to 'the civilised world' which is the place of international exchange; it is also apparent from the assumption Smith and Ricardo make of the non-existence of problems resulting from differences in the stages of economic development reached by the exchanging countries. Their analysis is perfectly static. From this consideration we deduce that they have in mind structurally similar countries. Our deduction is further reinforced by Ricardo's explicit reference to the possibility of the two countries inverting their specialisations, if the hypothesis is made of a technical innovation which causes the structure of relative prices to change in one of the countries. That inversion can only take place between economies structurally at the same stage of development.

That the model is a static one is also a result of the exclusion of increasing returns to scale. Both Smith and Ricardo wrote before the arrival of mass production by means of enormous fixed capital investment. Their manufactures are produced with the help of machines, but these have not yet assumed a leading role.[4] The entrepreneur is still little more than a large-scale artisan, who organises the labour of a small number of workers.

The division of specialisation among countries—wine from Portugal and France, wheat from America and Poland, manufactures from England—does not have, for Smith and Ricardo, important dynamic complications. They do not seem to realise

[3] D. Ricardo, *Works,* ed. Sraffa, Cambridge 1955, vol. I, pp. 133–138.
[4] This is noted by V. K. Dmitriev, in his *Economic Essays* of 1904 (a translation of which is in course of publication at the Cambridge University Press).

that the division of labour resulting from their scheme implies a faster rate of development for Britain than for those countries which do not specialise in the production of industrial commodities. F. Mauro has commented that their system of international economic relations is projected towards the past.[5] Exchange takes place among old countries, England, Portugal, the Hanseatic city-states which can potentially produce all the goods that are the objects of exchange. It is a trade that has its routes in the Mediterranean, the Baltic, the North Sea. The powerful breadth of the oceans does not touch this world. There is no place in it for dramatic changes. We have already excluded increasing returns. We must also exclude, as Ricardo indicates, the possibility of capital and labour moving from one country to another.

We must, in other words, exclude from the model the prime movers of modern economic history: great inventions, the differences in levels of development that have permitted colonisation, the huge migrations of Europeans to the new continents, the massive exports of investment capital to the new countries.

In the classical model there is only space for an international equilibrium mechanism based on movements of absolute and relative prices. The equilibrating medium is gold, flowing from one country to another. And gold—according to Ricardo—flows when there are changes in the conditions governing the production of commodities in one country, while they remain unchanged in the rest of the world. Following a very rigid version of the quantity theory of money, he asserts that gold flows cause prices to increase in the country which receives them so that technological superiority is neutralised by price increases, and equilibrium is regained.

That is the main reason for the classical economists' preference for the gold standard. The latter must exist in every country participating in international exchange in order for money to be neutral and for commodities to be exchanged according to the labour that is embodied in them and according to the principle of comparative advantage.

It is, however, a reason not based on absolutely watertight logic. When a functional relationship is established between the quantity of money and the general price level (and Ricardo does establish such a relationship), it does not make much difference whether

[5] F. Mauro, 'Towards an "Intercontinental Model": European Overseas Expansion between 1500 and 1800', in *The Economic History Review*, 1961.

the money is gold or paper. Money cannot be anything else but neutral. The working of exchanges and prices in all countries will nullify any attempts to exert influence on a country's economic conditions by manipulating the quantity of money existing in that country. The example of the effects of doubling a country's money supply, first analysed by Hume, is reproduced by Ricardo, who expresses complete faith in the international price mechanism. One last consideration can be made, but it does not have the advantage of being backed by quotations from Smith's or Ricardo's works. Ricardo's fight in favour of a return to convertibility for sterling, after the suspension of cash payments during the Napoleonic wars, can be thought of as an extension of his fight for *laissez-faire*. The classical economic system is based on the concept of scarcity pricing. The prices of commodities are inversely proportional to the latter's available quantities. The classical theory of rent, the Malthusian mechanism of equilibrium wages and the quantity theory of money all stem from that root. The classical economic system, however, is also based on the assumption that the costs of production determine the prices of commodities. Gold money is a commodity like all other commodities, produced at a cost that can be reckoned in terms of the labour used in the process of production. Paper money, on the contrary, when it is not kept convertible into gold (as Ricardo himself[6] showed was possible by using a gold exchange standard) is produced at virtually no cost and represents the most patent form of fiscalisation of economic relationships, and of public intervention in the economy, resulting in the distortion of existing private contracts.

In other words, if we can use a modern concept, that of *inside* and *outside* money, it would seem reasonable to attribute to Ricardo the opinion that gold, when it is used as the basis for the monetary system, does not constitute a case of *outside* money: gold, like all other commodities, is produced at a cost, and its value is conferred, according to the classical view, by the labour embodied in it and by its relative scarcity compared to other commodities. Its production, therefore, takes place analogously to the production of other commodities, and its value depends on the same motives that confer value on other commodities. The production of inconvertible money represents for Ricardo, on the other hand, the only

---

[6] On the gold exchange standard proposed by Ricardo, see R. S. Sayers' essay in his *Central Banking after Bagehot,* London 1957.

case of *outside* money. It is not a commodity, and is produced at virtually no cost; the State, by issuing it, does not become any poorer. The only principle that governs its value is the principle of relative scarcity (i.e. the quantity theory of money). Ricardo, therefore, fights his battle against inconvertible money to bring money back to the fold of the general theory of value, which regulates private economic relations.[7]

A hypothetical theoretical justification is thus the most we can produce to explain Ricardo's attachment to gold as the basis of the monetary systems of all countries. The Ricardian scheme of the causes of international trade, and the equilibrium mechanism he devised for international trade, have the extreme abstraction which we have already noted. That does not prevent Ricardo, however, from fighting for economic policy measures to be adopted by the government of his country: his rationale is the scheme itself, which is now alleged by him to regulate actual international economic relations. Unlike Smith, Ricardo makes little discrimination between reality and theory. On concluding his peroration on total freedom of trade, Smith had asserted that 'to expect, indeed, that the freedom of trade should ever be entirely restored in Great Britain, is as absurd as to expect that an Oceania or Utopia should ever be established in it'. That was so because 'Not only the prejudices of the public, but, what is much more unconquerable, the private interests of many individuals, irresistibly oppose it.'[8] Which, coming from the staunchest defender of private interest as the compass which unfailingly leads mankind to maximum welfare, is a distinctly pessimistic conclusion to make and one which reveals how well Smith was aware of the high level of abstraction of his system. But, for Ricardo, at least from what appears from his writings, theory and reality melt into each other. The mechanism of international equilibrium which he provides, working as it does through the quantity theory of money and the terms of trade,

[7] Moreover, he thought gold might be the best approximation to an 'unchanging standard of value'. As he wrote, 'May not gold be considered as a commodity produced with such proportions of the two kinds of capital as approach nearest to the average quantity employed in the production of most commodities? May not these proportions be so nearly equally distant from the two extremes, the one where little fixed capital is used, the other where little labour is used, as to form a just mean between them?' See *Works, op. cit.*, pp. 45–46.

[8] *An Inquiry, op. cit.*, p. 367.

ought to function in the short as well as in the long term; the terms of trade ought to move continuously, changing all the time the comparative advantage structure and immediately balancing the trade accounts of all countries. He does not offer any reason for trade among nations other than differences in relative prices, and no mechanism other than that just described to ensure the maintenance of international economic equilibrium.

An alternative model is offered by Friederich List. His main work, *The National System of Political Economy*,[9] is almost contemporary with Ricardo's *Principles*. But his influence on students of the international economy was as weak as Smith's and Ricardo's was strong. An examination of current Anglo-American textbooks on international economics will easily show List as one of the least-quoted authors.

Friederich List is the intellectual opposite of Smith and Ricardo. The latter try to establish political economy as an exercise in logic, a study of the internal consistency of abstractly formulated logical systems; the former attempts to immerse himself in the reality of economic history and to derive the most important lessons from it. His work, much more than Smith's, is an inquiry into the real causes of the wealth of nations. For him, economics is one of the arts of statemanship. He does not care about discovering the immutable laws that govern the actions of *'homo oeconomicus'*— What he wants to understand is how to get Germany on to a path which might allow her to become an economically powerful state in the shortest possible time, since he is convinced that economic power is the necessary precondition of political power.

His points of departure are opposite to those of Smith and Ricardo. To the latter, the *primum mobile* of economic activity is the individual's endeavour to maximise his own welfare, which brings him into competition with others for the command of scarce resources. To List, the *primum mobile* of economic activity is represented by man's desire to congregate in extra-familiar units. The basic feature of modern economies is the possibility of getting increasing returns by enlarging the scale of production, which is offered by manufacturing industry; whereas European agriculture, suffocated by rent, offers a completely opposite choice. It follows that the countries of temperate Europe, if they want to reach a

[9] F. List, *The National System of Political Economy*, Philadelphia 1857.

high level of development, *must* specialise in manufacturing. Since Great Britain, thanks to her past of intelligent protectionism, has managed to gain an enormous advantage in manufacturing over the rest of the world, other European countries *must*, if they want to develop, adopt protectionist measures, the strictness of which must be graduated in two phases: in the first phase, the need to import manufacturing techniques in order to learn them will make it expedient to import industrial products from Great Britain. Protection will thus need to be only moderate. In the second phase, when the industrial structure of the country has been built up, but is still not able to stand up to British competition, protection will have to be at its most severe, since the only available market is the national one. List was of the opinion that the future would not see European countries widening their mutual exchange of industrial products. He was convinced that the development of international trade would follow the mode of complementarity introduced by the colonial empires. From the temperate area manufactures would be exported to the tropical area, which would in its turn supply raw materials and agricultural products. The division of labour he prophesied is thus the one between the two areas. In the tropical area he included the south-western part of the United States.

He thus showed very clearly what he considered would be the two main avenues of development in the nineteenth century: manufacturing production, taking place at decreasing cost, would allow European countries to accumulate capital and grow fast; at the same time their need for raw materials and agricultural commodities would induce them to foster the development of the tropical area as Europe's complementary unit, i.e. as a producer of primary commodities and a consumer of manufactures. Only manufacturing production, however, took place at decreasing cost, so that Europe would grow much faster than the tropical area.

Adam Smith had considered increasing returns to scale; he had not, however, recognised the revolutionary implications of this feature of manufacturing production. Nor had he, or David Ricardo for that matter, drawn the conclusion that an imperialistic division of labour would obtain for the world as a whole, and a chasm would open between developed and under-developed countries. Smith on colonies is complementary to Smith on free trade. The imperialist model of development was imposed by force on colonies, he affirms. It is thus to be disapproved of, because colonials are not free to choose what they want to produce. The complementarity imposed on the tropical area does not seem to him to be a fundamental analytical element to be pointed out. In any case, his international trade model cannot include real complementarity among nations, but only actual or potential competition among states which have all reached the same level of development.

The greatness of List's analysis lies, on the contrary, in his full utilisation of the classical method of reasoning in order to reach economic policy conclusions of a kind which are the perfect opposite to the classical ones. We can say that by adding dynamism and history to classical analysis, List obtains a strategy for fast economic growth that is perfectly suitable to the socio-economic conditions of his country as well as of many other countries which want to undergo a process of modernisation. If we read List in the light of recent historiography,[10] we can clearly see—in his rejection of individual action as the basis for economic growth for countries other than Britain—his awareness of the impossibility of founding economic modernisation on a bourgeois revolution, i.e. on the English model, and of the ensuing need to find a different 'national way', based on collective action, i.e. by grafting a modernisation process on to a social context that has not yet known the rise of a 'liberated' bourgeoisie. List understands that in countries such as Germany modernisation must come as a 'revolution from above', which will permit the country to jump, as it were, over one historical phase, i.e. the destruction of the *ancien régime* effected by the bourgeoisie, which characterised the modernisation process in England.

That is why he attacks with such vigour 'the school', meaning classical economic theory and its basic principles. He understands the attraction that the classics exercise on the bourgeois groups existing in Germany. And he is convinced that the English revolution must not be exported, because it would mean crystallising for ever the hierarchical relations linking England to the rest of Europe in his time. In fact, if the European economies were made to go through a process which would involve the emerging of the bourgeoisie as the 'engine of growth', the cost of such an operation, in terms of time and resources, would be too high for them; whereas

[10] See, for instance, Barrington Moore, Jr. *The Social Origins of Dictatorship and Democracy*, Cambridge, Mass., 1964.

it had been bearable for the English economy, which had gone through the same process before the industrial revolution. In his time, List thought, the industrial supremacy of Britain and the powerful free trade policy which she tried to impose on the rest of the world, would tend to kill all attempts to build up national economies as powerful as, and independent of, the English.

The greatest disservice one can do Friederich List is to call him the 'arch-protectionist', in opposition to the 'arch-freetraders' Smith and Ricardo. List is not protectionist *à outrance*. He is a scholar who understands that "free trade" is not a revealed truth, but only a form of economic policy which, at the period he was concerned with, suited English economic growth but was damaging to other countries because it compelled them to crystallise their economic relations with Britain. If those countries wanted to modernise their economies, to become as politically powerful as Britain, he thought they should blend protectionism and corporativism, skip the bourgeois revolution, and base their growth on state intervention, a measure of autarky and a hierarchical relationship with under-developed countries.

Upon reflection, all today's industrialised countries seem to have followed Friederich List's recipe.

We must not neglect to mention another of his contributions: it was he who tried to place the teaching of the classical school in historical perspective. In a word, he said that the classics were liberal because liberalism suited England at the time. This suggestion has lingered on, never being completely disproved. Some years ago Lord Robbins declared himself convinced of the 'patriotism' of Smith and Ricardo. More recently it has been advanced[11] that Smith's free trade is the result of the coincidence of interests that existed between entrepreneurs and the landed aristocracy of his time, and that Ricardo's free trade is a testimony to the conflict between entrepreneurs and the landed aristocracy. It is noted that, in Smith's time, English exports consisted mainly of wool manufactures, made of English-produced wool, while at the same time England had a distinct technical superiority over the rest of Europe in agricultural production. In Ricardo's time, on the contrary, foreign wheat and corn competed successfully with English, and England exported cotton manufactures made of a foreign-

[11] For an intelligent and exhaustive appraisal of this view, see S. Sideri, *Trade and Power,* Rotterdam 1970, especially ch. IV.

produced raw material. There could be no agreement between gentry and entrepreneurs on trade policy.

We cannot deny that such remarks have a very suggestive appeal. Noting that about fifty years divide *The Wealth of Nations* from the *Principles of Political Economy and Taxation*, we see the British gentry changing in those five decades from free trade to protectionism and British merchants and entrepreneurs switching from free trade to protectionism and from protectionism back to free trade. One could say that if Ricardo had been Smith's contemporary, he would have been a protectionist and if Smith been Ricardo's contemporary he would have been a protectionist too, preoccupied as he was with the welfare of the gentry. They were able to promote free trade because, in the fifty years that separated their works, England went through the industrial revolution and the English economy needed free trade to keep growing. One cannot think of a better example of List's theory of the stages of economic growth. The great majority of economists who have, in the course of the last 150 years, had at their disposal both approaches, the classical and the Listian, have without hesitation opted for the former. The consequences of that choice have been grave. In 150 years an analytical orthodoxy has developed which is totally irrelevant to what concerns the causes and the modes of international trade; several decades have subsequently been spent by other writers in the effort to escape from its clutches and discover the theoretical limitations of classical trade analysis, which List had already pointed out more than a century before. What particularly concerns us here is that the study of the development of the international monetary system has all been conducted along the lines suggested by the classical model of international trade. A large intellectual superstructure has thus been erected, which proves very difficult to get rid of when one attempts, as I hope to do in this book, to study the international monetary system before 1914.

A classic example of that intellectual superstructure is provided by a famous quotation from the report of the Cunliffe Committee, which was set up in 1919 to analyse the functioning of the pre-war gold standard and to indicate how best to go back to it:[12]

When the exchanges were favourable, gold flowed freely into

[12] The Cunliffe Report is reprinted in T. S. Ashton & R. S. Sayers, eds. *Papers in English Monetary History*, London 1953.

this country and an increase of legal tender money accompanied the development of trade. When the balance of trade was unfavourable and the exchanges were adverse it became profitable to export gold. The would-be exporter bought his gold from the Bank of England and paid for it by a cheque on his account. The Bank obtained the gold from the Issue Department in exchange for notes taken out of its banking reserve, with the result that its liabilities to depositors and its banking reserve were reduced by an equal amount, and the ratio of reserve to liabilities consequently fell. If the process were repeated sufficiently often to reduce the ratio in a degree considered dangerous, the Bank raised its rate of discount. The raising of the discount rate had the immediate effect of retaining money here which would otherwise have been remitted abroad and of attracting remittance from abroad to take advantage of the higher rate, thus checking the outflow of gold and even reversing the stream.

If the adverse condition of the exchanges was due not merely to seasonal fluctuations, but to circumstances tending to create a permanently adverse trade balance, it is obvious that the procedure above described would not have been sufficient. It would have resulted in the creation of a volume of short-dated indebtedness to foreign countries which would have been in the end disastrous to our credit and the position of London as the financial centre of the world. But the raising of the Bank's discount rate and the steps taken to make it effective in the market necessarily led to a general rise of interest rates and a restriction of credit. New enterprises were therefore postponed and the demand for constructional materials and other capital goods was lessened. The consequent slackening of employment also diminished the demand for consumable goods, while holders of stocks of commodities carried largely with borrowed money, being confronted with an increase of interest charges—if not with actual difficulty in renewing loans and with the prospect of falling prices—tended to press their goods on a weak market. The result was a decline in general prices in the home market which, by checking imports and stimulating exports, corrected the adverse trade balance which was the primary cause of the difficulty.

When, as well as a foreign drain of gold, credit at home also threatened to become unduly expanded, the old currency system tended to restrain the expansion and to prevent the consequent rise in domestic prices which ultimately causes such a drain. The expansion of credit, by forcing up prices, involves an increased demand for legal tender currency, both from the banks in order to maintain their normal proportion of cash to liabilities and from the general public for the payment of wages and for retail transactions. In this case also the demand for such currency fell upon the reserve of the Bank of England, and the Bank was thereupon obliged to raise its rate of discount in order to prevent the fall in the proportion of that reserve to its liabilities. The same chain of consequences as we have just described followed, and speculative trade activity was similarly restrained. There was therefore an automatic machinery by which the volume of purchasing power in this country was continuously adjusted to world prices of commodities in general. Domestic prices were automatically regulated so as to prevent excessive imports; and the creation of banking credit was so controlled that banking could be safely permitted a freedom from State interference which would not have been possible under a less rigid currency system.

Under these arrangements this country was provided with a complete and effective gold standard. The essence of such a standard is that notes must always stand at absolute parity with gold coins of equivalent face value, and that both notes and gold coins stand at absolute parity with gold bullion. When these conditions are fulfilled, the foreign exchange rates with all countries possessing an effective gold standard are maintained at or within the gold specie points.

It is impossible to find a clearer and more complete explanation of how international economic relations were supposed to proceed and international economic equilibrium to be maintained under the gold standard. The basis, as we said, is the classical trade model. This is, however, enriched with important, if not fundamental, elaboration. The first is a distinction, which we owe to John Stuart Mill, between temporary and fundamental disequilibrium of the balance of payments. The second is the introduction of a new mechanism based on the changes in Bank rate operated by the Bank of England according to the rule discovered by Horsley Palmer in the middle of the nineteenth century.[13]

[13] On the Palmer Rule, see F. W. Fetter, *The Development of British Monetary Orthodoxy, op. cit.*

It is clear, however, that by removing, at least partially, the Ricardian assumption of factor immobility, in order to allow international shortage to take care of temporary trade imbalances, we do not get a very substantial modification of the Ricardian trade model. The Cunliffe report, in fact, kept terms of trade changes as the basic equilibrium mechanism. And it believed terms of trade changes to come about mainly as a result of changes in the money supply. As the banking system, not so important back in Ricardo's time, had by 1919 become paramount in supplying money, the Cunliffe Committee pointed to it as being responsible for changes in the money supply. The final effect, however, was the same as predicted by Ricardo, i.e. price changes. To introduce the Cambridge Equation as a substitute for the simpler Quantity Equation, as the Cunliffe Committee did in their report, makes very little difference. Marshall's and Hawtrey's contributions to the analysis (which consisted mainly in showing that the demand for bank credit on the part of commodity speculators was the main link between short and long term interest rates) are useful, but not very different from an 'inside' criticism, by which I mean one which leaves the classical equilibrium mechanism intact.[14] What is missing, in our opinion, is an analysis of the real essence of the pre-1914 international monetary system which tries to replace the central part of monetary orthodoxy with something new and more realistic.

Nor is this provided by the critics of the gold standard who wrote after the First World War, pre-eminently J. M. Keynes.[15] Keynes' *Tract on Monetary Reform* is a justification of the fiscalisation of monetary functions on the part of the State; an attempt to show that order is possible even without gold; that gold was sovereign in the developed part of the world only for a very short period and that, therefore, the system which was based on it cannot be considered as the optimum and primary objective of economic policy. But the analysis he provides in that book of the transmission mechanism linking money to prices, and of the equilibrium mechanism, is only an attempt to modify the orthodoxy 'from within'. Keynes does not try to introduce an analysis of the

[14] Alfred Marshall, *Official Papers*, ed. by J. M. Keynes, London, 1926, in particular, I, II, IV. R. G. Hawtrey, *Trade and Credit*, London 1929.
[15] J. M. Keynes' *A Tract on Monetary Reform* and *A Treatise on Money* have already appeared in the Royal Economic Society's publication of his collected works, London 1972.

international monetary system based on the complementary relationship established between developed and under-developed countries. His equilibrium mechanism is still based on changes in the terms of trade and works in a world of homogeneous and competing nations.

In *A Treatise on Money* he does not significantly change his line of argument. The Marshallian theme of commodity and stock exchange speculation is considered in depth, in the hope of finding a new link between Bank rate and long-term interest rates. To explain that link he goes back to the classics, to Ricardo in particular, through the mediation of Wicksell, and introduces a mechanism based on the difference between natural and money interest rates. In the first part of his Treatise, Keynes built splendid theoretical foundations for the passage of the Cunliffe report quoted above. It is still a declaration of profound faith in monetary orthodoxy, even if Keynes is the standard-bearer of the promoters of State intervention. State intervention is justified by a pessimistic view of the actual working of the orthodox mechanism, the existence of which, however, is never questioned.

With very few exceptions, modern students of the pre–1914 International Gold Standard have not added much to our knowledge. One of the exceptions is Arthur Bloomfield. In two essays[16] he demonstrated that, before 1914, national monetary authorities had a highly discretional monetary policy and that short-term international capital movements played an important role in keeping the international monetary system in equilibrium. By doing so he demonstrated the emptiness of the widely-believed myth, bolstered by the Cunliffe report and by the post-war advocates of a return to gold, that the gold standard worked automatically. Bloomfield had no difficulty in showing that central banks violated the so-called 'rules of the game' as frequently before 1914 as they have done since 1945.

Robert Triffin, another of the exceptions, limits himself to a series of critical reflections, points which he leaves for further discussion.[17] He contrasts the 'Cunliffe version' of the functioning of

[16] A. L. Bloomfield, *Monetary policy under the International Gold Standard,* 1880–1914, New York 1959; and *Short Term Capital Movements under the pre-1914 Gold Standard,* Princeton 1963.

[17] R. Triffin, *The Evolution of the International Monetary System: Historical Reappraisal and Future Perspectives,* Princeton 1964.

the pre-1914 International Gold Standard with some facts of economic history. The contrast reveals the shortcomings of classical trade theory as an instrument for interpreting pre-1914 historical reality. In that period, the major developed countries experienced parallel economic cycles, which shows clearly that the equilibrium mechanism did not work for them as classical theory would have it. That tendency was reinforced by the really remarkable parallelism shown by price-changes in the same countries. Moreover—he adds—wages never decreased to any significant extent, for any significant length of time, in any of those countries. They decreased much more in England in the 1920–22 recession, and in Germany and the US, in the early years of the great depression.

So far as capital movements are concerned, Triffin points out that if capital-exporting countries succeeded, up to a point, in controlling the flow by discount rate movements, capital-importing countries had huge difficulties when they tried to do the same: foreign capital flowed in during booms and out during slumps, without regard for the discount rates of those countries' central banks. In any case, as regards their importance in the equilibrium mechanism, Triffin believes capital movements to have far exceeded the changes in the terms of trade described by classical theory. New countries could use foreign capital to finance trade deficits for fifty years. England, on her part, experienced growing payments surpluses for the whole period, which were mainly caused by income flowing in from her past investments abroad.

After those remarks Triffin comes to some conclusions. He asserts that:

> The nineteenth-century monetary mechanism succeeded, to a unique degree, in preserving exchange rate stability—and freedom from quantitative trade and exchange restrictions—over a large part of the world.
>
> This success, however, was limted to the more advanced countries which formed the core of the system, and to those closely linked to them by political as well as economic and financial ties. The exchange rates of other currencies—particularly in Latin America—fluctuated widely, and depreciated enormously, over the period. This contrast between the 'core' countries and those of the 'periphery' can be largely explained by the cyclical pattern of capital movements and terms of trade,

which contributed to stability in the first group, and to instability in the second.

The adjustment process did not depend on any tendency toward equilibrium of the national balances of payments on current account.

The preservation of exchange-rate stability depended, however, on the impact of international monetary settlements—of the combined current and capital accounts—upon domestic monetary and credit developments.... As long as stable exchange rates were maintained, national *export* prices remained strongly bound together among all competing countries, by the mere existence of an international market not broken down by any large and frequent changes in trade or exchange restrictions.

Inflationary pressures could not be contained within the domestic market, but spilled out *directly,* to a considerable extent, into balance of payments deficits, rather than into uncontrolled rises of internal prices, costs, and wage levels. These deficits led, in turn, to corresponding monetary transfers from the domestic banking system to foreign banks weakening the cash position of domestic banks and their ability to pursue expansionary credit policies leading to persistent deficits for the economy and persistent cash drains for the banks. (Banks in surplus countries would be simultaneously subject to opposite pressures, which would also contribute to the harmonisation of credit policies around levels conducive to the re-equilibration of the overall balance of payments.)

By using Keynesian and pre-Keynesian analysis, and assuming a mechanism of banking multiplication in conditions of international convertibility, Triffin postulates a world, before 1914, in which international economic equilibrium was maintained by the harmonisation of monetary policies (and of economic policy in general) on the part of the major countries, which was achieved by (1) their mutual competition, and (2) the logic of the banking multiplier in conditions of convertibility, which was allowed to operate in each of them. Thus, in spite of the doubts he expresses whether the traditional adjustment mechanism is the key to the interpretation of the dynamics of the international monetary system before 1914, Triffin does no more, albeit with great effort, than repeat the conclusions reached in the Cunliffe report. Even the tone of his concluding remarks shows his intellectual capitulation to the myth of the monetary *belle époque*: 'In any case [he writes] the slow evolution which adjusted gradually the international monetary system of the nineteenth century to the economic requirements of peacetime economic growth ... was brutally disrupted by the outbreak of the First World War. The ensuing collapse of the system ushered in half a century of international monetary chaos.'

The image he evokes of a harmoniously working system 'brutally disrupted' by war, and the provocative title—'Half a Century of International Monetary Anarchy 1914–1964'—of his next chapter, which is carefully chosen to juxtapose the vision of order previously prevailing with that of the chaos which immediately followed, reveal Triffin's position as a qualified believer of the myth of the gold standard.

A recent attempt to re-interpret the same period of international monetary history has been made by D. Williams.[18] The title of his essay gives a precise lead to his main purpose. It is 'The Evaluation of the Sterling System', and it suggests that the pre-1914 international monetary system was really based on sterling rather than gold. Sterling was the key currency, and in particular the vehicle for international transactions on both current and capital account. Williams begins by asking the ritual question: how did the international monetary system really work before 1914. His answer is that the gold standard *began* as a sterling standard. England had deficits with Europe and the United States and surpluses with the Empire. Her banks in the Colonies and the City allowed long-term international investment to take place; this could continue only if money sent out of England as investment came back to England in payment for English goods exported. England, moreover, as the leading country in international finance, satisfied the demand for gold induced by rising incomes in the 'new' countries, and attracted gold from other European gold standard countries by aggregate changes in the Bank of England's discount rate. Thus, according to Williams, the international monetary system worked because the principal countries performed their roles, which he defines as follows:

[18] D. Williams, 'The Evaluation of the Sterling System', in *Essays in Money and Banking, in honour of R. S. Sayers,* ed. by C. R. Whittlesley and J. S. G. Wilson, Oxford 1968.

(1) England's role was as a long-term investor in the new countries;

(2) The new countries (including those that were part of the Empire) had the role of transforming British investment into demand for British exports;

(3) European countries, which were on the gold standard, held the system's ultimate gold reserve and had to allow it to be drawn upon via discount rate changes.

William's interpretation, although somewhat schematic, represents by far the most successful attempt to 're-live' the period, as far as monetary history is concerned. The roles he assigns to the various countries are, in my opinion, the correct ones: as will be seen they coincide with the results of my research. Some points are, however, missing in his analysis and I will try to elucidate these.

TWO

The World Economy after 1870

A large part of the traditional misunderstanding of the essence of the pre-1914 international monetary system derives from an insufficient knowledge, or a wrong interpretation, of the international economic history of that period. Thus at this point we have to make a brief excursion into late nineteenth century economic history to clarify its main themes.

For our purposes, it will be sufficient to concentrate on the economic events of three countries—Britain, Germany, and the United States. They were undoubtedly the leading powers of that period. The modifications that took place in the economic structures of those countries and in their relations with the rest of the world influenced the world economic history of that time. A vast bibliography is available on the subject. We shall merely analyse the points that are relevant in our context; for greater detail we shall refer the reader to specialised literature.

The four decades between 1870 and 1914 witnessed what has been called the 'Second Industrial Revolution'. The first had been largely a British affair. This is not the place to ask why that was so, but it is useful to remember that, by 1850, Britain had achieved absolute supremacy in the production and world trade of manufactures, particularly of those commodities produced in factories organised on capitalist lines. By this time, there was an enormous gap between the British level of industrialisation and that of any of her potential competitors. These years had also seen the triumph of free trade, a policy convenient for Britain, and also for those countries who wanted to import British-made machinery and know-how to increase their rate of industrialisation.

The Second Industrial Revolution, which began about 1870, was by contrast not at all a British monopoly. The First Industrial Revolution had been based on small factories, owned and run by individual entrepreneur families, a world of 'atomistic competitors'. Increasing returns to scale had scarcely begun to be felt, and when they were, they had largely come about through using machines to rationalise the activities of teams of workers engaged on the same production line.

On the other hand, the fulcrum of the Second Industrial Revolution was represented by new technology and heavy industry. In that sector the high ratio of fixed to circulating capital had begun to make the law of increasing returns more and more important. The importance of machine-based technology also resulted in the rapid economic obsolescence of vast stocks of perfectly good equipment. Consequently, ample financial resources were needed to enter into, and remain in, industrial production.

Because of these new conditions the 'comparative advantage' in building up new industrial sectors (such as steel, chemicals, electricity and electrical products) began to shift away from Great Britain towards Germany and the United States. Both those countries, literally following the British industrialisation 'recipe', had protected their infant industries from British competition behind high tariff walls. This had enabled both countries to operate relative price structures discriminating in favour of industrial products and against agricultural products and raw materials. Thus the redistributive process, which channelled resources from agriculture to industry and permitted rapid capital accumulation, had been allowed to work. Both countries, moreover, appeared particularly well equipped to meet the challenge of a Second Industrial Revolution, and this meant that they had to be able to build, and to run at the highest level of efficiency, a heavy industrial sector. Further, there had to exist external economies of a particular kind in the countries concerned: a labour force with a high enough level of technical education to build and man the machines, and to construct and operate organisational systems far more complex than those previously established. It seemed as if vertical, as well as horizontal, industrial concentration would be the only adequate organisational answer to the running of the Second Industrial Revolution.

Both Germany and the United States had these requirements. Their level of technical education, in the four decades under consideration, was always above that reached by English workers.[1] Giant industrial structures could, in those countries, be built without having to face the fierce resistance of a solidly established industrial *milieu* composed of small producers, as was the case in Britain. Vertical integration could be planned from scratch, rather than as the result of tortuous negotiation between existing firms or of epic take-over battles. In addition, the United States, as well as Germany, could benefit from an external economy such as had been available to (and fully exploited by) Britain, a century before: a huge growth in their respective national markets. Unification and the rapid natural growth of her population in Germany, and mass immigration into the United States, are phenomena of the period. Britain had conquered an empire, but she still had to make a market of it, and to keep that market to herself by means other than tariffs, as her free trade policy prevented her from imposing such restrictions.

In 1870, the population of the United States was 38 million; in 1909 it had become 89 million. The population of the United Kingdom had only risen from 31 to 45 million in the same period. In 1910 the German population was 65 million.[2] Great Britain was thus by 1910 only the third largest country in the West as far as population was concerned. In the same years many more of her absolute world records were demolished. Coal production, for instance, which in 1890 had been 140 million tons in the US and 88 million tons in Germany, compared to 182 million in Great Britain, had, by 1910, become 448 million tons in the United States, 264 million in Britain, and 219 million in Germany. In 1890, pig iron production had been 9.2 million tons in the United States, 7.9 million in Britain, and 4.6 in Germany. In 1910 it was 27.3 million tons in the United States, 10 million in Britain, and 14.6 in Germany.[3]

---

[1] As shown by A. L. Levine, in *Industrial Retardation in Britain, 1880-1914*, New York 1967, p. 73 ff.

[2] Population figures of the countries examined are taken from *Statistics for Great Britain, Germany and France*, National Monetary Commission, Government Printing Office, Washington 1910, and *Historical Statistics of the United States*, Government Printing Office, Washington 1957.

[3] Figures of production levels quoted by W. Mitchell, *Business Cycles*, Berkeley 1910.

In addition to losing these production records,[4] the British economy became, in the last decade of the nineteenth century, more specialised in the production of manufactured goods than it had ever been. British agricultural production had been severely hit by a series of bad harvests in the first five years of the 1890s, and this had merely been the final act in a decline that had already persisted for a decade.[5] Wheat-cultivated acreage decreased, as well as that used for the cultivation of other cereals. In 1884, 80 million bushels of wheat and 74 million bushels of barley had been produced. In 1890, 73 and 67 million bushels respectively had been produced. In the tragically low harvests of 1892, 1893 and 1895 only 58, 49 and 37 million bushels of wheat had been cropped. The yield per acre which had been around 29–30 bushels in the previous decade, had decreased in the three years of bad harvest to about 26 bushels.[6] The free trade policy, which had led to a crisis for British agriculture in the previous decades, gave it the *coup de grâce* in the early 1890s. Imports supplied British demand, so that prices could not increase to make up for lost home production. British agriculture, strained to its limits, did not recover. Increasing agricultural imports were the logical consequence. In 1884, imports had accounted for 50% of local wheat production. In 1913 local production had dropped to 50% of total wheat imports. The same happened with barley: while imports soared, local production declined. Maize imports doubled between 1884 and 1913.[7]

In the same period cattle and pig production remained level but sheep production declined. On the other hand, live animals and meat imports soared from a total of £26 million in 1884 to one of £56 million in 1913. During this period, therefore, Great Britain acquired more and more the features of an export economy. In 1911–13, British manufacturing production was 162% of what it had been in 1881–85, while her exports were 175% of what they

[4] The list of sectors in which, during that period, Britain lost her productive and technological supremacy is a very long one, and we refer the reader to specialised literature, a good review of which is given by Levine, *op. cit.*; to which a more recent bibliography can be added, which is to be found in S. B. Saul, *The Myth of the Great Depression*, London 1969.

[5] On the crisis of British agriculture, see S. B. Saul, *Studies in British Overseas Trade*, Liverpool 1960.

[6] Figures taken from B. R. Mitchell and P. Deane, *Abstract of British Historical Statistics*, Cambridge 1962.

[7] Data taken from Mitchell & Deane, *op. cit.*

had been. World manufacturing production had, at the end of the same period, become 310% of what it had been at the beginning, while world exports had only grown by 239%. In Germany, manufacturing production had increased, in the same period, by 363%, while exports had only grown by 290%.[8]

In 1899 Britain's share of world manufacturing production was 20·8%. Her share of world exports of manufactured goods was 38·3%. In 1913 her share of production had fallen to 15·8%, her share of exports to 31·8%. Germany's quotas had grown, in the same period, from 15·1% to 18·4% and from 20·4% to 25·6%.[9]

How had Britain been able to keep the largest individual share of world exports, while losing the top place in the production league? The answer to this question will undoubtedly form the most interesting part of our discussion, and, from our point of view, the most important.

Britain's foreign trade had undergone a profound transformation, particularly in respect of the destination of British exports; the process had begun during the 'great depression' which had perhaps hit British industry more heavily than its German or American counterparts,[10] which had been partially protected by their higher level of concentration, and by the greater involvement in industry of their countries' banking systems. When the slump reached its lowest ebb and business began to pick up, British industry was in a much worse shape than its direct competitors. In Europe, Germany had been greatly aided by the completion of the Continental rail network, which, in the immediately preceding decades, had facilitated a virtual unification of Continental markets as far as transport was concerned. In 1893, moreover, Count Caprivi had negotiated trade treaties with many Continental countries, with the result that tariff barriers against German products had been considerably lowered. All of which meant greater problems for British exports in Continental markets.[11]

And British exports did not even manage to resist competition

---

[8] Data quoted by Levine, *op. cit.*, p. 132.

[9] Figures calculated by A. Maizels, in his *Industrial Growth and World Trade*, Cambridge 1963.

[10] On the great depression, see S. B. Saul, *The Myth of the Great Depression*, *op. cit.*

[11] On Anglo-German trade competition in this period, the standard reference work is R. J. S. Hoffman, *Great Britain and the German Trade Rivalry, 1875-1914*, Philadelphia 1933.

in markets where Britain's rivals had no special advantages. On the American market, for instance, Britain had suffered a radical *défaillance*—as Table 2 shows (tables follow after the text).

The inability of British exports to 'hold down' the mounting wave of competition became even more evident in the next few years. In 1899, British manufacturing exports to the United States were 93 million dollars, out of a US manufacturing import total of 353 million dollars. Germany's were 66 million. In 1913, out of a total 414 million dollars, the British share was 110 million, the German 127 million.[12] Germany acquired a virtual monopoly in exports of chemicals, precision instruments and electrical machinery. In a sophisticated market like America, she had an easy time against Britain, who had not, for various reasons, managed to equip herself with an equally powerful *modern* industrial structure.[13]

Moreover Britain was also outdistanced by the United States in key areas of man and machine productivity: labour productivity grew from 1890 to 1907 at an annual rate of 2% in the United States, but only of 0·1% in Britain. In 1900–09 the output/labour ratio was very much higher in the United States than in Britain: the American ratio was 2·26 times the British in 15 key industrial sectors. And (in 1905–07) the value of output per horsepower of iron, steel, engineering and shipbuilding was 669 dollars in the United States, compared with 627 dollars in Britain. In 1909, the American industrial worker had available 2·88 horsepower, while his British counterpart, in 1907, had only 1·37 horsepower.[14]

Britain also demonstrated a decreasing ability to compete with German industry in her own home market. At 1913 prices, German exports of manufactured goods to Britain actually increased by more than 70% between 1899 and 1913.[15] They went up from 149 million dollars to 246 million whereas total manufacturing imports into Britain grew at a lesser rate—from 543 to 763 million dollars. At the same time, British exports of manufactured goods to Germany remained stationary at 121 million dollars (at 1913 prices), whereas total manufacturing exports to Germany rose from 292 to 406 million dollars, and United States exports of

[12] Data quoted by Maizels, *op. cit.*
[13] See S. B. Saul, *Studies in British Overseas Trade, op. cit.*
[14] See Levine, *op. cit.*
[15] Data on exports taken from Maizels, *op. cit.*

manufactured goods to Germany grew from 35 to 84 million dollars.

The British decline was also evident in European markets: as is clearly shown in Table 3, British exports to European countries either declined in absolute terms, or grew at a much more modest rate than total exports to those countries or German exports to those countries. When we examine the figures in detail, we note that British exports lost ground especially in new products, as we can see from Table 4.

British imports from those countries, however, kept growing unabated, so that the British visible trade deficit with Europe and the United States increased continually, as is shown in Table 5. In Latin American markets Britain maintained her supremacy; but there too it was seriously challenged by American and German competition, as Table 6 proves. In these markets British visible trade grew, in the 1890–1913 period, as follows: imports went up from £17·2 million to £73·7 million; exports from £28·4 to £54·0 million; re-exports from £1·2 to £2·5 million. From a surplus, Britain went into a deficit, due mainly to massive cereal imports (total imports from Argentina grew from £4·1 million to £42·5 million in the same period; while exports, in 1913, were only £22·6 million).[16]

We must now contrast this loss of British competitive power in the markets of most independent countries with the position of total supremacy which she managed to retain in trade with her Empire, where she maintained a virtual export monopoly. It had become a question of vital importance for her to be able to retain that position, since she had become dependent on the rest of the world for raw materials and agricultural products and could not offset these purchases against comparable sales of manufactured goods. As a source of food, the Empire was inadequate as is shown by Britain's trade deficits with the United States, Argentina and Europe. As a source of raw materials the Empire was not unimportant but it could not satisfy the mother country's needs altogether. Britain needed at all costs a market where she could count on a constant growth of trade surplus: a market which would, above all, be large enough to square her trade accounts with the rest of the world. The Empire, particulary India, was able to

---

[16] Data taken from Mitchell & Deane, *op. cit.*

provide her with the market she needed: Imperial territories
realised a large enough export surplus with the rest of the world
to be put at the mother country's disposal. Britain's retreat into
Imperial markets, and her staunch defence of the privileges she
enjoyed there, is one of the principal keys to an understanding of
world economic history in the 25 years of our period. The phenomenon can be amply demonstrated by a set of data on British
Imperial trade (see Table 7).

In these years, all Imperial territories were as firmly committed
to free trade as was their mother country. It is therefore vital to
discover how Britain managed to retain a monopoly in the Empire,
while simultaneously losing one independent market after another
to her competitors. Clearly Britain succeeded by means of 'non-
tariff protection'.[17] Tariffs were never important in the British
Empire (the ineffectiveness of the Canadian tariff of 1897 and of
the prohibition to export tin mineral from Malaya in 1902 has been
abundantly proved).[18] Non-tariff protection was, however, not too
difficult to impose. In the Empire proper (excepting the Dominions,
where private trading prevailed) foreign trade was for the most
part in the hands of the colonial authorities.[19] This was particularly
true in India, as Dr Bagchi has pointed out:

> The Government of India, with its political decisions, kept alive
> the conviction that 'British is best', a conviction not often shared
> on the free market. Britain's share in iron and steel imports into
> India on private account was declining before the First World
> War, mainly because European steel cost less. The Government
> of India, however, continued to buy only British-made iron and
> steel products, for all its needs; railways, moreover—either run
> by the State or by companies, based in London or in India, but
> controlled by British or Anglo-Indian firms—bought, with rare
> and insignificant exceptions, iron and steel railway equipment
> only in the United Kingdom. British railways producers had the

---

[17] This transpires from the consular reports of US Consuls, and is ascertained
by T. Wolfe in *Foreign Credits,* US Dept. of Commerce Publication, Washington 1912.
[18] By S. B. Saul, *op. cit.*
[19] Regarding colonies, this is attested by G. S. Graham, 'Imperial Finance,
Trade and Communications, 1895–1914', in *The Cambridge History of the
British Empire,* vol. III, p. 465, Cambridge 1967.

monopoly of the Indian market; several attempts to build locomotives on the part of Indian railways failed, although, when
the need arose, the railway workshops successfully built locomotives—for lack of official support.[20]

To this we must add, as Bagchi notes, the British policy of
'keeping the natives in their place', which meant keeping them
away from all levers of power, especially economic power. Bagchi
exhaustively shows how the British rulers deliberately prevented
Indians from becoming skilled mechanics, refused contracts to
Indian firms which produced materials that could be got from
England, and generally hindered the formation of an autonomous
industrial structure in India. Only British-owned industrial activities were allowed, and their owners showed their gratitude by
buying British-made products at prices that rose while those of the
exports from other industrial nations fell.[21] This particular aspect
did not bother British merchants in India, who could pass increased prices on to consumers.

The complete dependence of the Indian market was also assured
by the banking and monetary policy of the British Raj. The banks
established in Bengal and in Madras never had an Indian director
from 1876 to 1914; this was also true of all other large Indian
banks. Presidency banks, owned by British subjects, received
deposits from the government and from other public bodies without paying on them one *anna* of interest. In 1900, such deposits
represented a fifth of all bank deposits with Indian-owned banks.
No Indian had anything to do with the management of the Foreign
Exchange Banks, which financed the country's foreign trade.[22]

By such methods, Britain succeeded, in the period under discussion, in establishing a complex, delicate and vital relationship
with her Empire. The nature of this relationship is best explained
by reference to examples. Of Britain's total exports in 1913, according to Werner Schlote's authoritative study[23] the following
percentages went to the Empire:

[20] A. Bagchi, mimeograph on *European and Indian Entrepreneurship in
India, 1900–1930*, kindly made available by Prof. Bagchi.
  [21] As is very clearly shown in a graph constructed by Maizels, *op. cit.,*
p. 208.
  [22] Noted by Bagchi, *op. cit.*
  [23] W. Schlote, *British Overseas Trade from 1700 to the 1930s*, Oxford 1952.

Motor vehicles	67·4	Knives and cutlery	57·2
Copper & bronze ware	64·8	Soap	54·3
Electrical products	61·6	Dyes	48·8
Books	60·1	Arms & ammunition	48·8
Pharmaceuticals	59·9	Iron & iron ware	48·2
Locomotives	58·6	Tobacco products	44·5
Railway carriages	58·4	Machinery	32·5

These figures can be supported by further, more detailed, evidence: in 1910–11, India alone absorbed 38·7% of all British exports of finished cotton goods;[24] while from 1896 to 1913, British exports of finished woollens fluctuated as follows:

	Heavy all wool	Heavy mixed wool	Light all wool	Light mixed wool
1896				
(a) British possessions	17%	9	38	72
(b) Rest of the world	83	81	62	78
1913				
(a)	30	43	33	54
(b)	70	57	67	46

British locomotive production was divided as follows (in total units):

	Home	Foreign	India	Europe	Rest of Empire	Latin America	Others	Total
1860–89	5891	8979	3418	2480	1463	1037	581	14870
1890–1913	3711	13899	5542	770	3016	3090	1471	17600

And exports of British footwear were allocated as follows (in thousands of dozen pairs):

[24] The following data, concerning British exports of textiles, locomotives, shoes, engineering products, and shipping, are taken from the various essays contained in *The Development of British Industry and Foreign Trade Competition, 1875–1914,* ed. by D. H. Aldcroft, London 1968.

	Total	Australasia	South Africa	India	West Indies	Other
1895–99	661	195	246	36	55	92
1910–14	1304	270	841	150	41	462

The surprising ability of British exports to resist competition in Imperial markets, as compared with their weakness in the markets of independent countries, is demonstrated in the following table, in which are listed the totals of mechanical products exported from Germany and the UK, and their destinations. Figures are for 1912, and are expressed in thousands of pounds:

Export Market	France, Russia, Italy		British Empire		Argentina, Brazil, Chile (1911)	
Product	GB	Germany	GB	Germany	GB	Germany
Locomotives	50	896	1281	96	657	410
Pumps	79	181	250	18	49	43
Other engines	626	2143	1299	393	178	119
Agric. machinery	1073	1295	368	46	204	132
Boilers	241	162	642	1	195	35
Machine tools	209	1621	271	105		
Mining machinery	37	82	697	12		
Sewing machinery	901	944	319	151	408	212
Textile machinery	1792	1095	1431	28	26	9
Typewriters	11	118	8	7	4	23
Automobiles	436	1666	2153	317	226	443
Motor cycles	306	313	1384	266	53	24
Utensils	304	1077	1216	134	523	308
Railway cars	5	184	1120	59	1242	323
Arms and ammunition	205	211	2048	201	265	1027
Other machines	1032	3022	3581	257	946	1274
Totals	7037	15010	18066	1811	4650	4372

From a total of £973,000 worth of electric cables exported from England £661,000 went, in 1913, to the Empire. In the same year, out of a total of £2,632,000 worth of telegraph and telephone cable exported, £1,779,000 went to the Empire. Also in 1913, from a total of £283,000 worth of electric bulbs exported, £162,000 worth went to the Empire; while England imported £479,000 worth of electric bulbs, almost entirely from Germany.

Focusing our attention again on India, we may note that, between 1899 and 1913, imports of manufactured goods into that country increased as follows (in million dollars at constant prices):

Products	Country of Origin GB	Germany	World
Metal manufactures			
a) 1899	10	1	13
b) 1913	34	10	50
Machinery			
a)	8	0	9
b)	24	1	28
Transport material			
a)	8	8	9
b)	17	1	19
Chemical products			
a)	4	3	8
b)	9	5	17
Textiles and clothing			
a)	140	8	155
b)	197	9	226
Other manufactures			
a)	20	4	33
b)	35	8	54

Source: Maizels. *op. cit.*

In 1913, exports from Britain represented 80.4% of the total exports of manufactured goods to India, while the German share was 8.5%. By contrast, the German share of total exports of manufactured goods to Britain was 32.3%, and 30.6% to the US (compared to the 26.6% of Britain). The German share of all manufacturing exports to Latin America was 25.1%, whereas the English share was 31.3%; the German share in western Europe was 30.9% while the English share was 22.1%. Germany supplied only 5.3% of the total imports of manufactured goods to Britain's southern Dominions while Britain supplied 72.5%.[25]

The same trend can be detected in a sector of activity which was a traditionally British affair: merchant shipping. The number

[25] Data quoted by Maizels, *op. cit.*

of ships bearing the Union Jack, while decreasing in the independent ports of the world, increased in Imperial ports, as can be seen from the following table:

	% 1880	% 1900	% 1911
UK	70·4	63·7	59·9
Germany	38·1	26·9	23·0
Holland	49·8	41·7	30·5
Sweden	13·5	9·9	5·4
Belgium	59·4	44·6	44·1
France	40·6	40·8	36·1
Italy	34·3		28·7
Norway	11·8	10·9	9·8
Portugal	63·0	56·8	47·6
Denmark	11·4	7·8	5·1
USA	51·7	52·8	50·1
Japan		38·9	30·5
Argentina	37·8	29·3	33·5
Chile	79·9	50·1	50·7
Canada	65·4	61·0	69·9
New Zealand	88·0	91·8	96·8
South Africa	85·6	89·8	80·0
India	79·1	79·0	76·0
British Possessions	70·4	63·7	91·9*
			*(1905–08)

In a well-known article,[26] Gallagher and Robinson coined the definition 'free trade imperialism' to describe the imposition by the British government of the doctrine of free trade on unwilling trade partners in the age of British industrial monopoly, i.e. in the two decades following the first half of the nineteenth century. In my opinion, this definition may be aptly employed to analyse the international economic situation during the quarter-century before 1914. Although Great Britain was to an increasing degree being excluded from both the European and Latin American markets by Germany and the US, she nonetheless managed to create the export surplus she needed to square her international trade accounts by mono-

[26] 'The Imperialism of Free Trade' in *Economic History Review*, 1953.

polising the Empire markets, where her producers could off-load
the goods they had difficulty in selling elsewhere. While she kept
alive both the letter and the spirit of free trade within her national
territory, Britain allowed only the letter within her dependencies.

The evidence we have examined clearly points to the fact that,
in this period, the pivot of the international settlement system was
India. This is shown even more clearly by a diagram drawn by
Professor S. B. Saul[27] which is here reproduced:

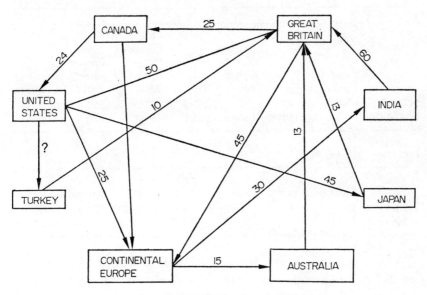

Arrows indicate direction of compensation

Figures are in £m sterling

At this juncture it will be valuable to introduce into our discussion a very important topic: long term capital movements. The
period under consideration saw a veritable boom in this type of
transaction. Most of the capital is known to have come from Britain, mainly in the form of re-investment of income earned on
previously invested capital.

Since British investment always preferred temperate areas of
recent settlement, it has often been stated that the economic explanation of Imperialism does not square with the facts. But this
statement must be reconsidered in the light of the wealth of detailed

[27] *Studies, op. cit.,* p. 6.

material, made available some time ago by Matthew Simon,[28] concerning new issues on the London Stock Exchange. After slightly reorganising the date, we arrive at the following table:

New Foreign Issues on the London Stock Exchange (Millions of £)

	Europe	N. America	S. America	Africa	Asia	Australia	Oceania	Total
1870–89	251	380·1	340·3	67·6	131·1	201·2	1·7	1272
1890–1914	244·7	997·1	470·3	345·0	423·8	227·4	7·1	2715·7

	Independ. Countries	British Empire	Regions of Colonisation	Tropics	Other Countries (Non-British Asia)	% of Empire within Total	% of Indep. Countries
1870–89	804·8	442	713·2	267·3	17·9	35·5	64·5
1890–1914	1497·6	1104·4	1636·7	623·1	186·0	43·5	57·5

Percentages of Total

	Europe	N. America	S. America	Africa	Asia	Australia	Oceania
1870–89	19·71	29·85	18·87	5·31	10·29	15·80	0·13
1890–1914	9·01	36·71	17·32	12·70	15·60	8·37	0·26

Although Simon gave the annual statistics from 1865 to 1914, he did not re-group them into sub-periods, as I have done here. Such a subdivision is useful, as it allows certain interesting observations to be made.

First, we can see the increased importance of investment in the British Empire in the period 1890–1914, as compared with the previous era. And second, we can see that investment in Europe and North America remained important throughout this period. The first of these facts is denied by Simon, who maintains that he is unable to find in his data any 'proof of a tendency to invest in that area, at the expense of independent countries'—although this tendency has been noted by writers such as S. B. Saul and A. R. Hall. In fact, according to Saul, 'the long period trend (for investment) was to abandon Europe in favour of raw material producing countries,

[28] M. Simon, 'The Pattern of New British Portfolio Investment, 1865–1914', in J. H. Adler, ed., *Capital Movements and Economic Development*, London 1967.

in particular those of the Empire'. What Simon does not realise is that the United States must be included among the primary producers. Our reorganisation of Simon's data also highlights the growth of the Empire's share in the period 1890–1914, compared with the previous twenty years. By contrast, the independent countries' share fell from 64·5% to 57·5%. The greatest relative dynamism is shown by Africa and Asia: the share of the former increased from 5·31% to 12·70%; the latter from 10·29% to 15·60%. Investment in Africa, in absolute terms, was in the latter period five times greater than in the former; investment in Asia four times greater. At the same time Europe's share of the total fell from 19·71% to 9·01%.

The data show, however, that in the second period, which is the age of 'great imperialism', investment in Europe and in North America was still 46·72% of the total of British investment overseas. If we add the 17·32% invested in South America, we get 64%. This marked preference of British capital for the independent countries would seem to constitute evidence of the 'non-imperialistic' nature of British investment. But that is not sufficient to deny the value of the so-called 'economic basis' of British imperialism. British capital went where it hoped to reap the highest return. The Empire seems to have offered better earning prospects to investors in the second period than it had in the first; at least, so our data seem to indicate. But it is clear that the best chances for profit existed in the temperate countries of recent settlement. British capital exporters realised this very well and their preference for those countries, which were those with which Britain had large visible trade deficits, created additional problems for the British balance of payments. The solution to the British payments equation was found, as we have seen, by creating and maintaining a trading surplus with the Empire, mainly with India. British imperialism was a complex phenomenon, from the economic point of view. Britain lost to Germany and the United States the race to produce and export 'new' products. She remained tied to 'old' products and found a sheltered market for them in the Empire. The Empire could pay for them because it sold primary commodities to the rest of the world. Thus Britain strove to keep her Empire industrially under-developed while she tried to bolster its ability to earn foreign exchange as an exporter of primary commodities. By so doing, she managed to exist without having to re-structure her industry and was able to invest her capital in the countries where it gave the highest return. To an increasing degree, British capital did not create a matching demand for British exports. British fiananciers were not compelled to 'tie' their loans to British exports because the Imperial outlet was always available for British products.

This complex arrangment, however, was two-edged. It allowed Britain not to be pressured into putting her industrial house in order and into earning good profits by engaging freely in international financial activities. But at the same time, by keeping the Empire, particularly India, under-developed, British industry became geared to a static, under-developed market, which could not absorb more than a certain amount of industrial commodities, while it generated higher and higher foreign trade surpluses with the rest of the world by selling primary commodities. It thus became necessary for Britain to control those surpluses, which really meant controlling the monetary policy of her Empire. How she managed to do so, we shall see in detail in the pages that follow.

THREE

The Spread of the Gold Standard in the World—
a short review

As in other respects, so also in this, the nineteenth century relied on the future permanence of its own happy experiences and disregarded the warning of the past misfortunes. It chose to forget that there is no historical warrant for expecting money to be represented even by a constant quantity of a particular metal, far less by a constant purchasing power. Yet Money is simply that which the State declares from time to time to be a good legal discharge of money contracts. In 1914 gold had not been the English standard for a century or the sole standard of any other country for a half a century. There is no record of a prolonged war or a great social upheaval which has not been accompanied by a change in the legal tender, but an almost unbroken chronicle in every country which has a history, back to the earliest dawn of economic record, of a progressive deterioration in the real value of the successive legal tenders which have represented money.

Moreover, this progressive deterioration in the value of money through history is not an accident, and has had behind it two great driving forces—the impecuniosity of Governments and the superior political influence of the debtor class.[1]

This long quotation from Keynes's *Tract* will be the guiding light for my interpretation of the development of the international

---

[1] J. M. Keynes, *A Tract on Monetary Reform*, London 1923, p. 9.

monetary system from 1870 to 1914. This was the time, especially
between 1890 and 1900, when a very large number of countries
attempted to get on the gold standard. The governments of countries as diverse as Germany, Austria, Hungary and Argentina all
tried their hand at monetary reform, and all in the pursuit of a
common objective, which was sometimes reached, but more often
missed. The move towards gold is the more interesting because it
involved such disparate nations.

Triffin recently observed[2] that the statement that the nineteenth
century was the century of great price oscillations has been proved
valid by exacting tests. From the beginning of the century until
1914 the downward trend of wholesale prices was clear and pronounced. Within that trend, fluctuations were frequent and profound. Upward and downward phases are easily identified. The
twenty-five years we consider here contained both a downward
and an upward phase. For our purposes, however, it is the downward phase, from 1873 to 1896, that matters most. It was during
this period that most of the monetary reforms took place whose
general aim was the adoption of the gold standard.

To what can this famous price-slump be attributed? Those
monetary economists who believed in the quantity theory had no
doubt: the years of falling prices had also been years of falling
money supply. If the *numeraire* was scarce, its value in terms of
goods had necessarily to rise, i.e. prices had to fall. To this *reductio
ad unum* made by the monetary school the passage of time has
not added conviction. Subsequent years have produced numerous
and varied alternative explanations of the 'great price depression'.[3]
It is worth rehearsing the most interesting of them. Before we do
so, however, we should recall what was said in the previous chapter: that the years of the Great Depression were also the years of
the Second Industrial Revolution, whose basic feature was the
mass production of industrial commodities. They were, in addition, the years of the transport revolution—of the combination of

[2] R. Triffin, *The Evolution of the International Monetary System, op. cit.,*
p. 12.
[3] The neo-quantitative interpretation of Milton Friedman has also been
offered. See his *Monetary History of the US 1869–1960,* written with A. J.
Schwartz, Princeton 1963. Friedman's quantity theory, however, reaches
such a level of refinement, that it really becomes a sort of Marshallian
demand for money theory. On this subject, see H. G. Johnson, 'Monetary
Theory and Policy' in *American Economic Review,* 1963.

steam and steel which revolutionised merchant shipping, and of
the penetration of railways into continents. All of which meant
lower prices for raw materials and finished goods, at least at the
wholesale level. The transport revolution brought huge cargoes
of New World cereals to European ports, thus disrupting European
cereal markets, as demand was not high enough to absorb the
increased supply. Prices slumped. The same thing happened to
the prices of industrial products when mass-produced articles appeared. The phenomenon was, it is true, less striking in the latter
case, as demand for those goods was much more volatile. There
were, however, other reasons behind the different behaviour of the
prices of primary commodities and industrial products. Market
structures, for instance, differed widely for the two classes of
goods. In primary commodity markets free competition reigned
even more than today, whereas the markets for industrial products
were dominated, to a very great extent, by a handful of producers:
Britain, Germany, the United States, France, Belgium, Italy. International trade in modern manufactures was still a basically
Anglo-German affair.

W. Layton, in his still very useful *Introduction to the History of
Prices*,[4] reckoned that between 1871–75 and 1894–98 the decrease
in price of products with a low value added was of the order of
40%. Leaders of his list were sugar (– 58%), petroleum (– 58%),
soda (– 54%), cotton (– 54%), tea (– 54%), silk (– 53%), wheat
(– 51%), wool (– 50%), iron in bars (– 49%), pig-iron (– 48%),
maize (– 47%), and tin (– 46%). Another 14 primary products
followed, including all basic minerals and textile raw materials,
whose price reductions ranged from 43% to 35%.

These data will exemplify the phenomena we have mentioned.
European agriculture was assailed and disrupted by New World
products. In reply, sugar beet was widely sown, with the result
that the price of sugar slumped, as we have seen. Iron was replaced
by steel; soda was being produced with the help of new technology;
and petroleum, thanks especially to J. D. Rockefeller's Standard Oil
Trust, was produced in hitherto unknown quantities. Enormous
mines were opened and began to produce huge quantities of the
principal raw materials.

The price of silver was every bit as much of a preoccupation.

4 London 1914.

In 1870, except for Great Britain, who had adopted the gold standard in 1821 by reintroducing gold convertibility, only Portugal had her currency tied to gold, which she had adopted as the only standard in 1854—undoubtedly because of her 'special relationship' with England. All the major European States, plus China and India, were on total, or at least partial, silver standards. The United States maintained the inconvertible currency they had introduced at the time of the Civil War.

Between 1814 and 1870, the price of silver had not been much of a problem: from $60\frac{11}{16}$d. in 1814 it had dropped only to $60\frac{9}{16}$d. in 1870. Nor had it ever gone below a minimum price of $59\frac{1}{2}$d. In the more recent period it had decreased steadily from the maximum of $62\frac{1}{16}$d., reached in 1859 (see Table 8). The gold/silver parity had, in the same period, shown almost the same constancy; oscillations had been experienced only at the time of the great gold discoveries in California (1849–50).

In 1872, however, the price of silver began to slump more and more rapidly. In 1876 it fell from $56\frac{7}{8}$d. to $52\frac{3}{4}$d. In 1880 it was $52\frac{1}{4}$d., in 1890 it had reached $47\frac{11}{16}$d., and in 1900 it was worth $27\frac{3}{8}$d. The gold/silver ratio followed the same pattern. In 1876 it was 17·88, in 1880 18·05, in 1890 19·78, in 1900 34·45.

In explaining the fall in the price of silver, the 'supply' factor must be taken into account; but its role should not be overemphasised. The annual supply of silver between 1811 and 1880 increased almost fivefold. But gold supply in the same period increased much more. In 1801–10 annual silver production was 50 times that of gold, in 1841–45 only 15 times, and in 1851–60 only 5 times. This drastic increase in gold production was not, however, accompanied by a decrease in the price of gold in any way comparable to the fall in the price of silver which took place in the last three decades of the century.

But the not very serious fall in the price of gold caused by the California discoveries was enough to convince several governments —those of Switzerland, the Kingdom of Naples, Spain, India and Belgium—to demonetise gold. In those countries silver was made the only standard: this decision made the solution of the opposite problem, that of demonetising silver, very difficult when the problem arose 20 years later. The decision to adopt a pure silver standard had in fact been taken on the eve of European industrialisation and of the international victory of the free trade principle. From 1851 to 1866 the international economy experienced a period of great prosperity, of rising prices, of fast increasing international transactions. The end came with the crash of the London finance house of Overend, Gurney. It was in that decade that gold became supreme as a means of exchange and of transaction. The growth of the unit value of transactions favoured its use. The difference between buying and selling points would have been much greater if silver, rather than gold, had to be transported to settle transactions among nations, or even between distant points within the same national boundaries. This was certainly an important element in determining the easy absorption of the much enlarged gold supply. On the other hand, it can be given as one of the reasons for only a slight increase in the gold/silver ratio when a much greater one was expected on account of the California discoveries. The beginning of European industrialisation also led to increased imports from Britain, the only country on the gold standard. Sterling acquired in this period its dominating status, as an 'international means of exchange', helped in no small way by British supremacy in banking and merchant shipping. General prosperity also allowed the silver crises to be postponed until immediately after the 1866 crisis. To the great chagrin of the silver standard countries, the beginning of depression coincided with a remarkable increase in silver production.

In the 1850s monetary authorities all over Europe had been principally concerned with the problems arising from the heavy arbitrage transactions that had taken place among France, Belgium and Holland. In 1850 Belgium had a stock of new silver coins, while the French silver coins were very worn (the loss in weight could be as high as 8%). It was therefore profitable to export French coins to Belgium, having bought them with gold coins, and use them there for the needs of trade, at a lower cost than would have been incurred if silver had to be minted into Belgian coins. Alternatively, French silver coins could be taken to Belgium, exchanged there at par for Belgian 'heavy' coins, and the latter exported to Germany or the Netherlands. These opportunities were not missed by speculators: Belgium saw about 85% of the coin she had in circulation disappear beyond her borders, to be replaced by 'light' French coin. French coinage also found its way into Switzerland, where 'heavy' coin was in circulation. Between 1861 and 1864, the strong demand for silver to be shipped to the East finally deprived Belgium of all her coin. In 1862, moreover, Italy adopted a monetary standard of the French type; her coin, however, contained only 0·835 pure silver, compared to the 0·900 contained by French coin. In a short time, Italian coin invaded France.

These difficulties played a large part in convincing European countries that they had to discuss monetary co-operation. In 1865, representatives of France, Italy, Belgium and Switzerland met in Paris at what was called the 'Latin Monetary Convention'. All the participant countries except France expressed a desire to adopt the gold standard. But France was opposed to this policy, so that the Latin Monetary Union, which sprang from the Convention, agreed to keep bi-metallism on a gold/silver parity of 1 to 15½, and to mint silver coins with a 0·835 silver content. The quantity of silver to be coined was fixed at 6 francs per inhabitant of each country. The Latin Monetary Union—it was agreed—would last 15 years.

Thus, on the very eve of the great fall in the price of silver, the nations of the Latin Monetary Union agreed on a policy that most of them did not like: Belgium and Italy had both expressed themselves in favour of gold. But what induced France, whose citizens had since 1848 shown so much greed for gold as repeatedly to embarrass the Bank of France, and which was already well endowed with gold, to demand a continuation of bi-metallism? The question is difficult to answer. The Bank of France was certainly not eager to be deprived of the discretionary powers it had been given by Napoleon, when he had founded it in 1803. And French high finance was in favour of bi-metallism. Both the House of Rothschild and the *Comptoir d'Escompte* instructed their directors to declare their firms' predilection for the double standard. It has been suggested that the double standard offered so many lucrative arbitrage possibilities that it would be unlikely that financiers would object to it.[5] And we cannot forget that those were the years of the greatest glory of the Second Empire, when it was the Emperor's express desire to see all Continental Europe united in a franc-area which would exclude and isolate Germany.

Even before the outbreak of the financial crisis precipitated by the fall of the price of silver, the Latin Monetary Union was shaken

[5] See H. Parker Willis, *The Latin Monetary Union*, Chicago 1900. On silver depreciation, it is interesting to read W. Bagehot, *On the Depreciation of Silver*, London 1877.

by a commotion which originated in Italy. On May 1, 1866, the Italian government declared the inconvertibility of its currency. This was the finale of the policy of financial expansion which Italy had pursued from 1859 to 1865. In anticipation of a large tax revenue from recently annexed territories, the Government of the former Kingdom of Sardinia had borrowed heavily abroad—a total of 1875 million lire—thus financing on capital account a current account deficit in its balance of payments of 1333 million lire. From 1860 to 1865, the government's revenues covered only 50% of its expenditure. Thus the Italian 'Rente', issued at prices ranging from 80% to 65% of nominal value, had by 1866 already fallen in the Paris Bourse to 54·08. Arbitrageurs immediately began to send it back to Italy in exchange for Italian gold and silver coin. The *cours forcé* seemed to the Italian authorities to be the only way out. Such a measure, however, was certainly against the spirit of the Latin Union. In addition, the repatriation of Italian government stock which, as we have seen, took place in exchange for

Movement of Precious Metals between France and Italy (millions of pounds sterling)

Year	Exports from France to Italy	Exports from Italy to France	Excess of French exports	Excess of Italian exports
1860	2,852	2,356	0,496	
1861	4,832	2,044	2,188	
1862	4,392	2,116	2,276	
1863	8,080	3,824	4,256	
1864	5,836	5,988		0,092
1865	6,688	5,784	0,904	
Total	32,080	22,055	10,028	
1866	3,064	9,108		6,044
1867	1,140	7,256		6,116
1868	2,740	2,816		0,076
1869	0,596	4,064		3,468
1870	0,352	3,522		3,200
1871	0,232	4,620		4,388
1872	0,320	4,212		3,892
Total	8,444	35,628		27,684

Source: *Report of the Royal Commission on the depreciation of silver*, HMSO, London 1876.

Italian coin, inundated France with Italian silver which, as we have also seen, contained less pure metal than its French counterpart. The outflow of precious metals from Italy and the inflow into France are documented in the table on page 45.

Very few people believed that the Italian government would, in the near future, recall its light silver coin in exchange for 'heavy' coin. Thus, even before the price of silver had begun its precipitous descent, the Latin Monetary Union had, because of Italian monetary policy, been disrupted by a crisis which revealed the artificial and archaic basis on which it was founded. The Italian monetary difficulties demonstrated the Union's basic shortcomings: it was supposed to unify several national monetary systems; but each country went on choosing the course it preferred in economic policy, without any attempt at harmonisation. The Italian monetary difficulties were, in fact, the result of the Italian government's expenditure of very large sums on its 'pacification policy' in the conquered South, on a new war with Austria, and on the building of a railway network—all of which, as we have seen, had to be done with only small help from tax revenues.

Another example of how the Latin Monetary Union was ill-equipped to unify its member countries' monetary systems was provided by the Franco-Prussian War of 1870. Again, arbitrage was rampant: masses of coins were exported from those countries which produced 'bad' coins, exploiting the high degree of monetary unity that had been achieved. But at the same time, and for the same reasons, the inflationary flow generated within the Union induced gold to flee its member countries altogether, so that they were left with only their inflated silver currency.

The fall of silver, which began in 1872, came, therefore, to aggravate an already difficult situation in the Union countries. In the whole Union, inflation made it possible to coin only 55.5 million francs in 1872, in five-franc pieces.[6] At the same time, silver began to be dumped on the markets of those countries that still permitted its free coinage. Germany had gone on the gold standard the year before, followed almost immediately by the Scandinavian countries. It is commonly held that she had managed to do so because of the war indemnity paid to her by France in gold. On the contrary, however, the indemnity was paid in bonds

[6] Willis, *op. cit.*

which were exchanged for gold in London, as we know from Bagehot and Willis. The Netherlands followed the German example in 1873. In that year, the United States forbade the free coinage of silver, and adopted a programme of official silver purchases. The East had, at the same time, reduced its absorption of silver. India imported only 4·7 million dollars' worth in 1870–71 and 3·5 million in 1872–73.[7] In 1869, the Madras mint had been closed, so that only the mints at Calcutta and Bombay were now operating. Persia had, at the same time, tried to put a brake on the outflow of gold resulting from the inflow of silver, by means of the Nasr-el-Dinh Sha decrees, which ordered the unification of all the mints in the country. In 1872, Japan also decreed the limitation of silver coinage to the Osaka mint. In the meantime, silver production doubled. From 1871 to 1875 production has been estimated to have been 2000 tons a year. Therefore, although gold production remained stationary at about 180 tons a year, the silver/gold ratio began to increase markedly.

The countries of the Latin Monetary Union, Austria-Hungary (which had, with a rare sense of opportunity, re-established silver as the *sole* standard in 1870), Russia, and the Eastern countries, became the object of all efforts of international arbitrage to deprive them of their gold, to export inflation to them through silver sales, and to make the exclusive value of their currencies slump. The largest part of the silver stream went, however, to flood the money supply of the Latin Monetary Union, both because its members were rich countries and because they were near to the greatest precious metals market, namely London. These countries, which owing to their internal problems had been compelled to resort to paper inflation, were, owing to the silver price slump, also obliged to accept silver inflation. To avoid the continuation of the latter at least, France and Belgium decided in September 1873 to limit the coinage of silver. What has been since known as 'limping bimetallism' was thus introduced in the Union; it was later to be codified. When the Latin Monetary Union held its conference in Paris, in 1874,[8] it clearly emerged that, although all members wanted to go on the gold standard, the 'limping standard' would

[7] See L. Laughlin, *History of Bimetallism in the US*, New York 1896.
[8] On international monetary conferences, see A. E. Janssen, *Les Conventions Monetaires Internationales,* Paris 1895, and J. Russell, *International Monetary Conventions*, New York 1898.

be retained as a compromise solution. One reason for this was that Italian silver coin was still circulating in large quantity in the Union; so had the Union adopted the gold standard, it would have had to ask Italy to redeem her silver coin—and, in view of prevailing Italian economic conditions, one could easily imagine what her reply would be.

The limping standard received its official sanction in the Union between 1874 and 1878. The price of silver had crashed in 1876; in the same year France had stopped silver coinage by law. Belgium had indefinitely suspended the coinage of the five-franc piece.

The only advocate of silver now left in the Union was, predictably, Italy. In 1878, at the International Monetary Conference in Paris, the United States tried in vain to bring the Latin Union back to bi-metallism. Belgium and France were too firmly against it, while the French government had just finished paying off its debt to the Bank of France, so that the *cours forcé* had come to an end. However, at the Latin Union Assembly the same year, Italy declared her intention of continuing to coin five-franc silver pieces. The Union grudgingly approved, provided no more than a total of 20 million francs were coined. But it was also agreed that the Italian was to be the last silver coinage. Subsequently, silver coinage was to stop for ever. The other members also contrived that Italy should put her signature to a joint declaration which stressed the necessity of redeeming silver coins that were in foreign hands. Italy signed, but was openly unenthusiastic about the declaration: about 100–120 million lire of her divisionary silver coin still remained in the hands of foreigners, in addition to an even larger sum in five-franc pieces. That mass of silver offered scope for diplomatic manoeuvring. It hung like a sword of Damocles over Italy, and was a 'persuasive argument' in the hands of France, the country that held most of the Italian silver. At the same time, her partners' fear that Italy might renounce her obligation to redeem her silver gave Italy the 'final word' on the Union's economic policy. The 1878 compromise is a good example of the delicacy of the situation. Italy managed to obtain her partners' approval for her to coin silver pieces, but still had to sign the final protocol that stressed the Union's adherence to the principles of *interruption* and *redemption*. And in 1879 the Union, which was due to expire that year, was instead renewed again, from fear of irresponsible Italian action in the silver coinage field.

However, the 'Italian problem' was soon to be solved politically, when the Tunisian question shattered Franco-Italian relations. Italy decided to shed the poor man's guise, and gave instructions to the Bank of France to collect all Italian divisionary coin held by foreigners, which would be redeemed at its face value. This marked the beginning of the ill-fated Italian attempt to return to convertibility. Cabinet ministers Magliani and Miceli presented their plan to return to convertibility in November 1880: Parliament duly approved it. The plan called for the launching of an international loan of 644 million lire to stabilise Italy's currency by redeeming her paper currency in circulation. The loan was to be subscribed in gold, for 444 million, and in silver, for 200 million. It would be paid for with Italian government stock, sold at 88·5% of its nominal value. 729,749,000 lire of bonds were therefore issued, which could be bought in Italian gold and silver or with foreign currency valued at fixed exchange rates. The loan was underwritten by two groups of financiers; one British and the other composed of Dutch, Belgian, German and Italian banks. French bankers refused (because of Tunis) to join in the operation, which was concluded between 1881 and 1882. Meanwhile, Italy had instructed the Bank of France to collect foreign-owned Italian divisionary coin. The Bank duly collected 79 million lire worth. Thus, on this peculiar form of 'currency change', Italy earned a profit of 20 to 40 million. The cause was that common to all currency changes—the coins were often in the hands of people who knew nothing of the possibility of redeeming them, or knew it but did not bother to use their knowledge.

The operation was, however, limited to divisionary coin. Another 300 million francs in Italian five-franc pieces remained in foreign hands, mostly in the Bank of France's vaults. Italy could certainly not afford to redeem such a large sum. As Italian-French relations worsened during the 1880s, Italy tried to cancel her debt, stealthily, by law. On February 22, 1881, Parliament approved the Abolition of Inconvertibility Bill under the terms of which, after January 1, 1886—i.e. after the expiry of the Latin Union—silver coins of foreign issue would no longer be legal tender in Italy, and provincial public treasuries would be instructed to accept them no longer. The same law ordained that Customs duties be paid in gold. On September 22, 1883, another law was passed, which decreed that at least two thirds of banking reserves should be kept in gold. In addition, banks were ordered not to accept silver in exchange for notes. It was a clear violation of the Latin Monetary Agreement. But it was the creditor, France, who held the knife by the handle. When mass redemption of the famous 300 million was threatened, the Italian government retreated, adopting a much more conciliatory attitude.

In spite of these difficulties the Latin Union still presented, at the International Monetary Conference of 1881, a united anti-silver front. Thus the defence of silver remained in the hands of Austria-Hungary, Russia and the United States, three countries which relied heavily on agricultural exports. The East was also in favour of silver. But India, as we shall see later, had to toe the line drawn for her by her British rulers. As for China and Persia, they had not yet joined the 'concert of nations'.

The case of the United States merits special attention. As we have seen, because of the disruption of the Civil War, the US had gone on the *cours forcé*, on which she would remain till 1879. As soon as the war ended, however, the American authorities began to organise the return of the dollar to gold convertibility. Before going on the *cours forcé* the country had been on a bi-metallic standard, with a preference for gold. But in 1873 Congress passed a Bill which suspended silver coinage. In the opinion of modern historians, that Bill was passed with the precise intention of putting the country on a pure gold standard after the return to convertibility. It had been presented, not surprisingly, by a Congressman from the Eastern seaboard, the industrial centre of the country. The suspension of silver coinage did not 'make news' until, a few years later, the American West entered the silver market as a major producer. American silver producers, who soon faced a falling world market, tried their best to dump their production on the United States Treasury, but the law of 1873 meant that the Treasury could no longer absorb it. The famous 'Silver Lobby' was thus born, which shortly included all the prophets of easy money, i.e. most of the representatives and senators from the agricultural West—a region forever in debt to the richer East, and therefore in favour of price increases which might help rid it of its burden of debt. The silver lobby was strengthened by a rather improbable alliance between great landowners, small farmers, owners of silver mines, workers and peasants, all convinced that their living standards were being lowered by a conspiracy of

Eastern financial interests, whose aim was apparently to make money as scarce and as expensive as it could possibly be. The degree of influence achieved by the silver lobby is demonstrated by the passing of two bills which introduced official purchases of silver: the Bland-Allison Act and the Sherman Act. The first was passed in 1878; the second in 1890 (and repealed in 1893). However, the silver party never did manage to obtain more than a programme of official purchases. The return to convertibility in 1879 put the country back on a pure gold standard. Moreover, while on the one hand the American government did concede something to the supporters of silver, on the other hand it began a campaign of official gold purchases to refurbish Treasury reserves —thereby causing the world scarcity of gold to increase. At the same time, the American government became the most eloquent exponent of a return to free silver coinage—in other countries. The United States promoted the convening of several international monetary conferences, at which her representatives tried to spread the bi-metallist gospel; always, however, with scant success.

The Sherman Act of 1890 may really be considered the swan song of the silver party. It was passed to persuade the South-West to accept the McKinley Tariff, which had been erected to reinforce protection of American industry. But by 1893 the Act had already been repealed. Henceforth, from its return to convertibility until 1914, the United States managed to amass an impressive gold stock, which was, as we shall see later, to have very serious consequences for international monetary equilibrium.

Following the Latin Union countries' adoption of the limping standard (which really amounted to the adoption of a gold standard plus a compromise solution for silver), the national and international defeats of the American silver party, and the great increase in silver production, the fate of that metal became very obscure indeed. Its price had been $52\frac{1}{4}$d. in 1880; by 1889 it had gone down to $42\frac{11}{16}$d. The national currencies that remained based on it thus lost 15% of their gold value, to which must be added a further 15% lost in the previous decade. At the same time, as we have noted, world prices of agricultural commodities slumped. Among the European countries, only Austria-Hungary and Russia remained tied to silver. Both were large exporters of agricultural products; and both were ruled by oligarchies deriving their power from land-ownership, who were therefore interested in maintaining the competitiveness of their products in world markets by means of a depreciating exchange. Continuous exchange depreciation constituted their last stand against the rock-bottom prices at which agricultural products were being sold by the United States.[9]

But even in those two countries the winds of change had begun to blow. In the 'dual monarchy' the conflict of interest was between the two components of the kingdom: Austria had started a process of industrialisation, while Hungary remained an immense granary. The former was bound to be against silver as much as the latter found it convenient to back it.

In Russia the conflict was not so clearly defined, territorially at least. A minority of innovators were shortly to install themselves in power; led by Count Witte, their aim was to build up a powerful industrial structure which would guarantee Russia's recognition as a major power in the international arena.

[9] On the monetary reforms of Austria-Hungary and Russia, there are two very good studies available, which are outdated as far as theoretical issues are concerned, but provide first-class factual evidence and comments inspired by unfailing common sense. They are Eteocle Lorini's *La Questione della Valuta in Austria Ungheria,* Turin 1892, and *La Riforma Monetaria della Russia,* Turin 1898. The author was sent by the Italian Treasury to observe the monetary reforms of other countries and report on them. He wrote two more equally valuable reports: *La Persia economica contemporanea,* Rome 1900, and *La Repubblica Argentina—e i suoi maggiori problemi di economia e finanza,* Rome 1902.

On Russian monetary reform see also M. Miller, *The Economic Development of Russia,* London 1926, ch. VI. On Austro-Hungarian and Russian monetary affairs, L. Yeager recently wrote an interesting if somewhat extravagant essay, 'Fluctuating Exchange Rates in the Nineteenth Century: The experiences of Austria and Russia', in *Monetary Problems of the International Economy,* ed. by R. A. Mundell and A. K. Swoboda, Chicago 1969.

On the main motives behind the Russian reforms, direct evidence is given by Count Witte in his autobiography. He added that, 'The reform was specially opposed by that section of the community which was interested in the export of commodities, particularly farmers. They held the erroneous idea that high prices due to the depreciation of the rouble were advantageous, but failed to realise that they had to pay correspondingly higher sums for imports' (Quoted by M. Miller, *op. cit.* pp. 106–107). Count Witte identified the groups against reform; but he did not distinguish between private and social interest, because the macro-economic loss from rouble depreciation coincided with the micro-economic gains of farmers and exporters.

In both empires, the promoters of industrialisation realised the need to put their respective monetary systems on the gold standard. Industrialisation, it was thought, could only be a speedy process if foreign capital intervened to stimulate it; foreign capital would come only if monetary stability reigned long enough in the capital-receiving countries—as income and perhaps the principal would have to be repatriated without losses. Silver could not guarantee monetary stability: there was no solution available other than the gold standard. Going on it would have meant a net loss of power for the landed aristocracy, and a net victory of creditors over debtors (the two consequences being, as will be realised, not mutually unconnected).

But it was the agricultural sector, in the Habsburg Empire, that was instrumental in supporting (and almost in initiating) currency reform. The first promoter of reform was in fact Wekerle, Finance Minister of the Hungarian Cabinet, who could count on a solid majority in the Budapest Parliament. Steinbach, his Austrian counterpart, would on the contrary have had difficulty in following his lead, because the majority the Austrian Cabinet enjoyed was only a slender one. To understand why the agriculturally minded Hungarian Parliament backed a currency reform that unseated silver, one has to remember that the year of the reform was 1892. As we have seen above, silver had, by 1889, fallen as low as 42d. an ounce; but in 1890 the passing by the United States of the Sherman Act induced a strong wave of bullish speculation. An international cartel had been formed, with the intention of controlling silver prices simultaneously with the introduction of the American legislation. By April, 1890, silver was back at 44¾d.; in August of that year, a week after the Sherman Act had taken effect, it jumped to 54⅝d. The cartel did not, however, manage to hold the price at that level for more than a month. In November it slipped down, to close the year at 47½d. A further decline had been prevented only by the massive purchases operated by the cartel, at the cost of huge financial outlay. Total demand had reached five million kilograms, as against four million kilograms actually produced that year. The difference had been more than covered by governments happily unloading their unwanted silver stocks on the market while the going was good. It was this huge de-stocking that transformed the defeat of the cartel into a ruinous rout: China alone sent 360,000 kilos of silver to the Indian market, while the Straits Settlements were flooded by 120,000 kilos. Rumania got rid of 25 million francs worth of silver, while Russia sold 10 million francs worth. It had been the cartel's aim to stabilise the price at the 'American par' of $1·29 an ounce (the equivalent of 59d.). But the maximum price they managed was 54d. The following two years were to see that price sink even lower. At the end of 1891 it closed at 54d.; at the end of 1892 it was down to 39d. In 1891 the Calcutta mint coined only 44·8 million rupees from silver sent from England and 21·2 million rupees from silver sent from China, compared with the 131·6 million coined in 1890. The price fell no lower only because Spain and Portugal bought 260,000 kilos and the United States 1,679,000 kilos.

The wild oscillations in the price of silver during 1890 inflicted heavy losses on Hungarian farmers. By the time they sold their crops, the gold premium had fallen from its previous level owing to bullish expectations about the price of silver. As international prices of agricultural commodities had remained unchanged, the revenue in Hungarian florins was reduced by more than 25% by the revaluation of that currency in terms of gold. The uncertainty that currency vagaries caused Hungarian farmers made them determine to link their fate to a currency less subject to oscillation: Count Wekerle's Reform Law correctly interpreted their feelings.

A further factor causing the Hungarian Parliament to favour putting the country on the gold standard was of a very different nature: the Austro-Hungarian State had in 1890 a short-term debt of 180 million florins, which fell on both governments of the Dual Monarchy. The debt consisted of 100 million of State notes and of 80 million of bills guaranteed by the government-owned salt mines. The latter part of the debt Hungary wanted Austria to bear alone, since she had incurred it alone before the Treaty of Union between the two countries. The Currency Reform Bill, placed before both Hungarian and Austrian Parliaments, therefore included an article proposing that a new stabilisation debt of 312 million florins be incurred, only 30% of which would be Hungary's responsibility. Hungary had in previous years amassed a gold stock of 50 million florins; she was thus much better placed than Austria, who had to find gold for 218 million. The ultimate Hungarian aim was, of course, to secure financial autonomy and to establish her own independent Central Bank. This she hoped to achieve by the Reform Bill.

Backed by such massive consensus, the Bill was approved by both Parliaments and implemented in 1892. It is worth noting that it did not include the abolition of the *cours forcé*: only the standard was changed, from silver to gold. The importance of this will soon be apparent.

The Russian currency reform took place four years later. Russia had been getting ready for it over a long period. When Germany and the Scandinavian countries had gone on gold, the then Russian Finance Minister, de Reutern, had already begun to limit silver coinage to the minimum, while at the same time increasing gold coinage and starting a policy of official gold purchases. By 1875 Russia had a gold reserve of 294 million roubles, 171 million more than in 1867, whereas during the same period, the fiduciary issue increased very little, from 709 to 797 million roubles. And in 1876 free coinage of silver had been suspended, while a gold standard experiment was conducted in Finland.

The transformation of the Russian system, begun by de Reutern, was carried on by Bunge and Wischnegradski, and full transition to gold took place under Witte. The actual timing of the reform seems to have depended on several favourable circumstances which Witte exploited to carry it through. The harvest had, in 1893–94, been 40% larger than the average for 1888–92. The tax on commercial profits, just introduced, had yielded a good revenue as it had been accepted without too much protest and was accordingly raised from 3% to 5%. Imports were growing; and customs duties revenue grew with them, especially from Europe, as a result of Witte's commercial treaties with France, Austria, and above all, Germany. Exports, too, were growing, gold production was on the increase, and the State-owned forests were yielding a large crop of wood.

The reform was of the same type as was implemented in other European countries in those years. A gold stabilisation loan of 100 million roubles was floated abroad against government stock sold at 92.30, which carried a 3% coupon. The terms were much less onerous than those at which the Russian government had been accustomed to borrow abroad. The loan was underwritten mainly in Paris; and its proceeds served to repay the debt the Russian government had incurred through its Central Bank, by the latter's issue of inconvertible notes. A further 65 million roubles of gold were purchased abroad by the government. £4 million of silver were also bought, to mint new silver coins. Finally, an *ukase* fixed the price of gold till 1898. The *cours forcé* was not repealed. Count Witte expressed the intention of putting gold into circulation, but only at a later date.

With the Russian reform, all the major European nations had thus, at the end of the century, achieved a remarkable homogeneity so far as their monetary systems were concerned. The gold standard had prevailed in most instances. In the continental countries, however, its features differed in detail from those of the English version, although most reforms had looked to the latter for inspiration. Gold convertibility had, in the various countries, reached varying degrees of completeness. For instance, Germany, who had reached an international economic position equal to that of Britain, allowed her citizens the prestige of a large gold circulation. So did France, the only country, with England, to be a creditor on capital account to the rest of the world. Germany and France, however, had furnished their monetary authorities with the ability to defend their gold reserves in case of need: the Bank of France could redeem its notes in silver whenever it deemed it necessary; the Reichsbank could issue fiduciary notes whenever it so wished and had to pay a tax only on such issues. The less economically powerful nations had transformed their metallic standard, but all had kept the *cours forcé* for their paper currency, as they rightly had little hope that gold would freely remain in their territories. Moreover, strategic considerations encouraged governments to build up defences against the possible outflow of their gold. Between 1890 and 1914, the political climate was often very tense, especially as far as the mutual relations of major powers were concerned. The need for a 'war treasure' had thus become a pressing one for most national authorities.

These selfsame reasons also induced the gradual transformation in most European countries of the gold standard into a gold exchange standard. The phenomenon did not escape Keynes' sharp eye: he explained the reasons for its cause in his masterly *Indian Currency and Finance,* published in 1913. The European nations and Japan were not, excepting France, creditors on capital account, as was Britain; nor did they have the latter's thoroughly developed banking structure. The English-type gold standard could not therefore be successfully imitated by them. Their Central Banks knew that it was not sufficient for them to alter their discount rate to cause gold to flow into or out of their countries. Unlike the Bank of England, they could not rely on a host of locally-based finance houses which could shift their resources from the home to the foreign market following any indication of change in discount rates. Monetary authorities, in the Continental countries and elsewhere, soon realised that they had to build a double line of defence—the outer layer consisting of foreign devises or foreign currency and short-term credits on foreign markets, the inner layer of gold reserves. As in the Bretton Woods System, countries that were basically long-term debtors had to equip themselves with short-term creditor positions, from which they could defend the parity of their currencies when threatened. Bloomfield and, more recently, Lyndert, have provided us with data on such countries' short-term credits, which, although incomplete, provide unambiguous evidence of the practice just described: forceful backing for Keynes' intuitions of 1913.

However, as was to happen with the gold exchange standards of the twentieth century, the *belle époque* was basically unstable and began to decline into a pure gold standard as the fateful year of 1914 approached. Of this, Keynes was again fully aware, and he considered it to be a dangerous involution. European monetary authorities, who had adopted gold as the sole standard, considered it as the reserve *par excellence* and saw their holdings of foreign currency as the means to protect it. The behaviour of the two forms of reserve indicates a very important difference: gold reserves grew much more than did foreign exchange reserves in the 15 years before 1914; at any rate, so presently available data would seem to suggest, and Keynes drew similar conclusions in 1913. Then, he condemned the *auri sacra fames* of European governments, as well as their propensity to run down foreign exchange reserves to protect their stocks of the ultimate asset, as pure idiocy on their part. However, he did not seem to grasp the most crucial aspect of the phenomenon he observed—namely that a stable gold exchange standard could exist only so long as the political sovereignty of the centre countries *vis-à-vis* the periphery remained unchallenged. That such is the case we shall abundantly prove in the next chapter when we review the monetary affairs of the British Empire, particularly those of India. Keynes' eulogy of the gold exchange standard, which he hailed as the international monetary system of the future, must therefore be considered as an *hepicedium*, a funeral song. In the following chapters, we hope to demonstrate that the 'guns of August' really demolished an international monetary system that had undergone 15 years of involution.

During the same period, the countries that would nowadays be referred to as 'under-developed' (i.e. the independent countries, most of which were then in Latin America) made repeated but rather ill-fated attempts to anchor their monetary systems to gold, in the wake of the industrial countries.

When we study pre-1914 monetary history, we find ourselves frequently reflecting how similar were the issues of monetary policy then at stake to those of our time. We have already seen that, following Keynes' interpretation, the debate on bi-metallism and silver may be regarded as a fight between debtors and creditors, industrial entrepreneurs and importers of manufactured goods struggling against producers and exporters of primary commodities. Both in all the European countries and in the United States, the three decades preceding the First World War witnessed industry prevail over agriculture, creditors over debtors. In some cases the traditional ruling elite was completely replaced at the helm of economic policy by a new class. In some other instances the *homines novi* succeeded only partially in their bid for power. The phases of the struggle were faithfully mirrored by events in the various monetary systems.

In Latin American countries, attempts to introduce the gold standard were doomed for precise reasons: as any industrialisation policy was, in these countries, generally absent, the debate on the gold standard—the debate between the supporters of stability and the promoters of inflation—followed rather different lines from those along which it moved in Europe. The ruling oligarchies of Latin America were composed of the owners of huge monocultural *latifundia,* who derived their income almost entirely from exports. They therefore had a vested interest in the continuous depreciation of their countries' currencies in terms of European currencies. As the national currencies depreciated, so the real income of agricultural labourers decreased, and so the *fazenderos'* real income increased, as the premium at which they exchanged their export proceeds for national currency went up. Labour costs were, in fact, met in local currencies. Foreign investors (that is, British finance houses and British private citizens) were, on the other hand, against depreciation and in favour of lasting monetary stability. The foreign owners of infrastructures, of mines, of *fazendas*, were interested in stability, as depreciation meant exchanging the profits they wanted to repatriate at unfavourable rates, thereby incurring a net reduction of returns on their investment. Those who had made hard currency loans to central or local Latin American governments were in the same boat as direct investors; not because they had foreign exchange problems, but because inflationary governments usually had difficulty in paying interest on, and repaying the principal of, hard-currency debts. The weaker voice of foreign immigrant workers joined in this chorus. They had to send money to families who still lived in their countries of origin, so they did not like to see the real value of their hard-earned wages eaten away by currency depreciation.

Where this chorus was strong enough to threaten the ruling oligarchies, stabilisation programmes were attempted. Such threats are, in my opinion, the key to an understanding of the motives behind Argentina's two attempts to go on the gold standard, and its actual adoption by Chile in 1892–95, Costa Rica in 1896, Panama in 1906, Ecuador in 1898, and Mexico in 1905. In all those countries, however, the ruling oligarchies' basic favour of monetary chaos was soon to prevail again, nullifying the effects of monetary reform.[10]

Japan was another matter: her adoption of the gold standard must be measured by the European yardstick.[11] The policy was calculated to bring Japan into the sphere of 'civilised nations', and was well suited to the country's prevailing interests. Swift modernisation and industrialisation had led to fast-rising imports; thus a strong currency would benefit the Japanese ruling class, especially as Japan was never a serious exporter of primary commodities.

Comparing Latin American monetary history with that of Japan is a fascinating exercise. Weak currencies were, as we have noted, well suited to Latin American power elites, while the opposite was true in the case of Japan. The Habsburg Empire and Russia were intermediate cases. Here, the economic interests of the ruling

---

[10] This is the interpretation of Lorini, *op. cit.*, for Argentina, and of A. G. Ford, in *The Gold Standard 1880–1914 in Britain and Argentina*, Oxford 1962.

[11] See H. Shinjo, *History of the Yen*, Kobe 1962.

class conflicted: whereas the newly-formed entrepreneurial class opted for a strong currency, the traditional landowners favoured a weak one. The conflicting interests were further tangled, since a self-styled entrepreneur was often himself of landowning stock. In these countries monetary reform largely stemmed from other causes, as we have shown above.

We have now reviewed the principal motives behind the transition to gold made by most countries in the period from 1870 to 1914, and the different forms that transition took in the various instances. From the dawn of the new century to the outbreak of the great European war, the adoption by most countries of some kind of gold standard had brought about a state of affairs which after the war would surely have been called a 'golden age'.

The international monetary system, as it developed in the course of our period, did not however possess—except to a very small degree—those features which were attributed to it by a bevy of post-war economists: men who were really seeking a magic formula to resurrect the pre-war world from its ruins. In none of the cases reviewed did those who implemented monetary reform have the slightest intention of linking their countries to an international monetary system which would then automatically produce a kind of international economic meritocracy, based on differences in prices and interest rates among the various nations. In reality, we have seen how silver was used until its inflation became intolerable; how, by going on to gold, countries tried to defend themselves against the immense slump in the price of primary commodities and silver. Where the ruling class could benefit from a depreciating standard, they kept silver in the saddle; and they never tried to change to gold—except, of course, for the wrong reasons. When they did decide in favour of such a change, it was sometimes in order to obtain political credit in their countries or hard-currency loans abroad; but more often their arm was simply twisted by other forces that, temporarily at least, challenged their supremacy. And, just as they had easily adopted gold, the ruling classes as carelessly repudiated it when, during and after the Great War, it did not suit their interests to retain it. However, nineteenth century public opinion did not create the Gold Standard Myth; nor did it believe in an *ubi consistam* of eternal duration as was claimed by Keynes in the passage quoted at the beginning of this chapter. After the Great War, it was the utopian jeremiads of a few daydreamers which were responsible for the distorted image of the pre-1914 gold standard that has been so commonly accepted ever since. But the present study clearly shows that international economic events followed a pattern which could not possibly be called automatic. The various governments adopted such economic policies as they deemed would best serve the interests of the ruling classes. They favoured fixed exchange rates when they were expedient and progressive devaluation when it appeared possible. Nor were they afraid to change course whenever they felt it was necessary. Moreover, uncertain and even downright self-contradictory economic policies were adopted—as they often are nowadays. It would therefore be misleading to postulate any important qualitative differences between the monetary policies of the period under review and those of our own time.

FOUR

Indian Monetary Vicissitudes—an interlude

The study of the monetary policy of the British Raj is interesting even if conducted merely for its own sake; it is certainly most useful as a component of our analysis. As has emerged in the second chapter, India had assumed in the 25 years under discussion the role of a protagonist of the international settlements system: her trade surplus with the rest of the world and her trade deficit with England allowed the latter to square her international settlements on current account. This enabled her to use the income from her overseas investment for further investment abroad, and to give back to the international monetary system the liquidity she had absorbed as investment income.

This, however, was not the only reason why India had an important place in the international monetary system. The reserves on which the Indian monetary system was based provided a large *masse de manoeuvre* which British monetary authorities could use to supplement their own reserves and to keep London the centre of the international monetary system. India had played a similar role in the period immediately preceding, when she had stemmed world inflation by absorbing huge quantities of silver which would have otherwise glutted the Western markets.

It is a common belief that India was always the silver standard country *par excellence*. This belief, like many others, has been proved to be false. Silver was imposed on India by the British.[1]

[1] On the establishment of the silver standard in India, see S. V. Doraiswami's perceptive book *Indian Finance, Currency and Banking*, Mylapore 1915, pp. 1–20.

The East India Company, which ruled India in the first decades of the nineteenth century, chose silver as the standard of value in 1806. In 1816 the Company forced silver rupees into circulation in Southern India, displacing the 'golden pagodas' of the Madras Presidency. This policy had a clear aim: to extract gold from circulation at a time when gold production was stationary and demand, especially because of the resumption of cash payments by the Bank of England, was running high.

In 1835 the government of India declared the silver rupee legal tender in the whole country; silver and gold rupees were coined at a 15:1 parity. Silver did not, however, become the sole standard until 1853, when Lord Dalhousie demonetised gold, forbidding its use for payments to the Treasury. This measure was adopted —at least so available sources state—in order to protect the flow of payments made by the government of India to the metropolis, at a time when gold prices were sagging as a result of the Californian discoveries. Moreover, in 1862, the government of India ordered that bank-notes issued by the Presidency Banks be withdrawn from circulation to be replaced by government-issued banknotes; thereafter, note issues were to be a monopoly of the Indian government. The notes were given a metallic reserve as guarantee, which was called the Paper Currency Reserve.

The monetary history of the British Raj was affected from the beginning by two major opponents: the businessmen (plantation-owners, industrialists, merchants), and the Raj itself. As was to be expected, the former were concerned to see India go, and remain, on a continuously depreciating standard, as their economic calculations were not very different from those we have attributed to the *compradores* of Latin America. On the other hand, the government of India wanted to maintain the country on as strong a monetary standard as possible; its main preoccupation was to appropriate the hard currency needed to cover the 'Home Charges' arising every year. The Home Charges consisted mainly of interest on debts to England incurred by the Raj, pensions of former Indian civil servants living in England, payments to the War Office for the upkeep of the Indian Army (and of the whole Imperial Army), and purchases of materials in England on the Raj's account, mostly effected through the government stores.

The two opponents' interests therefore conflicted; and from this conflict stemmed most of what may be called Indian monetary policy under the British Raj. However, during the period we are studying a third interest emerged—the India Office, the branch of British metropolitan administration whose job it was to supervise Indian affairs from London. At its head was the Secretary of State for India, a senior minister in the British Cabinet. Indian monetary policy, then, was the outcome of the interplay of these three separate centres of power.[2] As the period drew toward its close the power of the India Office grew, and its decisions were the ones that increasingly determined the course of Indian monetary history. In these years, the Office's staff included the best brains of the Civil Service—among them J. M. Keynes and Basil Blackett, men who had enjoyed a training in political economy far superior to that experienced by the average British entrepreneur or Indian civil servant. It was the India Office which demonstrated that the gold exchange standard was the monetary system best suited to India's needs. They were fully aware of the part played by the Indian monetary system in keeping both the British and the international monetary systems in equilibrium.[3]

When silver prices began to slump the conflict of interests that rent the expatriate commercial community and the Raj became more acute. As early as 1875, a report to the British government stressed the need to adopt a gold standard in India. In 1878, the Indian government submitted a proposal to close the mints to silver coinage, in order to induce the rupee to rise to 2 shillings. The proposal was studied by an ad hoc committee but was rejected in 1879. Over the next ten years the government of India continually urged Britain to allow her to adopt a gold standard; and in 1886 there was an official request to authorise the closing of Indian mints to silver coinage. But the India Office was adamant. Silver had fallen from 48d. to 45d. in one year; but in that decade the power of the British commercial community was unchallenged. Exchange stability was therefore unthinkable for the rupee. Continuous cur-

---

[2] And contemporary observers, from the Indian Currency Committee of 1895 to Alfred Marshall, saw it in these terms. The evidence given by Marshall to the Gold and Silver Commission, and to the Indian Currency Committee of 1898, is particularly noteworthy. On the second occasion, Marshall clearly identified the conflicting interests of the Indian government and of the exporters.

[3] See J. M. Keynes, *Indian Currency and Finance*, London 1913, and Basil Blackett's unpublished memorandum in the Public Record Office (Treasury Files T. 170 19), reproduced as an appendix to the present book.

rency depreciation—it was authoritatively argued—was the only remedy against world-wide falling prices, the only way of keeping Indian exports competitive in world markets.

After the failure of the official silver price support policy of the United States government and the forced demobilisation of the speculative positions of the 'silver corner', silver quotations, as has been noted, really crashed. In 1892 the London price had fallen to 39d. So the government of India reiterated its request to reinforce the rupee by closing the Indian mints to silver coinage—as had been done, for the same reason, in Austria-Hungary. The Secretary of State for India decided to submit the proposal to a committee, to which he appointed, among others, Sir Reginald Welby, General Richard Strachey and Bertram Currie: two financial experts and an 'old India hand'.[4] The committee's report was published on May 31, 1893. Without doubt it is the most lucid pre-Keynesian document on Indian monetary problems. The clarity of its analysis and the honesty of its approach to the problem are remarkable, particularly when compared to the sycophancy of later, similar documents. Seen in the light of the conflict of interests between British merchants and the Raj, it clearly emerges as a document inspired by a 'public' vision of Britain's responsibilities toward India.

The report began by noting, without beating about the bush, that the basic problem with the Indian monetary system stemmed from the fact that:

> the Government of India have yearly to remit a large sum to this country in discharge of their gold obligations. In 1873–74, before the fall [of silver] commenced, the amount remitted was £13,285,678, which at a rate of exchange of 1s. $\frac{10}{351}$ d., was represented by RX £14,265,700. During last year [1892–93] the amount remitted was £16,532,215, which, at the average rate of exchange in that year, viz. 1s. $\frac{2}{895}$ d. required payment of RX 26,478,415. If this could have been remitted at the exchange of 1873–74 it would have needed only RX 17,751,920. The difference is thus RX 8,726,495 (p. 7).

[4] *Report of the Committee Appointed to Inquire into the Indian Currency,* HMSO, London 1893. It is generally known as the 'Herschell Committee' as Lord Herschell, the Lord Chancellor, was its chairman.

The government of India's difficulties were made worse, the report hastened to add, by the fact that the fall in the exchange rate had brought protests from the government's own employees, both civil and military. They received their salaries in rupees, and asked for compensation for the losses suffered from the fall. Many of these officials, the report noted, had families to keep, and children to educate, in England—to whom they had to send gold. Several private companies had already agreed to similar requests from their employees. Up to that moment—the report went on to say—the difference between the value of the rupee and that of gold had been financed out of increased taxes; in particular, a tax on salt had been introduced. Thus the weight of fiscal imposition had been transferred from the shoulders of one class of Indians to those of another, the poorer class, who already suffered the greatest from the increases of rupee prices due to the falling exchange rate. In fact, the report noted, if price increases were followed by a slower increase of wages, they would necessarily harm the working classes.

The committee asserted that, if silver kept falling, the additional rupees needed to remit unchanged amounts of gold could certainly not be obtained by stiffer taxes. Land-tax rates were either fixed or could be reviewed only every 30 years. Income tax (which hit only those incomes above middle-class level) would need to be doubled to supply the necessary amount—which would 'produce great discontent amongst those who are capable of appreciating and criticising the actions of the Government, and of promoting agitation when they are prejudicially affected' (p. 15). 'Representations that a great increase of taxation was due to what has been erroneously called the "tribute" paid to this country would add sensibly to the danger, and afford an inviting scheme for agitators,' the committee warned openly (p. 15). Even if a falling exchange rate for the rupee were to stimulate exports, the committee considered that this would not benefit India as a whole—although it could temporarily benefit the entrepreneur at the expense of the labourer since wages rose more slowly than prices. Exports had been no less when the rupee had been stable than when it had fallen. It was also contended that exchange rate stability discouraged British investment from going to India; but this again, said the committee, was contradicted by experience. The committee also recorded the feeling of many that 'by making silver the standard and keeping the Indian mints open to silver the Anglo-Indian Government have attracted to India that depreciating metal, and have thus made India purchase, at a comparatively high cost, an enormous quantity of it which is now of less value than when it was bought' (p. 13).

And it went on to note that, since a large part of the savings of Indian peasants were represented by silver trinkets, by closing the mints to that metal the value of coins in terms of silver trinkets would increase, and the Indian *ryot* would lose much of his savings.

Weighing all the elements that it had found relevant to the controversy, the committee concluded by expressing itself in favour of a closure of the mints to private silver coinage. It supported this proposal by noting that Austria, who had applied comparable measures, had seen her currency fall in the twenty years from 1875 (the year of the closure) to 1892 from 100 to 92·98, while the rupee had, in the same period, fallen from 100 to 67·04.

But while the committee supported such a closure, it qualified its support of the introduction of the gold standard in India by the condition that gold should *not* be introduced into that country's circulation. A gold currency was not a necessary requisite of the gold standard; the experience of many countries showed that clearly. For a country like India, which did not have a well-developed banking system, a gold circulation would have represented a heavy and unnecessary economic sacrifice: the lack of any widespread use of banking cheques would have meant that a huge quantity of gold would be required for everyday use.

Having obtained the authoritative support of the committee, the government of India forged ahead with its plan, and closed the mints to private silver coinage in 1893. American pressure at the Brussells Conference did not succeed in changing this official British policy in India. A small concession to pure gold standard supporters was made in the form of an order to the treasuries in India to accept payment in gold sovereigns at the rate of 15 rupees to 1 sovereign. But, as Keynes later pointed out, the mint closure had been ordered by law, while the second measure was merely an administrative measure which could be repealed *ad libitum*.

The Law of 1895, then, sanctioned the priority of British interest over Anglo-Indian commercial interest. A trend was thus set which would have maintained until 1914; but when gold was discovered in South Africa the mother-country again stepped in actively to manipulate Indian monetary affairs. Between 1893 and 1898, the government of India had carried on with its programme of monetary stabilisation. In addition to the already-mentioned closure of the mints to private silver, the Indian government had refrained from coining silver rupees itself. The rupee began to rise in terms of sterling; by 1898 it had reached 1s. 4d. This revaluation caused Anglo-Indian merchants to protest angrily. At the same time, Indian public opinion was in favour of an early introduction of gold into circulation, a measure which was seen as a means to partial liberation from British financial domination. The Imperial government appointed another commission,[5] who pronounced in favour of a gold money supply for India. British financial circles, headed by Lord Rothschild, had expressed their approval of such a measure.[6] As has been seen, gold had begun to flow from the Rand to London in ever-increasing quantity, and the possibility that the market might be glutted, and the price fall, seemed every day to become more real. The Imperial government accepted the commission's proposal, and therefore ordered that sovereigns be freely coined in India at a rate of 16 rupees to one sovereign. Accordingly, in 1900, Sir Clinton Dawkins, permanent under-secretary to the Treasury, declared that a branch of the Royal Mint would be established at Bombay to coin sovereigns. In the same year the Gold Standard Reserve was established, which would receive the profits made by the government of India on the silver rupee coinage and would also serve as a necessary buffer stock to gold circulation.

Gold circulation was, however, to remain but a pipe-dream in India, at least before 1914. Soon after the British government had approved its implementation the Boer War broke out. As we shall see later, the Boer War represented for sterling a real watershed. Confidence in London, the *sancta sanctorum* of international finance, began to falter, which had immediate repercussions for

[5] The Indian Currency Committee, appointed in 1898 under Fowler's chairmanship.

[6] In his evidence to the committee, Alfred Marshall also expressed his approval, although with the inevitable qualifications which always accompanied his utterances. He considered that a *stable* monetary standard favoured the expansion of trade, and made it clear that exporters were certainly favoured by progressive depreciation, but exports were not necessarily encouraged (*op. cit.*, p. 301). He also declared himself against the introduction of gold into Indian circulation. He clearly understood that the majority of the countries which had gone on the gold standard had already transformed it into a gold exchange standard, by buying foreign short-term securities to build a first line of defence around their gold reserves (*op. cit.*, p. 303).

Indian monetary affairs. As the Bank of England's gold reserve fell to an all-time low, the decision to introduce gold into Indian circulation began to look peculiarly ill-timed. Had it been implemented, a considerable quantity of gold would have flowed to India from London or elsewhere. It was imperative that the decision be postponed; so the Treasury and the director of the Royal Mint engaged in subtle dilatory tactics. Their correspondence with the India Office on the subject, subsequently published, makes interesting reading. At the time when Sir Clinton Dawkins had made his declaration, the Indian government had conducted an experiment: it had put five million pounds of sovereigns into circulation in India, following the advice of the 1898 commission. This experiment had been carefully monitored by those who saw the Bank of England reserve falling to a dangerously low level. On August 15, 1899, the deputy director of the Royal Mint had already opposed the idea of opening a Bombay branch to coin gold: he compared the scheme with the mints that had been opened in Australia, emphasising that the motive for opening them was the finding of gold in Australia: they had never been intended to mint coins for internal use in Australia, but only for export. Gold production in India being scarcely one tenth of what it was in Australia, the reasons that had motivated the establishment of mints in Australia were not applicable to India. There was consequently no need to open a mint at Bombay. The deputy director's opinions were, however, overruled, the above-mentioned declaration was made. Preparations began for the construction of the Bombay mint. But the deputy director was undeterred; he ordered that construction work be suspended, as he expressed differences of opinion with the engineers over the size and location of the Mint Building. On this subject, a thick file of correspondence between London and Delhi built up in the course of the next year. Then in May, 1901, the deputy director, fearing that technical difficulties might at last be overcome, opened fire directly on the validity of the project. He wrote that much had changed in the two years that had elapsed. The gold standard now had a strong foothold in India, so there was no longer any need for the Indian government to press its intention of making gold the main monetary standard. Moreover, India produced less gold than had been expected, and sovereigns freely flowed in from abroad when needed; so the personnel of the proposed Bombay Mint 'would have been kept idle for the greater part of the year, at considerable cost to the Indian Treasury.' But his arguments failed to convince Lord George Hamilton, the Secretary of State for India, who ordered that work on the Mint should continue. In justifica- tion, the Treasury reproduced an almost exact replica of its previous arguments. Meanwhile, gold-mine owners in Southern India, tired of witnessing this lengthy exercise in inter-departmental prevarica- tion, negotiated long-term contracts with London gold merchants to deliver their produce to that market. When this fact was brought to the attention of the India Office the latter could only reply by post- poning their project indefinitely; the Secretary of State issued an order to that effect in February, 1903, without deigning to provide any explanation of his sudden *volte-face*.

The British Treasury had thus brilliantly achieved its objective; at the same time, another event took place which was to make the Indian monetary system rely even more heavily on a gold exchange standard. It will be remembered that a Gold Standard Reserve had been established. By December 1901, it had amassed £3,447,317, of which £2,439,093 in gold was held in India and £1,008,424 in British government stock was held in England (see Table 9). At the end of the first quarter of 1902, however, the whole Reserve was transferred to London and invested in British government securities.[7] The British authorities then used it to buttress the fall in the price of Consols resulting from the financial demands of the Boer War.

This measure marked the beginning of the most interesting phase in the monetary affairs of pre-war British India: the management of Indian financial policy passed into the firm grip of the India Office, who transformed it into a docile instrument of British monetary policy.

It is worth recalling that, from 1900 to 1914, the Indian economy experienced remarkable growth. In 1893–94, Indian exports had been £70,877,900 (see Table 10). By 1902–03 they had grown to £85,877,900; and by 1912–13 they had become £164,364,800. As the table shows, Indian visible imports, while doubling in the same period, remained steady at $\frac{2}{3}$ of exports. Since, as we have just seen, the Indian trade surplus had grown so much, it became essential for British governmental and financial circles to make sure it was properly financed. The difficulty lay in making India absorb from £40 to £60 million worth of British financial instruments every

[7] Marshall stated: 'when one country invests into another country's securities, I call that lending to the other country' (*op. cit.*, p. 316).

year (when Bank of England gold reserves never reached £35 million). As we have shown above, India's foreign trade was structured so that it realised a large deficit with Britain but a large surplus with the rest of the world; it was thus a basic element in the balancing of Britain's international accounts. By preventing India from transforming her annual surplus into gold reserves, the India Office contributed in no small way towards keeping British interest rates lower than would otherwise have been the case. The mechanism worked as follows: in 1902, as seen, the Gold Standard Reserve was changed into British government securities—Treasury Bills, Exchequer Bonds, Consols. This trend continued until 1914. British government securities in the Gold Standard Reserve's portfolio grew from £3.5 million (at market value) in the first quarter of 1902 to £16 million in the first quarter of 1912. In addition, the India Office began to place money from the Gold Standard Reserve, at call and at short-notice, with finance houses in the City of London. This began in 1908, when £1,131,223 sterling was so deposited which grew to a maximum of three million in the first quarter of 1910—only to diminish to £1,500,000 sterling in later years. Throughout those fifteen years the prices of British government securities fell continually, which caused a net capital loss for the Gold Standard Reserve of India. Moreover the maximum rate of interest on funds lent to the City was 2%.[8] It is valuable to bear

---

[8] This fact emerges from the interesting evidence given by M. de Webb, President of the Karachi Chamber of Commerce, to the Royal Commission on Indian Finance and Currency: Cmd. 7070, HMSO, London 1913, Appendix XXI, p. 550 ff. De Webb, an English *pied-noir*, was interested in an independent Indian monetary system; being himself an entrepreneur in India, he consequently thought that an independent monetary system would allow him to borrow money in India at less prohibitive interest rates. He also considered the high taxation rate imposed by the Indian government to be totally unjustified, in view of its ability to show a budget surplus every year.

Since 1908, de Webb maintained that London merchant bankers and stockbrokers had borrowed very high sums from the India Office. He gave a detailed list of borrowers and the sums they had borrowed; the idea was—so de Webb considered—to establish permanent credit lines at short-term interest rates. He also gave a detailed list of joint-stock banks which had borrowed from the Indian government at rates lower than the market rates.

De Webb's evidence reveals the tendency towards independence that was developing among the British in India, just as it had done in the Dominions. On that tendency see also S. B. Saul, *op. cit.* and Graham, *Cambridge History of the British Empire*, p. 486.

in mind that the greater part of those funds was lent to leading banking houses, whose most eminent representatives formed the Financial Committee advising the Secretary of State for India on these very matters; prime commercial paper was held as collateral, as was the practice in Lombard banking. Thus English banks were able to borrow from the India Office at 2% and reinvest on the London market at 3%. But this was not all. The Indian government's broker, a private firm in charge of such transactions, was paid a commission that increased proportionately as these transactions grew in size. During the period in question the broker amassed revenue to the amount indicated in Table 11.

To this mass of money flowing from India to London through the management of the Gold Standard Reserve should be added the money accruing from the permanent Indian surplus. After 1893, the value of the rupee had become stable, mainly as a result of the above-mentioned measures. It became essential to British interests that it did not follow the logic of exchange, and thus increase in value *vis-à-vis* sterling as the trade surplus grew. As is shown in the table, several stratagems were devised to prevent it from so doing. First, silver was sold to India, to the tune of £4 million a year for ten years. By putting into circulation rupees of fixed silver content, the Indian government realised the remarkable profits that enabled it to accumulate and invest the Gold Standard Reserve. A good share of the surplus was, despite all efforts by the British, transferred into sovereigns and gold bars, while about fifty per cent was financed by imports of Council Bills—a device which was extensively used by the India Office to keep the rupee on a stable course.[9] It was a system which had been devised previously but which only came into its own during our period. As we have seen, the Indian government was continually obliged to transfer sums to London in gold to pay the Home Charges;[10] they had therefore to find that gold. In order

[9] On the mechanism of Council Bill transactions, the classic is Keynes' *Indian Currency and Finance, op. cit.*, p. 102 ff, which was largely duplicated in the *Final Report of the Royal Commission on Indian Finance and Currency*.

[10] The Home Charges had experienced a considerable increase in value. As regards their legitimacy, it is amusing to read Marshall's evidence to the Indian Currency Committee of 1898. Marshall maintained that India had found in British rule a cheaper form of government than any other she could have. 'Were it an expensive Government,' he stated, 'I think our presence in India would not be justifiable' (*op. cit.*, p. 291). It should also be remembered,

to get it, they sold in the City bills that entitled the buyer to an equivalent sum available, in rupees, in India. These bills were usually bought by importers of Indian products, who used them to make payments in India. However, it was convenient for them to buy bills only when their gold price was lower than the cost of making payments by shipping gold—the alternative method. Initially, the price of Council Bills was determined by their supply, which was in turn strictly limited to the value of the British payments the government of India had to make. But after the rupee was stabilised, and the Indian trade surplus had begun to grow, that close correlation was broken. Although the Indian government never needed more than £15 million for its British payments in the ten years before 1914, the India Office during the same period sold £241 million worth of Council Bills (if we exclude the fiscal years 1907–08 and 1908–09, when the rate of exchange of the rupee fell following a check in Indian exports owing to the world slump, we find that £220 million worth of Council Bills were sold, against gold requirements of £120 million, which Keynes estimated the government of India would need over 8 years).

This difference between the gold requirements and the actual sales of Council Bills is explained by the India Office's policy of pegging the rupee's exchange rate. Council Bills were sold in weekly auctions at the Bank of England; and the proceeds of those sales were deposited with the Bank, which was also banker to the government of India. By selling an appropriate quantity of Council Bills, the Secretary of State for India succeeded in preventing the export of gold to that country, since the low price of the bills would make it advantageous to use them for payments in India. The Bank of England, saddled with a host of difficulties (as we shall see better later on) depended heavily on the arrangement it had with the government of India, particularly when the latter's account reached huge dimensions after the disproportionate sales of Council Bills.

---

he continued, that 'For instance, we export to India a great number of prime young men. If their value were capitalised, as it would be if they were slaves, it would be several thousands of pounds apiece. We bring them back afterwards, if they come back at all, more or less shrivelled and worn out. Those are vast unreckoned exports. India complains she sends us a tribute of goods for which we have given no return. We have given a return for many of them in the shape of men in the prime of life, who, on the whole, I think are very cheap for the purpose' (*op. cit.*, pp. 312–13).

The account was therefore eminently stable, and the sums deposited in it could be used by the Bank for ordinary commercial lending, which led to handsome profits. So, when the India Office began to lend money to City finance houses, the Bank of England staged what amounted to an open rebellion against the move. The then Governor, Mr. Cole, harshly criticised it in his evidence to the Royal Commission on Indian finance and currency. The decision, he said, played havoc with the Bank's efforts to keep the money markets in equilibrium. Moreover, he added, lending to institutions other than the Bank of England meant a lower revenue for the government of India;[11] he did not, however, condescend to explain the reasoning behind this claim. The 2% interest rate the India Office received in the City was not the ruling rate, but it was 2% more than could be got from the Bank of England, who paid no interest on deposits.

The management by the India Office of Indian monetary affairs, in the decade before the Great War, generally elicited violent criticism from all sides. As we have seen, the Bank of England openly voiced its dislike. In India, British merchants and industrialists were no less despondent. In a period of prosperity such as India had never known in the recent past, they could not bear the country to be kept in a state of financial under-development just to suit financial interests in the metropolis. At every harvest season Indian interest rates would shoot up to unbearable levels. Moreover, they opposed what was considered undue government interference in their affairs, especially as far as taxes were concerned. They considered fiscal pressure to be unduly high, in view of the fact that the Indian government's budget was every year in surplus and the country had a trade surplus year after year; in addition to which the government had a substantial credit balance, as shown in Table 12. Indian public opinion was equally at odds with the India Office monetary policies. They thought it was in contrast with high fiscal pressure; they also realised the advantage, from the point of view of national sovereignty, of a pure gold standard over the gold exchange standard which India had been given. Nor did they understand how it could benefit India to drain her resources in order to send money to a country who invested all over the world.

[11] See the evidence given by Cole, Governor of the Bank of England, to the Royal Commission on Indian Finance and Currency, and Blackett's previously mentioned unpublished memorandum.

For the Indian bourgeoisie, the gold standard became a national-
istic and anti-imperialistic slogan.[12]

The India Office's conduct of Indian monetary affairs was at the
centre of one of the gravest political and financial scandals in
English social history. In 1912, the government of India, through
the India Office, secretly bought a very large quantity of silver,
using the services of Samuel Montagu & Co., the largest bullion
broker in the City. The secrecy of the operation was intended to
prevent the speculative price rises that would inevitably have taken
place if the Indian government's intention had been made public.
But, as Keynes wrote, 'the head of that firm was unfortunately tied
by close family links to the Under-Secretary of State for India'. After
the scandal exploded, the whole financial policy of the India Office
was subjected to violent criticism in the House of Commons, in
the Press and in India. Those who had brought the scandal to light
were not, perhaps, uninterested in bringing down Lloyd George's
reformist Cabinet. The government was compelled to appoint a
Royal Commission to inquire into the matter. But their report,
published on the eve of war, did not receive much attention: there
were graver matters in hand. The report expressed the Commission's unqualified approval of the conduct of the India Office
and its warm support of the gold exchange standard as the system
best suited to India. The report, and the evidence accompanying it,
presented an account of Indian monetary history in minute detail,
together with the opinions of a large number of experts. My account
of the story has been no more than a reading of those documents
in a different light.

[12] For an expression of this state of mind, see Doraiswami's already mentioned book; and also S. K. Sarma, *Indian Monetary Problems*, Madras 1911.
It is interesting to note that at the time of the great depreciation of silver,
Indian 'responsible public opinion'—to use the words of the Herschell Com-
mittee—had passionately fought for the free coinage of silver. For further in-
formation on Indian monetary affairs, and for other views than those here
expressed, see D. Tripathi, 'The Silver Question: India and America' in
Journal of Indian History, 1966; K. N. Chauduri, 'India's International
Economy in the Nineteenth Century: a Historical Survey' in *Modern Asian
Studies*, 1968; and D. Rothermund, 'An Aspect of the Monetary Policy of
British Imperialism' in *The Indian Economic and Social History Review*,
1970.

FIVE

The British Financial System in the Age of the International Gold Standard

Britain entered the second half of the nineteenth century with a currency the principles of whose issue and control were still in dispute, a banking system still unitary, dispersed and fragmentary, a bill market of rudimentary organisation, and a mechanism of public finance which had hardly changed for centuries. It ended the period with a highly centralised banking system based on joint-stock banks operating through branch networks; with a central bank which controlled not only domestic credit but also the gold reserve for international payments and which was the chief arbiter in the working of the international gold standard. Ancillary to this there was a discount market, developed along highly specialised lines for the handling of short-term paper and playing a highly specific role in the general banking system.[1]

In this chapter, I shall do no more than try to qualify some of Scammell's assertions. It is difficult to find a better summary than that sketched above of the profound transformation the British financial system underwent during the course of the period under consideration. It would not be an exaggeration to define that process as a 'financial revolution'. Britain was the first among developed nations to experience it, just as she had been the first to experience both the agricultural and the industrial revolutions. One of the prime movers in the financial revolution was certainly the joint-

---

[1] W. M. Scammell, *The London Discount Market*, London 1968, p. 59.

stock, limited liability deposit bank. In Scotland it had already prevailed over other forms of financial organisation by the first half of the nineteenth century. In England, its tumultuous growth in the second half of the century was favoured by the very law which Parliament had passed to regulate banking activity once and for all: I refer, of course, to Peel's Act of 1844. The facts are known:[2] Peel's Act translated into concrete terms the conviction that inflationary situations resulting from over-lending could be successfully prevented by strict regulation of the note issue. Accordingly, the Bank of England was allowed to issue only a very limited amount of its notes against the Government Stock it held. Any other amount had to bear a one to one relationship to gold in the vaults of the Bank. The Act split the Bank of England into two separate departments: the Issue Department, which held the gold and silver reserves and all Government Stock, and which issued notes against those assets in the quantity prescribed by the Act; and the Banking Department, where the Bank, as laid down by the Act, conducted its formal banking business.

The Bank's ability to intervene in the money market as a central bank strictly depended, therefore, (1) on the size of the reserves held in the Issue Department, and (2) on the reserve of bank notes in the Banking Department, i.e. on the Bank's *liquidity*.

Peel's Act was intended to be a definitive turning-point in English banking history, and was supposed to be followed by continuous stability, as opposed to the alternating credit booms and crises that had preceded it. Agreement on the common ground of monetary stability had been easy for the representatives of landed interest and those of the up and coming middle class of merchants and entrepreneurs.

Peel's Act was an elaborate weapon; but its victim was already dead. Its authors had, in fact, completely overlooked the need to regulate the major source of dynamism in English banking: the deposit bank. The capillary collection of deposits by means of a branch network was, as has been noted, already a reality in Scotland at the time of the Act. Such activities, helped rather than hindered by the Act, expanded rapidly in England, exploiting a loophole in

---

[2] On this subject, see Sir Henry Clapham's classic, *The Bank of England, A History*, Cambridge 1966, vol. II, p. 186; and the older book by A. Andreades, *History of the Bank of England*, London 1909, which devotes more attention to Peel's Act and its consequences.

the credit austerity that resulted from severe limitation of the note issue. At that time, credit in England consisted mainly in short-term lending to trade and industry, which was effected by the banks' discounting of 'real' as well as 'financial' commercial paper. Until Peel's Act, banks had exchanged their notes for the bills presented by their customers. But after the Act British banks swiftly changed *en masse* to the Scottish system, henceforth crediting the sums that proceeded from the discounts into their customers' accounts; those accounts could be drawn upon by *cheques*.

The efficiency of the new system had been well proven in Scotland, where, according to all the sources, the economy of notes was great, as the velocity of circulation was made, by the use of cheques, very high indeed. Grafted onto the powerful British economic system, deposit banking grew unfettered until the outbreak of the European war, apparently to the satisfaction of everyone—at least, Parliament was never called upon to modify its legislation of 1844. Now we have introduced the deposit bank as the protagonist, we must turn our attention to the other main actors of our piece: the other British financial institutions.

The Bank of England we have already discussed. We must now delve deeper into its history. The Bank was a revolutionary institution, having been founded in the aftermath of the victory of the bourgeois revolution of 1688. It was founded to finance the revolutionary government, and in particular the loan that government had floated. The Bank succeeded in placing the loan among City merchants and thus their stake in revolutionary finance encouraged them to oppose the return of the Pretender, who would certainly not honour the debts of the revolutionary government.

As with other trading companies that were founded at the time of the Republic and Protectorate, the Bank of England began as a private company, though it did enjoy a 'special relationship' with the Government. The Bank took the form—then a privileged one—of a joint-stock company, which enabled it to gather a capital which, at that time, was considered enormous. Its management was entrusted to a Governor, chosen from a board of directors which was recruited *una tantum* from representatives of the most prestigious trading houses of the City and subsequently refurbished by co-optation.

The Bank of England, then, was from its inception a unique institution. It was financed by British capital and managed by a host of London merchants (mostly of foreign birth or descent), and it was guaranteed a monopoly on large-scale banking, as it was the only bank whose shareholders were allowed to enjoy limited liability. It was also granted a monopoly over banking and monetary transactions on the Government's account, and its notes were raised to the status of legal tender in England, a status shared with gold and silver coined by the Royal Mint.

As late as the mid-nineteenth century, the Bank of England was still the largest bank in England, a giant surrounded by dwarfs, who exercised its will (which amounted to the country's monetary policy) directly, without recourse to sophisticated methods. Its discount rate was, for all practical purposes, the market discount rate, a state of affairs that remained until the time of Bagehot: as he remarked, 'at any normal time, there is not enough money in Lombard Street to discount all the bills in Lombard Street, without having to take money from the Bank of England'.[3]

This meant that the Bank was at that time the main buyer of bills, which were placed in its portfolio to await maturity. The Bank obtained bills both from its private clients and from the bill brokers, a peculiarly British brand of financial intermediary, whose fast growth was to constitute the first challenge to the Bank's financial primacy. As Samuel Gurney, founder of the House of Overend, Gurney, declared to a Parliamentary Commission, 'My business is usually what is called a bill broker, a merchant of money, who takes it from those who have a surplus, and distributes it to those who need it.'[4] From the financial point of view England was still a country of counties. Branch banking had not yet spread everywhere, and the agricultural counties, whose banks collected more deposits than they could lend locally, were still distinct from the industrial counties, whose banks needed more money than they could collect locally to discount the bills of local merchants and entrepreneurs. This was, as Bagehot noted, the reason behind the development of bill brokers, who took parcels of bills from banks in Lancashire to banks in Norfolk, Suffolk or Hampshire. They did not guarantee those bills; neither did they accept them—they were purely intermediaries working on commission. But the brokers' position gradually changed from middlemen to buyers and resellers of bills

[3] W. Bagehot, *Lombard Street: a Description of the Money Market*, London, Kegan Paul, Trench & Co., 1882, p. 114.
[4] Quoted by Scammell, *op. cit.*, p. 115.

in their own right, for which they came to need capital. This was obtained from banks, especially from the Bank of England; money was borrowed at very short notice or at call, giving bills as collateral, as was the practice of 'Lombard banking'. A further step was made when the brokers began to discount bills, i.e. to accept them directly from their signatories or from the banks of the industrial counties, and to hold them until maturity. They themselves thus began to shoulder the risks of the 'safe end' of the operations, and were compelled to arrange their business so that each working day they had enough bills maturing to match their cash-flow requirements.

In the limited sphere of banking activities conducted in mid-nineteenth century England, the bill brokers were begun to be seen as dangerous competition by the Bank of England. They were encroaching upon the very branch of business on which the Bank throve: the discounting of bills from all over the country. Moreover, they worked on borrowed funds. But it was precisely because of the development of this web of financial interconnections that the Bank of England could control the level of interest rates. However, the Bank, as a typical monopolistic institution, was not used to accepting competition as a fact of life. From 1850 to 1866, British financial history records several skirmishes between the Bank and the brokers, which resulted in crisis in 1857 and in financial catastrophe in 1866.

The crises were world crises. The first came as the result of an investment boom in Europe, financed from very scant resources, which were used to their utmost (and beyond), by industrial banks such as the *Crédit Mobilier* of the Pereire brothers—which had to keep performing the miracle of reconciling short-term deposits with long-term loans. The second was caused by the protracted American Civil War, which induced a severe cotton famine in Europe. In Britain, the fight to the finish of the Bank of England and the bill brokers proved to be a third, equally important flashpoint.

Among the bill brokers of the fifties, the discount house of Overend, Gurney had come to prominence. No other financial institution had yet attained the heights they had risen to, excepting the Bank of England. So conflict between the two giants seemed inevitable, particularly as their business had become very similar in nature. But in the course of the crisis of 1857 the Bank of England lent the brokers more than nine million pounds, while lending the banks only eight million.[5] However, such generosity towards the brokers resulted from its fear of the political repercussions that a refusal of full assistance would have. At the outset it had opposed a flat refusal to Overend, Gurney's request of unlimited assistance.[6] But the delay in assistance caused the brokers' position to worsen, thus making the crisis graver. By the time the storm was over, the two institutions were at daggers drawn. In 1858, the Bank decided to close its discounting facilities to brokers, and to admit them only to advances. Overend, Gurney, for their part, began a series of operations designed to embarrass the Bank: for instance, they deposited about £2 million with the Bank, only to withdraw the whole sum at one time. The Bank 'paid with a smile', but was not amused. The slumping world market did not help the two giants to find a peaceful *modus vivendi*. Money was cheap and plentiful, so competition for commercial paper became keener, and profit rates were depressed.

After their experience with the Bank during the 1857 crisis, the brokers began to hold reserves. But why did they not keep them at the Bank of England? This question was asked by Walter Bagehot in *The Economist*.[7] It was the beginning of Bagehot's career as a self-appointed mediator between the Bank and the rising financial institutions who were coming to challenge the former's primacy—a career that ended only with his death in 1878. According to Bagehot, the brokers preferred investing even in Consols to depositing their reserves at the Bank. Then in April 1860 came the 'confrontation' episode of the £2 million, which was blown up into a veritable scandal. The Government was asked to intervene following a question in the House by a member who was a Bank of England shareholder. Mr. Gladstone did intervene, *ad cognoscendum*, by asking both the Bank and Gurney's for explanation. In the end it was Gurney's who backed down and returned the two million pounds to the Bank. Mr. Gladstone, the arch-enemy of money-power, who had invented the theory of the balanced budget mainly in order to remove the Government from the Bank of England's clutches, reported impartially to Parliament on the subject, refusing to condemn the brokers; in private he congratulated the Bank on this

---

[5] Bagehot, *op. cit.*, p. 288.
[6] Clapham, *op. cit.*, p. 228.
[7] Clapham, *op. cit.*, p. 241.

happy conclusion while using the occasion to remind the Bank of the fact that it was an eminently public institution.[8]

The final defeat of Overend, Gurney at the hands of the Bank of England occurred on May 10, 1866; on which day the great discount house declared itself bankrupt with debts of over £5 million. Under a new generation of directors, its management had gone too far into the minefield of low liquidity financial bills while still getting its money at call and short notice. The Bank watched its rival fall without making any attempt to come to its rescue: on the contrary, it implemented a six-month 'dear money' policy specifically to make Gurney's fall inevitable. Only after its rival had gone under did the Bank go to the market's rescue by extending unlimited assistance to anybody needing it, to allay the panic induced by Gurney's failure. The Bank even obtained a letter from the Chancellor of the Exchequer authorising it to suspend cash payments if necessary—a conventional measure in times of grave crisis, whose repeated use in the course of the nineteenth century had occasioned the observation by European critics of *laissez faire* that the English government had to bail out liberalism at the least sign of a storm.

The crisis of May 1866 was a purely British affair as far as its causes were concerned; but it had violent repercussions in all financial markets. On May 10 the Bank rate was at 8% whereas the discount rate was 5% in Vienna and 4% in Paris. The Bank's decision to leave Gurney's to their fate even at the price of a City panic must be judged by modern observers with much greater severity than was shown by contemporary writers like Bagehot. Bagehot overlooked the competition feud that had generated the crisis, rather stressing that Overend, Gurney had deteriorated beyond recovery; and he acclaimed the Bank's role as a lender of last resort. But modern observers should pay more attention to the cost of the crisis in terms of real resources, and to the fact that the Bank was left a free hand to bring about at least indirectly the failure of the 'Norwich Upstarts', the corner house of Overend, Gurney. On the occasion of the Baring Crisis, when a family who had provided a score of directors for the Bank's board was at the centre of the storm, the Bank was to react very differently.

The disappearance of the largest discount house did nothing to

[8] Clapham, *op. cit.*, p. 246. On Gladstone's relations with the Bank of England, see also Clapham, who uses unpublished sources made available to him.

resolve the most serious internal contradiction in the British financial system, which had survived the 1844 Bank Act: the Bank of England was born a private company as regarded ownership and was to remain so for 150 years; but it was called upon to perform public as well as private business functions. The Bank had always undertaken public transactions on the Treasury's account; but was now additionally asked to be the last resort lender to the whole financial system, which involved keeping a large cash reserve. At the same time it had been allowed to pay its shareholders a dividend on the operations of the Banking department, i.e. on private banking transactions. So its capital—as Bagehot acutely noted—was not really risk capital. The Bank of England could hardly fail, as it was proved and accepted by hallowed tradition that the Government would intervene to bail it out of any situation. All the same, the proprietors and directors of the Bank of England looked with growing unease and envy at the fat profits being reaped by other private banks in the second half of the century. They did not as yet consider their role with equanimity (indeed, they would not do so until 1914 or even later); but saw their function as consisting in the maintenance of reserves, at high cost, for the whole financial system, while simultaneously competing for funds with other financial institutions and rescuing the latter should the need arise—although it was much better for the Bank to let them fail and thus regain a monopoly over collecting deposits and discounting bills.

The Bank Act, which separated the Bank's two functions but at the same time left their running in the hands of the same people, had accomplished only one half of the necessary reform. The other half, namely the elimination of the Bank's private banking operations, would come only after the First World War. Right through our period, until the very summer of 1914, the British financial system suffered from the instability resultant from having a central bank which was also a commercial bank. A series of partial and temporary equilibria were pragmatically negotiated; but the basic instability remained, latent in times of financial peace, but very evident whenever crisis broke out. Most pre-1914 financial crises were at least partly caused, and certainly aggravated, by the Bank of England's institutional schizophrenia.

After the fall of Overend, Gurney the British financial system had a period of uneasy peace. From 1848 to 1866, Bank of England deposits remained stable at about £7 million; but in only four years from 1852 to 1856 the deposits collected by the five largest joint-stock banks shot up from £14,460,000 to £29,250,000.[9] Whereas the Bank of England (as another consequence of having to keep a reserve) never paid interest on deposits, the other banks did. After the disappearance of Gurney's corner house, commercial banks began to appear—a real challenge to the Bank in the money market. By opening branches all over the country, they gradually eliminated traditional bill-broking functions: banks now kept branches in both the saving and the investing counties. In addition, inter-bank money flow was much enhanced; both by the joint-stock banks' admission to the London Clearing House, previously open only to Country Banks, and by the Bank of England itself joining the Clearing House in 1864. The joint-stock banks' habit of keeping their clearing house balances at the Bank of England dates from this year.

The 1860s saw the beginning of the process which was, in the course of the next decades, to make the City the most important *international* financial market. These were the years of the victory of free trade and the great expansion of international trade. British capital had already financed development in new countries for decades; now it was called upon to finance the increasing movement of commodities across borders and oceans; an activity which was destined to absorb until 1914 a large part of Britain's financial resources.

In *Lombard Street*, Bagehot acknowledged the importance of the process of internationalisation undergone by the City. After 1870, the French defeat and the consequent inconvertibility of the Bank of France's paper demoted Paris from her previous position as the most dynamic international financial centre. And Berlin, even though enriched by the French indemnity, showed no ambition to take over that position: Germany had at that time no capital to spare from her gigantic industrial development.

It was thus left to London to control the flow of international capital, which by the seventies had already begun to gather momentum, prompted by the search for maximum freedom and highest profit. Which meant much increased overseas calls on the Bank of England's reserves. Prior to 1870, gold could be obtained from Paris, but now the Bank of France's inconvertibility had closed that source; while Berlin soon made it clear that its recent gold

---

[9] Data from Mitchell & Deane, *op. cit.*

acquisitions were to be kept intact at all costs. So the Bank of England, disregarding Bagehot's advice to use its discount rate as the main instrument of monetary policy, preferred to adopt the so-called 'gold devices'—to influence the London gold price by various tactics, depending on the Bank's needs.[10] But it could have scarcely acted otherwise during the seventies, since gold was not flowing as freely as discount rate policy required for smooth working.

Bagehot clearly realised the direction of prevailing trends in the City; he did not however take them all into account. In *Lombard Street* he devoted almost no space to the international transactions bill brokers and merchant banks were already engaging in when the book was published: he dealt only with the traditional practice of loans by merchant banks to foreign governments. But we know from Scammell that international transactions were already over-shadowing all others in both types of institution.

We have already noticed how bills had lost their pre-eminence in British home transactions; at the same time, however, the Bill on London had become the main means to financing international trade. It was this transformation that saved the bill brokers, as it gave them the breathing space which had been denied them by the spread of current account financing for international trade. The world-wide use of the Bill on London was also responsible for stimulating the development of merchant banks as a component of the British financial structure.

The merchant banks were foreign firms which had, in earlier centuries, established branches in London purely for merchanting purposes. They had allowed their foreign suppliers to draw short-term bills on them, which enabled the suppliers to receive cash before the commodities they sold reached their destination. The bills would be discounted by banks, once the merchant houses had *accepted* them—that is, acknowledged the legitimacy of the claim made on them. But the Bill on London, which began life as the representation of an actual mercantile transaction, was soon to be transformed into a purely financial instrument, as had already occurred with internal trade bills. Sometimes a fictitious real transac-

[10] Detailed descriptions of the gold devices are provided by the *Interviews on the Banking Systems of England, Scotland, France, Germany, Switzerland and Italy* of the National Monetary Commission, US Govt. Printing Office, Washington 1910; and by R. S. Sayers, in his justly celebrated *Bank of England Operations, 1890–1914*, London 1936, pp. 71–101.

tion was recorded in the Bill; though more often the transaction was unspecified. At the same time, London merchant houses became acceptors of bills rather than actual debtors. They accepted foreign bills on commission, which could then be discounted by bill brokers or banks; thus allowing the drawee to finance his London transactions (which did not necessarily involve British firms, or the movement of merchandise to, or from, Britain). When the bills matured they were paid to those who had discounted them by the merchant houses which had accepted them, and the houses were in their turn reimbursed by the drawee.

Thus, a completely new mechanism of international finance came into existence in the last quarter of the nineteenth century, which was based almost exclusively on London. The centrepiece of the mechanism was the joint-stock banks, which supplied the cash required by the bill brokers to discount the bills accepted by the merchant banks, and which had also begun to discount bills themselves. Now that sterling was the international currency *par excellence*, British banks could easily use their discretion to choose between home and overseas financing: when the home market was quiet, they naturally tended to prefer the international market, where they could make their resources available at low cost—either directly or through the bill brokers. But if the sterling circuit should be closed anywhere in the world by an individual wanting to turn the paper he had received into cash, then the Bank of England would lose gold.

A new dimension was therefore added to the Bank's problems. When money was cheap and plentiful in London, the market discount rate fell so low that it induced gold exports; the Bank was then compelled to stem the outflow by raising its discount rate, and to make those rises effective in the discount market, it had to borrow money at artificially high prices.

So, during the eighties, a financial mechanism had again come into being independent of the Bank of England, jeopardising its supremacy once more. With the development of the current account system, liquidity creation had ceased to be the Bank's prerogative and had become a function mostly performed by the joint-stock banks. As no legal requirements existed compelling the latter to keep a cash reserve, every penny they collected in deposits was put to the fullest and most advantageous use. The joint-stock banks regarded the money they lent to the discount market and to Stock

Market brokers, at call or at very short notice, as their liquidity reserves. A huge credit pyramid was thus erected on the exiguous (Sca⊢) cash reserves kept by the Bank of England. Banking costs were reduced to the lowest level yet experienced (or for that matter to be experienced). On the other hand banking profits were maximised, owing to the extreme economy of cash on which the British system operated. But at the same time, monetary policies became very difficult to enforce—except when money was in short supply (usually for reasons that had as little to do with the bank rate as with sun-spots). Britain had succeeded in erecting a modern credit system, comprising a Central Bank that held the system's reserves, a powerful network of joint-stock banks, and a host of other financial institutions specialising in putting to the greatest use the money they borrowed from the banks. An essential link was, however, missing: the banks were under no obligation to keep deposits with the Central Bank, or even to keep a cash reserve. In practice they did both, but only to suit their convenience: there was no attempt to follow what would today be called a macro-economic policy. In the absence of statutory reserves, and since public debt did not exist in sufficient quantities to constitute a *masse de manoeuvre* for monetary authorities, the Bank of England lost most of the power to control the money market that it had formerly enjoyed.

But the eighties were not to see a period of feuding between the Bank of England and the joint-stock banks such as the nineties would witness. It was a decade of basic agreement between the Bank and the money market. From 1880 to 1890, the three types of institutions mentioned above all throve on fast-developing business. Discount houses (heirs to the bill brokers) and merchant banks prospered on the financing of foreign trade, as they utilised the 'raw material' created by the joint-stock banks; these in turn continued to expand and grow in size. Only the Bank of England was shut out of the magic circle, but its Board of Directors was composed of men who were very much involved in the City's prosperity: they were for the greater part merchant bankers who accepted Bills on London and underwrote or placed loans floated by foreign public authorities. The code of impartiality which the Bank's Charter laid down for its directors, which Bagehot had so highly extolled, was therefore violated. Directors were still merchants; but the merchandise in which they traded was short-term credit.

The profound transformation undergone by British finance caused the establishment of a new, unstable balance of power, whose precariousness would be soon demonstrated by the Baring Crisis of 1890.

At the centre of this crisis (which is, amid the many fascinating incidents in our review of British financial history, perhaps the most intriguing) was the House of Baring, the most illustrious of the London merchant banks. Lord Revelstoke, its head, had fallen prey to the fatal long-term investment fever that was claiming so many of his counterparts all over the world. Using money borrowed on short terms of repayment, he bought large portions of the bond issues floated by Argentine central and local governments.[11] But when revolution broke out in Argentina, the value of *cedulas*, as these bonds were called, promptly plummeted, and Lord Revelstoke had to meet his rapidly-accumulating debts with a portfolio the value and liquidity of which had sunk to a very low level. This was not, however, another 'Norwich yokel' case, where the Bank of England was challenged. 'The House of Baring', Max Wirth wrote soon after the crisis,[12] 'lent to princes and sovereigns when Rothschild was still a clothes-trader in Frankfurt'. It would therefore be accorded privileged treatment.

The Chancellor of the Exchequer was at that time Lord Goschen, formerly a Director of the Bank and himself a merchant banker. The Bank's Governor was Lidderdale, a man of action who would powerfully influence the course of British financial history.

Already in June–July 1890, doubts were expressed about the liquidity position of the larger accepting houses, soon after news of the Argentinian revolution arrived in the City and the *cedulas* fell to very sacrificed prices. When business picked up after the summer recess, the rumours became more insistent. They were echoed in Goschen's diary: for example, on October 7 he wrote: 'Went to the Bank; things queer. Some of the first houses talked about, Argen-

[11] It was, according to Sir Alec Cairncross, Baring's refusal to underwrite issues, and their preference for outright purchases, that brought about the 1890 crisis. See his *Home and Foreign Investment*, Cambridge 1953, p. 92.

[12] From 'The Crisis of 1890' published in the *Journal of Political Economy* in 1893. A study of the 1890 crisis by L. S. Pressnell has recently been published: 'Gold Reserves, Banking Reserves, and the Baring Crisis of 1890', in *Essays in Honour of R. S. Sayers, op. cit.* It is a very accurate piece of work but often clouded by the *caritas patriae* which so often animates historians writing about their home country.

tine, etc., have created immense complications. Uncomfortable feeling generally. Money, the Governor says, not likely to get cheaper....'[13] The Bank rate had indeed kept growing, from 3% in April to 5% in September; but what is more important, the market rate, much lower than the Bank rate until shortly before, had now risen to the latter's level—an event without parallel in recent years.

The great houses Goschen referred to, especially Baring, were sending out distress calls to their colleagues and to private bankers to get liquidity. Bertram Currie (of Glyn's, then the largest English private bank—whom we have already met in our chapter on India), played a leading role in the resolving of the Baring Crisis. He wrote,[14]

The first intimation of any trouble in the affairs of Messrs. Baring Brothers & Co. was conveyed to me by Mr. S. Brunton, the broker, on October 13th, 1890. He came with a message from Lord Revelstoke, to say that the firm required a large sum of money, and that it was difficult for them to appear in the market as borrowers. Before replying to this proposal I told Mr. Brunton to ask Revelstoke for a statement of the bills payable and receivable. He returned with the answer that the acceptances of the firm amounted to 10 million £. Stg. and the bills in portfolio to 9 million £. Stg.

Thereupon Glyn and Co. made an advance to Messrs. Baring of £500,000 on the security of stock in A. Guinness & Co. Ltd., standing in the names of various partners in the Baring firm. Subsequently, a further sum of £200,000 was advanced on Canada Government Treasury Bills, and £50,000 on Securities sold for delivery on the Stock Exchange.

Evidently the £750,000 obtained by Revelstoke from Glyn's went some way towards allaying fear, since Goschen was able to note in his diary on October 25th: 'Things have quieted down in the City and the fate of some of the largest houses is no longer discussed.'[15] The truce was however short-lived: on November 6th, Lidderdale raised Bank rate to 6% after the Bank of Russia had withdrawn

[13] See A. D. Elliot, *The Life of G. J. Goschen*, Vol. II, London 1911, p. 169.
[14] See R. Fulford, *Glyn's 1753–1953*, London 1953, p. 209.
[15] Elliot, *op. cit.*, p. 169.

one million pounds, in gold, and a withdrawal had been announced by the Bank of Spain. We know of the former from Clapham,[16] and of the latter from Hamilton.[17] Hamilton wrote in his diary:

> I was at the Bank to-day receiving tenders for Treasury Bills. I found on arrival that the Bank rate had just been raised to 6% owing to a withdrawal of gold yesterday and further expected withdrawals on account of the Bank of Spain. The rates at which Bills could be issued were, of course, very high, though not so high as was generally expected. I hesitated a little whether to allow the whole amount; but in view of the probability that things may become still tighter before they are easier, and of the expediency of supporting the Bank, I took the whole in three months' Bills, though the average rate we had to pay was fully 5 per cent . . . by far the highest rate to pay in any circumstances. There is certainly great uneasiness in the City; and I asked the Governor how far the rumours about the difficulties of sundry big houses had real foundation. He said he was frightened about one house, and he did not mind telling me confidentially it was Murriettas.

Thus, unless he wanted to purposely mislead Hamilton, on November 7th Lidderdale did not yet know of Barings' difficulties. Together with the Bank, the Treasury by pumping money out of the market, was in fact making things even more difficult for Barings.

Two days later on Sunday November 9th, Goschen received a

> mysterious letter from Governor of the Bank hoping I should be in town early tomorrow—very alarming.[18] [He promptly obliged and] found him in a dreadful state of anxiety. Barings in such danger that unless aid is given, they must stop. X. came in while

---

[16] Clapham, *op. cit.*

[17] Sir Edward Hamilton's *Diaries* are kept in the British Museum (48654 726D). Hamilton was a brilliant civil servant, who had been private secretary to Lowe and Gladstone when they were at the Treasury. A great expert in City affairs, he collaborated with Goschen, especially in the conversion operation of 1889, about which he published a slender volume: *Conversion and Redemption*, London 1889.

[18] Elliot, *op. cit.*, p. 169.

I was there; almost hysterical. Governor and he both insisted that the situation could only be solved if Government helped.

Liabilities on acceptances	£16,000,000
„ on deposits	£4,000,000

Assets showed about £12,000,000 more or less available and un-realisable securities, but a surplus behind if time were given. They must be helped by four millions. Bank would give one million, if Government would give the same. Others, such as A. S. Rothschilds, Glyn's, and banks, must find the remainder. Picture drawn of the amount of acceptances held by various banks, which would have to stop. All houses would tumble one after the other. All credit gone. I entirely understood their reasoning, but re-membering action taken in France when Comptoir d'Escompte was in difficulties, I said the great houses and banks in London must come together and give the necessary guarantee.[19] This was declared impossible if the Government didn't help. The very summons to help would produce catastrophe. [...] From Bank I went to..., hoping to induce them to come forward. I found...in a blue funk, very much demoralised.... suggests the Government should say that they would save Barings. Pre-posterous.... less wild, but everything 'must go crash unless Government helped.' I alone could save the situation.

Lidderdale had been informed of Barings' plight when he accepted Everhard Hambro's invitation to go to his office to inter-view the Barings.[20]

Goschen offered to send the Governor a letter authorising him to suspend the Bank Act. The Governor, however, refused—even

---

[19] Goschen here refers to the crisis of March 1889, which dramatically arose out of large-scale speculation on the price of copper by the *Société des Métaux* of Paris, under the aegis of the *Comptoir d'Escompte*. When the attempt failed the *Comptoir d'Escompte* suspended payments, but was temporarily pre-vented from going bankrupt by the voluntary co-operation of other French bankers, headed by the Paris branch of the House of Rothschild. The total collapse of the French banking system was thus averted, though a grave crisis, also aggravated by the suspension of work on the Panama Canal (which was financed largely in Paris), could not be avoided. See Max Wirth, *op. cit.*, and *The Economist*, Commercial History for 1889.

[20] Clapham, *op. cit.*, Vol. II, p. 328.

though the Bank's reserve (only £10,815,000) was altogether
inadequate to weather the storm threatening the City. Instead, he
asked Goschen to persuade Rothschilds to approach the Bank of
France for a gold loan. Goschen was completely against involving
the Government directly in the crisis. Parliament would have to be
asked to authorise it, in which case everything would come out and
panic would strike the City. But, barring direct financial intervention, Goschen put himself completely at the disposal of the City's
inner circle—to which he belonged anyway—with the aim of
securing, in alliance with the Governor, an adequate guarantee
underwritten only by merchant bankers, to which joint-stock banks
would only later be asked to contribute.

The same day, Goschen asked Rothschilds to request gold from
the Bank of France. Rothschild did so; and an immediate and
positive reply was received. One and a half million pounds were
offered by the Bank of Russia and two million by the Bank of
France, on the security of an equivalent amount of Treasury bills;
which, of course, the Treasury made immediately available.

Still on the 9th, Goschen sent a message to Bertram Currie requesting him to come to the Treasury at 4.30 p.m.[21] There he told
him of Barings' difficulties, and of Lidderdale's proposal to give
Currie and Hoskier (a partner of Brown, Shipley, and a friend of
Revelstoke's) the task of reviewing Baring's position and expressing
an opinion on it. Currie accepted the job but refused Hoskier as
colleague, proposing instead B. B. Greene, a former Director of the
Bank over 80 years old. Goschen accepted Greene, who went with
Currie to Barings' Counting House in Bishopsgate, to check the
note on the situation that Lidderdale had been given by Revelstoke
on Barings' ledgers.[22]

On November 12th, N. Rothschild and the Governor went again
to Goschen, urging the Government to grant direct financial
assistance. Goschen, however, after consulting with Salisbury and
Smith, again refused it, reiterating his offer to suspend the Bank
Act and grant any other form of unofficial assistance.[23] Meanwhile
Hamilton simultaneously organised an issue of Treasury bills to the
Bank so contrived as to avoid further disturbing the market:

[21] Fulford, *op. cit.*, p. 210.
[22] Fulford, *op. cit.*, p. 210.
[23] Elliot, *op. cit.*, p. 170.

We nominally raised two millions from the Bank by Treasury bills; with the proceeds of the sale of Bills we paid off an equivalent of our temporary loan from the Nat. Debt Commissioners on redemption account; and with the money repaid they bought Consols from the Bank at the certified price of the day. So the Bank got Bills in lieu of Consols; and the Nat. Debt Commissioners got Consols at a very favourable price in lieu of their temporary loan to the Treasury.[24]

It was another tangible sign of the Government's decision to go a very long way to help the City, only stopping short of a direct financial guarantee.

In the City, all sorts of rumours circulated. The solvency of all the great houses was doubted, but there was as yet no word about Barings in particular. The Press showed great moderation, except for the *Standard's* financial correspondent, who—as Hamilton noted with disdain—'is always giving offence to everybody and must be an exceedingly ill-conditioned man'. Hamilton much appreciated such moderation, 'for they must know somebody has gone wrong and they might by blowing indiscriminately upon houses in innuendo fashion, greatly aggravate the situation.'[25]

On November 12th, Goschen was informed by N. Rothschild that the Bank of France had made another £1 million in gold available, requesting again the issue of Treasury bills as security.

On November 14th, a Friday, Bertram Currie went to see Green. They agreed to inform the Government that their analysis of Barings' account revealed a substantial surplus. At 5 p.m. Currie was asked into the Governor's office at the Bank, where the greater part of the members of the Bank's Committee of Treasury had gathered. The Governor said he had informed the Committee of the content of Currie's enquiry into Barings' finances; on the basis of Currie's findings he was ready 'to recommend the Bank of England to undertake the liquidation of the Baring estate and to contribute one million £. Stg. to a fund for guaranteeing the assets, provided that a sum of not less than 3 millons was contributed by other parties.'[26]

[24] Hamilton, *op. cit.*, November 12.
[25] Hamilton, *op. cit.*, November 12.
[26] Fulford, *op. cit.*, p. 211.

I then rose [Currie reported] and said that, as an evidence of my belief in the correctness of the estimate which, in conjunction with Mr. Greene I had made of the assets, the firm of **Glyn and Co.** would contribute £500,000 to the fund, provided that Messrs. N. M. Rothschild & Co. would become responsible for a like amount.

At that moment it was announced that Lord Rothschild had arrived, and I was asked to see him. When informed of the circumstances of the case and of the condition which I had made, he hesitated and desired to consult his brothers, but was finally and after some pressure persuaded to put down the name of his firm for £500,000. Mr. H. Raphael, Messrs. Gibbs, Morgan, Brown, Shipley & Co., and others joined in the guarantee for sums of £200,000 to £250,000.

Hamilton reported that Rothschild must have thought he had already done enough for Baring by purveying foreign gold. At all events, we have it on Hamilton's authority that 'it was not until the Governor of the Bank had intimated that "we can get on without you" that the Rothschilds put down half a million'.[27]

The joint efforts of Goschen and Lidderdale had succeeded in prompting the Sancta Sanctorum of the City to close its ranks and defend its interests. Only the following day, November 15th, were the joint-stock banks asked to contribute to the Fund, which rose, with their help, to 18 millions.[28] Gurney was asked to contribute, but refused—in spite, Hamilton noted, of 'all his millions, made out of the business which Barings brought out with such Eclat, because Revelstoke with the best intentions had put him in to some Argentine securities'.[29] It is tempting to guess that Gurney, the eternal City outsider, might have compared the treatment meted to Barings by the Establishment with that which his firm had received at the same hands in 1866.

By this stage, Hamilton considered that he had lived through a most memorable week: 'What with financial crisis, the wreck of *HMS Serpent* off the coast of Spain involving the sacrifice of nearly 200 lives, and a terrible railway accident near Fenuton, this week has been really a week of horrors.' He concluded by reflecting that,

[27] *Diaries, op. cit.,* November 15.
[28] As stated by Currie, in Fulford, *op. cit.,* p. 211.
[29] *Diaries, op. cit.,* November 18.

after the storm was over, most people had shown sympathy to the Barings. There was a 'feeling in John Bull for the fallen and moreover not a few are sorry to think that the downfall of Barings means the indisputed supremacy of the Jews in the commercial world'.[30]

However, this was by no means the most important consequence of the Baring crisis for the British financial system. It also proved to be the swan song of the power of the Bank of England and of the merchant banks. Barings were prevented from going down and taking other houses with them; but this was made possible only by a series of expedients—all traditional instruments of policy had been abandoned. Bank rate was not used (it remained at an undramatic 6% throughout the crisis). Gold was obtained only by involving the Government in both the negotiation and the guarantee, which was in the form of Treasury bills. As we have seen, the Treasury went to the lengths of organising a somewhat devious operation to make the Bank's assets more liquid; and the joint-stock banks were called in to help only after the Inner Sanctum had reorganised its ranks.

This last point, in particular, shows how well aware the financial ruling class was of the deep rift that had opened within Britain's financial system. The City's Inner Sanctum—the Bank of England and the accepting houses—realised that, in order to save themselves from the ruin following Barings' bankruptcy, they could count only on themselves and on assistance from the Government, several of whose members were also financial experts. All the outer layer of the financial system had to remain excluded from the crucial part of the deal, and even the existence of the crisis had to remain unknown to them as long as possible.

If we analyse the situation, we have to agree with the financial elite's assessment. No help could be expected from the joint-stock banks: they had in 1890 only just emerged from a period of great dynamism, concentration and huge capital investment. From 1881 to 1886, their capital had increased from £35,521,000 to £39,838,000; by 1891, it had grown to £50,751,000. They had opened new branches at a frenzied rate: there were 2413 branches in 1881, 2716 in 1886 and 3383 in 1891.[31] High capitalisation often leads to a re-

[30] Hamilton, *op. cit.*, November 16.
[31] Data taken from J. Sykes, *The Amalgamation Movement in English Banking 1825-1924*, London 1926.

duced rate of return on capital; the British banks were therefore engaged, from 1886 to 1890, in a desperate attempt to keep both profits and dividends high. They employed several methods; for example, they decreased the reserve/capital ratio from 52·5% to 47%. But above all they tried to maximise profits, in a period when good commercial paper was hard to come by (as was only to be expected, seeing that the world had not yet begun to recover from the 'great depression'), by pouring a huge amount of money into the Stock Exchange in the form of short-term loans to brokers. These loans, on the prudence of whose granting procedures most observers had their doubts,[32] were extended on the collateral of stocks to be delivered on future dates or on fortnightly repayment. Moreover, according to *The Economist*, the stocks accepted as collateral were often of dubious quality. And the effect of the loans on the Stock Exchange was enhanced by the reform of the Stock Exchange accounting system, which allowed brokers to hold much lower supplies of working capital. A pound lent to a stockbroker would now go much further towards financing Stock Exchange transactions.

Therefore, in the autumn of 1890, the joint-stock banks were recovering after five years of frantic expansion. Their liquidity position had been progressively worsening since 1889. The effects of the European speculation crisis of 1889 had been felt, and, in addition, in the same year Goschen had pumped liquidity out of the system through his Debt Conversion operation. In the autumn of 1890, the situation was aggravated by the progressive rise in interest rates and the depression of Stock Exchange values. Pressed for liquidity and for profits the banks had reduced the balances they kept at the Bank of England. In 1878, out of £500 million of bank deposits, the Bank of England held only £10·8 million. By 1889, while the banks' total deposits had grown to £630 million, only £11·7 million was with the Bank.[33]

So the Bank of England could scarcely count on help from a

[32] See for example *The Economist*, October 19, 1889, and also several other articles in that journal during the period, denouncing the 'foul play' on the Stock Exchange resulting from the large amount of credit granted to it by banks. These denunciations were taken up by Max Wirth, *op. cit.*

[33] Figures given by Mitchell and Deane, *op. cit.* Clapham's figures differ: he gives a minimum of £8·3 million and a maximum of £14·1 million in 1878, and a minimum of £9·4 million and a maximum of £15·2 million in 1889.

banking community so profoundly affected by its own internal transformation and by the bad shape of world economy in general. In the event of a panic, the joint-stock banks would inevitably act in a totally egotistic manner and engage in a *sauve qui peut* operation which would have involved every bank attempting to amass as much cash as it could by whatever possible means—recalling it impartially from the Stock Exchange, the discount houses and the accepting houses. Had the plans to save Barings been revealed to the banks, they would probably merely have rushed all the faster to gain liquidity.

So the Inner Circle decided to go it alone: to prepare their defences by relying only on trusted friends. How well-founded their fears were is demonstrated by the Bank of England's accounts during the week of the crisis. Compared to the previous week the Bank had £7,069,000 more of 'other securities', while bankers' deposits had increased by £6,079,000. 'These moves', commented *The Economist*, 'show how great has been the desire on the part of the bankers, and of others, to be ready for any emergency, and how largely they have used, to that aim, the Bank of England's facilities.'

The Baring crisis, like the crisis of 1866—and indeed most others—revealed very precisely the shape of Britain's financial structure, and the lines along which it was developing. Arising from the crisis, a general conviction grew in the Inner City that it was necessary to attract joint-stock banks into the Establishment: otherwise, enclosed in their 'ghetto' they would enjoy only 'power without responsibility'. This status induced them to behave in a way which was, for the Establishment, distasteful in normal times, but would have been lethal had another crisis, of similar gravity, shaken the City. There was no guarantee that, in a similar crisis, the City would be lucky enough to have the equivalent of a Lidderdale at the Bank's helm, a Goschen at the Exchequer, and a house of Baring's unique prestige in the doldrums.

But even Goschen could find no other solution to the problem than to exhort (to order would be a more apt verb) the joint-stock banks to permanently raise the amount of their deposits at the Bank of England. He also expressed the intention of revising the Bank Act to make the bank-note issue more flexible. Nothing, however, came of it. The *cours forcé* did not arrive in Britain until the summer of 1914.

The joint-stock banks took Goschen's advice and increased the balance they held at the Bank of England.[34] For his part, Lidderdale drew bitter conclusions from the crisis about the power of the Bank in the money market. As we know from Goschen's diary, he wanted to be reappointed for another term of office: his success in shoring up Barings secured him the re-election he sought. Accordingly, when he had obtained it, he launched the Bank on a programme of revanche intended to recover at least a part of the discount market. Unfortunately his policy conflicted directly with the interests of the joint-stock banks.

The basic and implicit contradiction in the British monetary system thus re-emerged in all its clarity. Bagehot had noted that the non-remunerative task of maintaining a reserve was entrusted to the Bank of England, together with the unwritten understanding that the Bank's proprietors would not risk their capital since the Government would always bail them out. Lidderdale had, however, no intention of keeping to the precise cost-benefit analysis Bagehot had outlined. Instead, he acted as a private banker, trying to snatch a share of the market from the competition's clutches.

Even before the Baring crisis, Lidderdale had shown that he intended to take this approach. He had promised Hampshire County Council that he would pay interest on a part of their deposit with the Bank: this promise had been induced by the fear of losing their account. In June 1890 Lidderdale had reached a similar agreement with the India Council: a sum of £32 million, the proceeds of a loan the Council had floated in order to repurchase a railway in India—a loan which they did not intend to use for another six months—was lent to the Bank[35] at a rate of one per cent below Bank rate when the latter was at 3% and 1½% below Bank rate

[34] In 1889, total deposits with joint-stock banks had grown by one third from 1879, while joint-stock banks' deposits at the Bank of England had increased in the same period by 50%. At the same time, gold in the Issue Department of the Bank of England had increased from £20·5 to £30·3 million, and the reserve of notes in the Bank of England's Banking Department had risen from £12·5 to £19·3 million. But in 1898, Alfred Marshall could still write that it was not the joint-stock bankers but 'the Directors of the Bank of England, helped by Lombard Street in general, [who] had earned the gratitude of the nation by increasing that ultimate reserve' (*op. cit.*, pp. 323–4); he therefore apportioned merits in opposite proportion to that allocated in this study. But we have access to the relevant data, then unavailable: further proof that a full assessment of the City's finances was impossible for extraneous observers.

[35] Clapham, *op. cit.*, p. 347.

when the latter was above 3%. This arrangement subsequently became common practice and was extended to many other Bank clients.[36]

On July 24, 1890, the Bank's directors had ruled that bill brokers, discount companies, money dealers and other similar institutions could, with the Governor's consent, be allowed advances and the discount of paper of up to 15 days' maturity, at a rate not below the published rate.[37] A historic decision, since it contradicted the Bank's own ruling of 33 years before which had excluded Overend, Gurney from its facilities.

In the course of the following years, paper of longer maturity was gradually admitted to its discount window, in order to lure bill brokers back to the Bank. The reconquest of the discount market was pursued with the enthusiastic approval of the then manager of the Bank's branches, Ernest Edye, who wrote a memorandum[38] reiterating the need for a radical transformation of the Bank's business clients from a clique of public institutions which tended to generate only unprofitable business towards a purely private trading clientele. The policy bore substantial fruits: in 1889, securities and advances counted for £33 million in the Bank's accounts, and by 1899 they had risen to £89 million.[39] At the same time, under the guidance of H. G. Bowen (in charge of those operations from 1893 to 1902), the Bank went on to invade another joint-stock bank preserve: loans to the Stock Exchange. Fortnightly loans began to be extended in ever increasing amounts to stock exchange dealers, at much higher rates than were charged in other Bank operations. The annual amount of such loans soon reached about £2 million.

The return to the role of a commercial bank by the Bank of England began under Lidderdale's governorship and continued after he had completed his extended term of office.[40] These policies were highly successful when judged from the point of view of the Bank's proprietors. The Bank's dividend rose from 7% to 10% in 1897 and remained at that level until 1904. However, from the point of view of monetary policy, or the Bank's ability to control the money market, Lidderdale's policy was highly disadvantageous.

[36] Clapham, *op. cit.*, p. 347.
[37] Clapham, *op. cit.*, p. 357.
[38] Clapham, *op. cit.*, p. 370.
[39] Data from Clapham, *op. cit.*
[40] Though he remained on the influential Treasury Committee of the Bank.

During the nineties, joint-stock banks continued to develop at an even more rapid pace than before. From 1880 to 1889 there had been 50 take-overs; from 1890 to 1899 there were 152.[41] Joint-stock banks' deposits had grown from £500 million in 1880 to £640 million in 1889, and stood at £850 million in 1899; in 1914 they were worth £1226 million. Bank of England deposits in the whole period rose from £33 to £99 million, but the percentage of bankers' balances among the Bank's total deposits grew out of all proportion, from £11 to £47 million. Up to 1899, however, it kept decreasing (£10 million out of £49·6 million total in 1899). In the same period, the income accruing to the Bank from discounts, advances and short-term lending increased as follows:

Year	£ Income from Discounts	£ Income from Advances, Short-term loans
1880	62,000	138,000
1889	90,000	257,000
1899	120,000	356,000
1913	336,000	324,000

Source: Clapham, *op. cit.*

The Bank's efforts to increase profits were sufficient 'to destroy any hope of systematic collaboration' between it and the joint-stock banks.[42]

The process of concentration had reduced the joint-stock banks' numbers to a handful, and had dramatically increased the financial power of the survivors. How could Lidderdale's effort be anything but vain, when against the £40 million the Bank collected in the private market stood the £1100 million of joint-stock bank deposits? Every joint-stock bank had attained a position of financial power many times greater than that of the Bank. So, in order to maintain its control over monetary policy, the Bank would have had to follow a course precisely opposite to the one it in fact elected to pursue: in other words, it would have had to withdraw from competition, and perfect 'moral suasion'—to persuade the joint-stock banks to co-operate in shaping the monetary policy best suited to

[41] Sykes, *op. cit.*
[42] Clapham, *op. cit.*, p. 372.

London's interests. On the contrary, however, the Bank continued until the very end (the 1914 crisis) to give battle on terrain which Bagehot had long before advised it to abandon, and on which it met with an endless chain of defeats.

It won, it is true, in some skirmishes. For instance, it secured large deposits from the government of Japan; but these were clearly 'political' deposits. The bitterest defeat suffered by the Bank in the same period was certainly due to the joint-stock banks' ability to divert towards them and the money market the surplus funds of the government of India. As we have seen earlier, the Bank's bitterness over this defeat was so great that it induced Mr. Cole, then Governor, to abandon all restraint in his evidence to the Royal Commission on Indian Finance and Currency, and to plunge into a violent attack both on the banks and on the Government who allowed their despicable activities.

The situation of growing anarchy was caused by the swift rise of joint-stock banks, merchant banks and discount houses, and also by the progressive reduction in the Bank of England's ability to control the money market. This anarchy reinforced the 'natural' alliance that had always tied together the Bank of England, the accepting houses and the discount houses. Joint-stock banks were therefore totally excluded from official monetary responsibility. It is difficult to imagine a more perfect exercise in anachronism. This dichotomy was the leitmotiv of British financial history from 1890 to 1914; it had first been played by the whole orchestra during the Baring crisis, and was now being played with a frightening *crescendo* during the 25 years that followed. The British financial system developed, in the course of those years, along the path dictated by its internal 'logic'. All financial activities tended to concentrate in the hands of a few olygopolistic enterprises. In the years immediately preceding the war, we see joint-stock banks replacing merchant banks even in the latter's most specialised function, international accepting business.

The interpretation of the British financial system set out in this chapter runs directly contrary to that projected by Walter Bagehot. The system did not, as he thought, grow into a myriad of highly-specialised finance houses dominated by the Bank of England's towering presence; on the contrary, a handful of 'all-purpose' banks emerged whose financial power suffocated the City's inner circle—the Bank of England, the merchant bankers, the discount houses.

The Bank of England had even to suffer the ultimate indignity of a plan to establish an alternative gold reserve. The meetings of the Secret Gold Reserve Committee, formed and dominated by the mightiest and most arrogant of joint-stock bankers, Holden of Midlands, must be regarded as an attempt to gather a 'Constituent Assembly' of joint-stock bankers; the Committee proposed to carry their independence of the 'Great Lady' to the ultimate extreme, i.e. to expropriate her of the most sacred of her functions.

The process was interrupted by the war, which returned to the financial establishment a large part of the power it had lost to the newcomers. But this should not obscure the main directions the City took during this period: directions which it is essential to understand before we analyse the development of the international financial system in the same period.

SIX

The International Financial System,
1890–1914

From 1890 to 1914, the international financial system developed along lines not very different from those regulating the development of world production and commerce in the same period. In finance, as well as in other economic activities, the general characteristic of the period is the cumulative loss of importance on the part of Britain, especially if we compare it with the two immediately preceding decades. In the two earlier decades, London's domination of world financial markets had been absolute: Paris had disappeared; Berlin had not yet come to the fore. New York, the financial capital of the debtor-country *par excellence*, was still relatively undeveloped as far as international financial transactions were concerned.

But the next two decades witnessed the blooming of giant financial institutions in each of these countries. At the same time, the gold standard came into use throughout the developed world. Those two phenomena caused repercussions for the international financial system which we must now review in detail.

From 1870 to 1890, London's dominion over international finance had required the working of the international financial mechanism to be uncomplicated. The superiority of Britain's financial system over those of other countries had been reaffirmed by the growth of joint-stock banks, and had given London the ability to monopolise the financing of international trade. As we have said earlier, London possessed all that was necessary to operate unchallenged in the international field. Sterling had prevailed over all other currencies as the most stable and efficient vehicle of trade. The London accepting houses had assembled unique experience in assaying commercial paper from all over the world. The growth of British deposit banks placed at the City's disposal a huge quantity of funds which could be used to finance worldwide trade.

In a monocentric system such as the international financial system then was, there was no question of foreign nations losing confidence in Britain, since Britain was herself almost the only source of the 'raw material' processed by the City. The central phenomenon of the period was the progressive loss of financial power suffered by the Bank of England in the discount market.

The next two decades saw the simultaneous manifestation of two further factors: the continuation of banking concentration in Britain, which we have already mentioned; and the emergence of financial centres competing with London. During these years the international financial scene acquired the polycentric features which it would retain until the outbreak of the Second World War: three new centres grew to prominence in these years in addition to the main ones of London, Paris, Berlin and New York. It is here proposed, however, to concentrate on the development of the four leading centres.

LONDON

Events in the City are of especial interest during this period. London kept her traditional monopoly over the gold trade; and gold flowed in successive waves from different countries—Australia, the Klondike, South Africa. London was still the only place where gold could always be obtained, but at a price. In the gold market, Bank of England reserves formed a buffer stock, absorbing surpluses and making good deficits. The Bank, in order to protect its reserves, made use of controlling devices such as Bank rate, the gold devices and open market operations. The latter were made easy, in the later part of the period, by the growing amount of Public Debt to be placed on the market. As we have seen, these were the years when a basic change occurred in the structure of international settlements: Britain shifted her exports towards the Empire while the Empire developed a strong tendency to be in surplus with the rest of the world. Substantial amounts of cash became available to colonies and dominions which were duly invested in London. According to Lindert's calculations,[1] in 1913 British possessions in Africa, Asia, and Australia held about 150 million dollars deposited in London, of which 136·3 million belonged to the government of India. The London money market also had another very important source of foreign deposits, namely Japan. The Japanese government and the Bank of Japan had between them 101·7 million dollars deposited in London in 1913; the Yokohama Specie Bank had 86·8 million. A large proportion of these dollars should, however, be regarded as politically-motivated deposits: in 1902 Lord Lansdowne signed a convention with Japan opposing Russian expansion in the Far East. According to the convention, each of the two countries agreed to go to war to support the other in case one or both of them were to be attacked by an alliance of two powers.[2] The convention became a treaty in 1905; Japan became a guarantor of Britain's presence in India and Britain a guarantor of Japanese presence in Korea.

Another politically-motivated deposit was maintained in London by the National Bank of Greece: in 1913 it was 10 million dollars. Other European monetary authorities also kept money deposited in London: in 1913, there were about 100 million dollars of which the Bank of Russia owned 23·7 million and the Reichsbank 14 million. We would call such deposits 'intervention money' (as was also the case with part of the Japanese funds), which was kept in London as it was the only free gold market.

In the last two decades of our period London succeedeed in maintaining her supremacy in the short-term sector of the world money market, i.e. in the financing of world trade. In 1914 Keynes calculated that international trade bills financed by London stood at 350 million pounds.[3] His figures are still accepted by modern authorities. Other financial centres also went into the business of accepting and discounting foreign trade bills. None of them had, however, managed to become serious rivals to London by 1914. This is testified by many witnesses, among whom we can trust

---

[1] P. H. Lindert, *Key Currencies and Gold, 1900–1930, Princeton* 1969.

[2] On the Convention and the subsequent treaty, see A. P. Thornton, *The Imperial Idea and its Enemies*, London 1959, particularly p. 144 ff.

[3] Lindert, *op. cit.*, casts doubts on the accuracy of Keynes' calculations, but his Ph.D. thesis is as yet unpublished. Until his arguments are available Keynes' figures stand unchallenged.

especially Jacob Riesser[4] (who admitted the German Reich had a long way to go to match Britain in this field) and the American specialist A. J. Wolfe.[5]

London also remained the paramount market for public loans flotation by the governments of new countries, which did not necessarily mean that the ultimate buyers of such loans were British (we shall see later the importance of foreign customers on the London Stock Exchange). But the borrowers kept a good share of the money they had amassed for loans, depositing it with the loans' underwriters (usually a merchant bank). This system was described by Hartley Withers as 'a deliciously simple system by which borrowers . . . became lenders'.[6] Withers also reported the observation of an American banker, A. B. Stickney, about the system's peculiar qualities: 'It will sound like a paradox, but it is literally true that, by her splendid banking organisation England receives interest on millions and millions of her own debts to other countries'.[7] That was because British banks knew how to put to profitable work the greater part of the money deposited with them by other countries' residents and public bodies.

PARIS

In the twenty years before 1914 Paris completely regained its position as an international financial market, second only to London in its ability to absorb foreign loans. During this period the three largest French banks experienced an impressive growth of deposits (current accounts increased at the Crédit Lyonnais from 376 million francs in 1890 to 1235 million in 1912; while the *Comptes de cheques* at the Société Genérale grew from 150 to 448 million, and the *Comptes de cheques et d'escompte* at the Comptoir National d'Escompte grew from 89 to 611 million).[8]

The growth of deposit banking meant that a very large supply of funds was placed at the disposal of the great French finance houses;

[4] *The German Great Banks*, his monumental work translated into English and published by the US National Monetary Commission in 1910.
[5] *Foreign Credits, op. cit.*
[6] H. Withers, *The Meaning of Money*, London 1911, p. 97.
[7] *Op. cit.*, p. 98.
[8] Data taken from E. Kauffmann, *La Banque en France*, Paris 1914.

at the same time foreign stocks and bonds were absorbed by a large proportion of the French bourgeoisie. The largest part of her foreign loans went to the Russian government for purely political reasons; this was to ensure that France did not have to bear alone the whole of the German military threat on her borders. Russia, like Britain's long-term debtors, thus became a short-term lender in Paris. In 1913 the Russian government (again according to Lindert's figures) had 221·8 million dollars deposited in Paris, a *masse de manoeuvre* that the Russian government's agents in Paris employed to influence the French Press into organising a thinly-disguised publicity campaign to lure the French public into buying more and more Russian bonds, and to secure the friendship of prominent French politicians for Russia.[9]

Other governments also kept deposits with French banks: in 1913, the Bank of Greece had 19 million dollars, the Italian Treasury 7·5 million, the Reichsbank 5·4 million and the Bank of Japan 13 million. Meanwhile, the Banque de France acted as the keeper of both the country's gold reserve (its traditional role) and the world's ultimate gold reserve. The French gold reserve grew from 50 million pounds in 1890 to 74 million in 1899 and to 130 million in 1910, following the increase in French circulation. By 1903, France had 458·9 million dollars of gold reserves, to be added to a gold money circulation of 509·4 million dollars. World total gold assets were, in the same period, estimated to be 2614·8 million dollars. Among the European nations, only Germany had more gold in circulation. French paper money, on the other hand, totalled only 177·9 million dollars.[10]

However, as the last decade before 1914 wore on, the Bank of France showed greater and greater reluctance to play its part as repository of the world's ultimate gold stock. As the international political climate daily deteriorated, France could scarcely look on the departure of her gold reserves with equanimity: we shall return to this point later on.

---

[9] A fact which we learn from A. Raffalovich. See his *L'abominable venalité de la Presse*, Paris 1931. Raffalovich, one of the best-informed financial commentators in Paris during the pre-war period, had been almost continuously in the pay of the Russian government.

[10] See the tables at the back of the book.

BERLIN

Berlin's growth as an international financial market (even more than the other great financial centres) is inextricably linked with the development of the German Great Banks. The Deutsche Bank, for instance, was founded, in the glorious year of 1870, to promote the development of Germany's foreign trade transactions. According to the Bank's charter, the Company's objective was 'to conduct business of all kinds, particularly in order to extend and facilitate commercial relations between Germany and other European countries, and between Germany and overseas countries'.[11] Until the Deutsche Bank was founded, German foreign trade was wholly dependant on English intermediaries as far as finance was concerned. German firms' acceptances, calculated in marks, had, because of that currency's instability, been discounted at rates that compared unfavourably with the rates at which sterling-calculated paper was discounted. The Deutsche Bank was therefore concerned to change such a disadvantageous situation. It opened an agency in London, the German Bank of London, with the objective of financing German bills in Lombard Street. By the eve of the Great War, German exporters had succeeded in substituting marks in their transactions with Latin America and, more generally, in their transactions with the foreign branches of German merchant houses. Similarly, they were using marks in transactions with Europe and Russia; but they had to stick to sterling in transactions with the British Empire, Portugese Africa and Japan, and to French francs in Egypt, Morocco and Asia Minor.[12]

The 'nationalisation' of German export trade finance took place as a natural consequence of the growth of German banks. The great Hamburg merchant houses became, like their British counterparts, intermediaries in foreign trade between bankers and industrialists. Merchant houses, being financed by the banks, could pay exporters *cash* (at 30 days), taking upon themselves the risks involved in ex-

[11] Reported by Riesser, *op. cit.*
[12] As reported by Wolfe, *op. cit.* On the development and main features of pre-war German banking, the classical interpretation reference (apart from Riesser) is that of P. Barrett-Whale, *Joint Stock Banking in Germany*, London 1931.

tending credit to the foreign buyers of German goods. But by 1914 the merchant houses had already gone into decline: the symbiosis of banks and industry was almost complete. Industry was now in a position to finance its own exports through the banks that headed the cartels; it could also use credit very effectively to increase market penetration.

According to Wolfe, German exporters were very flexible in determining the length of the credit they allowed their foreign customers. They took account both of the local conditions in the various markets and of the expediency of using credit terms as a method of sales promotion. In countries such as the United States, German exporters dealt mostly in cash or at very short term. But in Latin American countries maturity could be extended to six months and sometimes even to twelve; in Central America and the West Indies the usual length of credit varied from four to nine months; in China and Japan from three to six months; in South Africa, the Dutch Indies and the Straits up to six months; while in North Africa and Asia Minor it could be as extended as nine months.[13]

It is therefore hardly surprising that, when reading the reports of British Consols, we find mentioned among the main reasons for the success of German exports the length of credit, compared with British practice. German exporting houses also frequently managed to persuade foreign clients to keep deposits with them or with German banks (on which, according to Wolfe, the clients received a 6% interest rate).

In Berlin, as in the other main financial centres of Europe, large sums were deposited by the countries who received long-term loans from Germany or were significantly involved in trade with Germany. In 1913, according to Lindert, Chile had 34·8 million dollars deposited in Germany, the Russian monetary authorities 53 million, the Italian Banks of Issue 17·8 million, Sweden 15·4 million, the National Bank of Romania 10·5 million and the Bank of Austria-Hungary 8·3 million. Total official funds in Berlin amounted to 152·3 million dollars in December 1913.

Although the Reichsbank amassed a very large gold reserve, it never reached the size of the Russian or French gold reserve. But gold did circulate widely in Germany—by 1903, the German gold circulation was 668·6 million dollars, overshadowing both paper

[13] Wolfe, *op. cit.*

and silver. This was certainly ample reason for the Reichsbank's attachment to its gold. Thus Berlin's response was always slow when London called for gold, by varying Bank rate; discount rate differentials between the two centres had to grow very large before gold moved out of Berlin. Often, writers report, there was no question about price: gold just did not move. We can easily understand the Reichsbank's attitude to gold when we remember that Germany had developed her banking system enormously. Major bank deposits had (according to the *Deutscher Oekonomist*) grown as follows from 1883 to 1913 (figures are expressed in millions of marks):

Year	Creditor Accounts	Deposits	Acceptances and Cheques
1883	495·5	250·5	346·8
1893	934·3	387·2	531·5
1903	2248·3	1261·3	1300·2
1913	5331·6	4392·5	2450·6

On the other hand, the assets of the German banks were much less liquid than those of their English or French counterparts. Then there was the German public's preference for gold, which we have already noted. All these factors adequately explain the behaviour of the German monetary authorities—although they certainly did not make the working of the international monetary system any smoother.[14]

NEW YORK

The workings of the American financial system are perhaps as crucial to an understanding of international finance in our period as their British or Indian equivalents.

For it was during these years that the United States became an

---

[14] On discount rate differentials between Berlin and London, see O. Morgenstern, *International Financial Transactions and Business Cycles*, NBER, Princeton 1959. On the Reichsbank's monetary policy, an interesting mimeographed study has been written by K. Bopp, *Reichsbank Operations 1876–1914*, University of Pennsylvania, Philadelphia 1953.

economic giant: the greatest in the world. It is here proposed to summarise only the more important features of that economy.

(1) America was the only leading nation to export both agricultural commodities and manufactured goods, though agricultural commodities still prevailed. This American pre-eminence in world agricultural markets, coupled with the seasonal pattern of agricultural exports, meant that international finance faced the annual problem of meeting the heavy surplus in the US trade balance resulting from its agricultural export proceeds each last quarter.

(2) America was the only leading nation to import capital from abroad (excepting Russia, who was at that time well behind the Western countries as far as economic power was concerned).

(3) America was the only leading nation without a central bank: its monetary and banking systems were most unusual.

The United States still remained a country where, although industry was taking giant strides, economic life was still mainly organised around agriculture. According to the census of 1900, out of 29 million people employed, 10 million were still in agriculture. In the same year agriculture produced 20% of the country's GNP.[15] Primitive banking habits were still prevalent among the American farming population, cash being preferred to bank deposits.

Industry was at this time still exclusive to the East; agricultural production was mostly confined to the South and West. Financial activity, and the organisation of foreign trade, were therefore concentrated in the East, even though the greater proportion of exports came from the South and West.[16] The imports and exports of the City of New York alone in 1900 and again in 1910 represented about 50% of the country's foreign trade.

In the spheres of both internal finance and international finance, this economic polarisation presented a number of very peculiar problems. In order to comprehend them, it is necessary to consider the main features of American banking.

There were four types of bank: national banks, state banks, savings banks and loan and trust companies. All were engaged in

[15] See the US Historical Statistics, *op. cit.*

[16] Mentioned by C. A. E. Goodhart in *The New York Money Market and the Finance of Trade 1900–1913*, Cambridge, Mass., 1969. This book is useful especially for its summary of the evidence on American trade and financial practice, which is not now easily available elsewhere. I shall use Goodhart's descriptions quite extensively in the following pages.

similar banking activities, but were subject to different institutional rules. The national banks, founded after the National Banks Act of 1864, were under federal control; the other banks were subject to varying state regulations. While national banks specialised in current accounts, the others had a large percentage of total deposits in the form of time deposits. National banks enjoyed the privilege of note issue; but they paid for that privilege by submitting to federal rules—which were much stricter than state rules. The result was that, with the decreasing importance of notes as compared to deposits—which took place throughout the United States—the national banks, handicapped by stricter regulations, achieved a more modest growth-rate than the other banks, who were under looser state control. As in England, it was an institutional feature that determined, in the United States, the course of banking development. The law of 1864 had clearly been intended to place national banks as the heart of the American financial system; but it was no more successful than Peel's Act. The American banking system bypassed the law to advance in a dangerously anarchist fashion. On the one hand, the national banks maintained a large part of the banking system's total reserve. They had to keep a 25% reserve/deposit ratio if they were situated in 'central reserve cities' (New York, Chicago, St. Louis); if they were situated in 'reserve cities' their reserve rate was still to be 25%, but a part of it could consist of deposits with national banks in central reserve cities. National banks in other towns had to keep a 15% reserve ratio, 3/5 of which could consist of deposits with national banks of the two other categories.

State banks had no legal reserve requirements. Consequently they kept very low reserves (only 4% to 5%), supplemented by a 'line of first defence' composed of highly liquid assets, mostly short-term loans to the New York market (known as call loans) or deposits in national banks.

An enormous web of inter-bank deposits was thus spun by the American banking system. It connected the tens of thousands of provincial banks (by 1909 the United States had no less than 22,491 banks) with each other and, ultimately, with the New York banks. In 1909, the latter only numbered 153, yet they collected 25% of total 'non inter-bank' deposits, and held 15% of all banks' capital and almost one third of the total reserves. But even though they were very powerful, the New York banks were still only commercial banks; they had no capacity to create reserves for the rest of the banking system. The only immediate source of cash for the whole American banking system was the New York money market, where the New York banks placed a large part of the money deposited with them by other banks. Any liquidity shortage, no matter where in the country it occurred, was communicated to the New York money market, where the New York banks operated mainly by means of Lombard loans (i.e. loans against the collateral of stocks quoted on Wall Street) and by purchasing American commercial paper (which required only one signature, instead of the two required in European practice). The New York banks' placement decisions were of course the main determinants of the level of interest rates on the New York money market.

The monetary base was in the American system composed of gold and silver coins, the national banks' notes, gold and silver certificates, national banknotes (the 'greenbacks'), and the 1890 issue of Treasury banknotes. Of all these components, only gold coins and the national banks' notes had any dynamic possibilities; supply of the others was rigid.

Another important feature of the US financial system was the large amount of monetary base that almost permanently resided in the vaults of the Federal Treasury.[17] Owing to historical reasons (which are highly interesting but are too intricate to discuss here) the main American interest groups had agreed on having a Treasury independent of the banking system. This Treasury could, if it wanted, redeposit the money it received as federal revenue with the banking system; but it often refrained from so doing, for fear of enraging some section or other of the public. Even if the Treasury were to deposit its public revenue with national banks this would not greatly change the situation since national banks were required by law to hold as great an amount of federal bonds as public deposits.

Being linked to the American productive structure, the American

---

[17] The basic source of Goodhart's information about the working of the American financial system is the many volumes produced by the massive inquiry into monetary affairs conducted by the US Congress National Monetary Commission. This body was appointed after the 1907 crisis, which was purely American in origin. The monographs relevant to our context are: O. M. W. Sprague, *History of Crises under The National Banking System*, and E. W. Kemmerer, *Seasonal Variations in the Relative Demand for Money and Capital in the United States.*

financial structure was incapable of adequately facing the difficulties caused by the agricultural seasonal cycle. Most American crops were harvested between August and November; and harvests caused money to move from New York towards the agricultural areas. In November and December the flow would continue in the same direction, because of the need to transport the produce. In January–February, there would be little agricultural activity; then, in March–April, money was again drawn from New York to pay for seeds. Three months of complete agricultural inaction would then follow before the cycle began again with the wheat harvest.

So the demand for money became seasonal, too. But the American financial system was not able to take this in its stride without dramatic consequences. When money flowed out of New York, it tended to remain in the provinces for quite a long time, since farmers did not go much for deposits. It was therefore necessary to wait until they actually spent the cash they had earned on Eastern-produced goods; then the provincial banks returned the money they received from the shop-keepers to New York.

Such a cycle is common to all countries where agricultural production predominates in some regions while industry and trade prevail in others. In most countries, however, branch banking tends to even out the imbalance of regional payments, and central banks inject new liquidity when part of the money supply leaks from the system owing to farmers' primitive financial habits. But in the United States there was neither a branch-banking network nor a central bank. When money went West, the New York money market had no means of recovering it, at least from the States. It had to try and obtain gold from overseas. The trade surplus the United States enjoyed year after year, from its industrial self-sufficiency and agricultural exports, should have induced large gold inflows. In reality, however, much less gold than might be expected actually entered the States; so it must be assumed that most of it stopped in London. This was because a very large part of the United States' foreign trade was financed in sterling, in London, since London accepting houses had great experience in the American market and US bills were ineligible for discount in Europe, as they only carried one signature. American bankers were thus thoroughly familiar with London finance; and since the sterling/dollar exchange fluctuated as exports or imports prevailed—according to seasons—they lent in London when the dollar was strong and borrowed in London when it was weak. Thus in both cases they took advantage of the possibilities for gain afforded by the existence of a net interest differential between the two financial centres (*net* in the sense that it still existed after exchange rate differentials were taken into account).

The existence in New York of a large forward exchange market thus caused imbalance: when New York experienced an outflow of money towards the South and West, the situation was not fully restored by the gold inflows that agricultural exports should have induced. There were inflows; and their size was large enough to constitute a grave and perennial disturbance to Britain, where the gold came from. But the inflows were in no way as big as they needed to be to balance supply and demand in the New York money market. Interest rates were therefore the only means by which the market could be stabilised. Interest rates rose in New York to scarcely credible seasonal heights—even 125% was recorded. As there was no central bank to control the market, any seasonal imbalance could combine with exogenous disturbances to produce a panic which might shake the whole United States financial structure to its foundations.[18]

The United States affected the international financial system in other ways as well. We have already seen how United States bi-metallism was the cause of more than one international financial crisis. After the States went off the silver standard, it became the largest source of demand for monetary gold. The regulations of the national banks required that gold had to back all note issues. In addition, the United States Treasury began to accumulate gold to put the huge but rather precarious American banking system on a solid foundation. This policy represented a real threat to the work-

[18] We may usefully contrast the American banking system between 1890 and 1914 with the English banking system as it developed in the twenty years before the publication of Bagehot's *Lombard Street*. According to Bagehot, the agricultural counties of Britain produced an excess supply of savings and the industrial counties an excess demand for savings. The gap was bridged by the rise of bill brokers. In the United States, on the other hand, agriculture was as much, or more, in debt as industry, and not at all integrated in forms of *finanz-kapital*. Moreover, as we have seen, banks had to keep their reserves as deposits at higher ranking banks; so bill brokers could not solve the problem. Only a few New York banks were in a position to act as lenders. As there was no lender of last resort, the system had to be constitutionally unstable.

ing of the international monetary system: the Treasury stored gold in fantastic amounts but was not then able to put it automatically at the disposal of the American banking system, or to send it back to the London gold market—in which case there would be a scarcity, and the Bank of England would raise Bank rate. Compared to the American Treasury, the gold-reserve conscious European central banks seemed very international in outlook. They could do no more than put a spanner in the gold-flow mechanism when it suited them. But between the United States Treasury and the gold market there was no two-way mechanism: the former simply purchased, in vast quantities.

We have not considered a further element: the American public, which absorbed gold at an amazing rate. The United States population, it must be remembered, grew from 60 to 90 million during our period. Even had their liquidity preference and income per head remained constant, 50% more gold would have been needed. As it was, income per head enlarged spectacularly. The public demand for gold therefore followed suit. Monetary gold in the hands of the public amounted to 639 million dollars in 1890; by 1911 it had risen to 1,753 million dollars. The proportion of gold in the total money supply increased from 39% to 49% in the same period, despite an even larger increase in paper currency. At the same time, a powerful shift from currency to bank money began to take place. In 1890, currency in the hands of the public totalled 888 million dollars, while bank deposits were 3,020 million and savings banks deposits were 1,375 million. Until 1900, the growth in bank deposits was not sensational: in that year, currency in public hands amounted to 1,191 million dollars, bank deposits were 5,187 million, and savings bank deposits were 2,128 million. By 1913, however, although public currency had decreased to 1,881 million dollars, bank deposits had grown to no less than 13,519 million, and savings banks deposits to 3,732 million.[19] At the base of the pyramid were the gold reserves of national banks, state banks and the Treasury. These increased as shown in Table 13. A notable shift in emphasis took place between 1899 and 1910; whereas the gold reserves of the banking system remained stationary, Treasury gold reserves almost trebled. Thus the Treasury began to

[19] Bank deposit data are taken from M. Friedman and A. J. Schwartz, *A Monetary History of the United States, op. cit.*

play the principal role, amassing and protecting the nation's reserves. From the point of view of the efficient functioning of both American and international monetary systems, this shift was certainly not very advantageous. The US Treasury was by no means the lender of last resort of the American system; once it acquired gold, it just sat on it.

In a preceding chapter we have seen how monetary authorities, in developed as well as less developed countries, engaged in serious and often repeated attempts to place their respective monetary systems on a gold basis. Most of them met with only scant success. We must now consider the consequences these attempts had on the working of the international monetary mechanism, and how the latter was modified.

The different national laws establishing a gold standard in various countries often had a common feature: they all decreed that the country's monetary base should at all times be tied to the monetary authorities' gold reserves by a fixed ratio. But commercial bank deposits were seldom fettered by these laws. Bank deposits were almost automatically assumed to follow the changes in the monetary base. Consequently, two phenomena frequently recurred.

(1) Monetary authorities, in a period of economic expansion such as the two decades between 1896 and 1914, were induced by the real economic growth in their countries to expand the supply of money; they therefore came to need both an unceasing supply of gold and a standard policy to defend their existing gold stock from calls made on it from abroad.

(2) The growth of commercial bank business, unchecked as it was by any fixed reserve rations, was truly enormous in most countries. The concentration of banks, the establishment or development of clearing mechanisms, the reduction of the percentage of coins and notes (as compared to bank deposits) in the total money supply in public hands—these factors all contributed to growth.

In these two decades, gold reserves undoubtedly began to be concentrated in central banks. We can see how the process developed from the table on page 118.

It is evident from the table that the concentration of gold in the central banks' vaults took place at the expense of publicly-held gold, which is all the more remarkable when we remember that industrial consumption of gold was also growing considerably.

The proportion of central banks' gold among total gold stock rose from 20% to 29% between 1889 and 1899; by 1909, it had become 34%. Official gold reserves were growing *vis-à-vis* total gold money supply: in 1899 they represented 31%, in 1899 52%, and in 1909 59·8%.[20]

Year	World stock of gold (1)	World monetary gold stock (2)	Monetary authorities' gold reserves (3)
1889	1383	711	296
1899	1759	958	503
1909	2545	1446	866
		(in millions of £)	

Sources
(1) *First Interim Report of the Gold Delegation of the League of Nations*, Geneva 1930 (Table 14).
(2) *Ibid.* (Table 15).
(3) *Royal Commission on Indian Finance and Currency*, HMSO 1926, Appendix XXX (Table 13).

Should this concentration of gold in central bank vaults to be approved or disapproved, from the point of view of the smooth functioning of the international monetary system? Keynes considered it a positive development. In *Indian Currency and Finance* he expressed the opinion—to which he held all his life—that a world monetary system entirely based on fiduciary money should be the ideal objective of policy-makers. He was certain that, if it were in the hands of monetary authorities, gold would be more easily available to balance the international monetary system than if it were left in private hands. Keynes' opinion may be contested: when left in the hands of the public, gold can be freely exported by gold merchants should its price rise sufficiently to convince people to get rid of it; in the hands of monetary authorities, gold reserves become (as Keynes himself noted) a piece in the international power game, a mythical symbol; and their decrease is seen as a sign of financial insecurity and political weakness. This is exactly why monetary authorities, during our two decades, could not tolerate any reduction in their gold reserves and tried (in the best mercantilist fashion)

[20] By 1913, according to Triffin's data on monetary authorities' reserves and Kitchin's data on world gold money, the concentration of gold money in the hands of monetary authorities was still increasing: by then, the authorities held two thirds of world gold money.

to boost them by all available means. Since they were unable to adopt a flexible approach to reserves, they were compelled to protect them by foreign currency deposits in strategic world financial centres.

The transformation of the international monetary system into a gold exchange standard, which took place during the same period, should be viewed in this light. The monetary authorities of gold standard countries had to defend their gold reserves during the oscillations that took place between the 'gold points'. They could do so only if they had a *masse de manoeuvre* of foreign currency deposits, which could be used to intervene in both spot and forward foreign currency markets. Gold parity was therefore defended for precise economic reasons. Against the already mentioned advantages of such a policy must be weighed the cost of keeping additional reserves, in order that we may see the situation through the eyes of the *belle époque* monetary authorities. The greater liquidity preference that monetary authorities in smaller countries showed in this period was, from the point of view of the countries where they held their deposits, an advantage. Great Britain, and to a lesser extent France and Germany, could afford to spend more abroad, both on current and on capital account, than would have been possible had peripheral countries not preferred international credit to real resources.[21]

This meant that the greater countries could keep investing in the lesser. The balance between short-term indebtedness and long-term credit was often maintained bilaterally; but multilateral financial transactions were also juggled to obtain an overall balance of payments. A major country could invest in a peripheral country to more or less the amount of short-term deposits it received from that country. That was often the case with British investments abroad.

The pre-1914 international monetary system was highly dynamic: it could have not been otherwise with an equally dynamic international political situation. The two systems in fact moved in the same direction. We have seen (Chapter 5 above) how the Bank of England lost her monopoly in the London money market, and how

---

[21] This assumption is made on the basis of evidence from Bloomfield, Lindert and Triffin, and of my own findings, suggesting that monetary policy was, in its main objectives, as discretionary under the gold standard as it has since been.

an olygopoly situation developed in Britain as a result of banking concentration. The same process also took place in the wider monetary field. London lost some of her power to control the international financial system to Paris and Berlin. An olygopoly situation thus arose in the international financial system; and 'Suzerainty' networks were established between the three leading nations and peripheral countries. It was a highly unstable system, since a gold exchange standard could only be stable when short-term creditors had absolute confidence in the (major) country where they kept their reserves. Such a degree of confidence could only be reached when the lesser countries were politically or economically subservient. British possessions were dominated in this way. Should they have a surplus, they were denied the right to choose between gold and sterling; they had to deposit any surplus, in sterling, in London. At the same time London held deposits of independent countries, who could exercise the right to choose between gold and sterling whenever they wanted; which was a major disadvantage. Japanese deposits, for instance, were politically negotiated, and it is probable that other countries similarly used London deposits as an instrument of foreign policy.

The largest source of weakness for London was, however, the 'American Account'. The United States deposited the greater part of its seasonal surplus in London, but London paid dearly for this American preference for sterling. The United States used the London money market as its central bank, as it did not have one of its own until 1913. London thus had to absorb all seasonal oscillations in the American demand for money and to cope with all the US crises that resulted from a combination of seasonal and exceptional disturbances. Moreover, the United States was not another India: it certainly deposited a part of its surplus in London; but, at the same time, it absorbed gold like a huge sponge—national and state banks and the public all amassed the metal, especially in the decade before 1914. The US Treasury was, however, the principal glutton. The combined gold reserves of the Treasury and the national banks grew to be a huge proportion of world official reserves: in 1889 they were worth 81 million pounds out of a total of 296 million; in 1899 they stood at 124 million out of 504; and in 1910 they totalled 273 million out of 867. The reserves of the three centre-countries combined (Great Britain, France, Germany) were worth no more than those of the United States alone. In 1910 the

States even overtook them, contributing 273 million pounds against their 200 million (see Table 13).

America's role was thus crucial. During the whole of our period, she was the largest exporter of primary commodities and was industrially highly developed, but from the point of view of central banking, the States remained at the level of a colony; moreover, most of her foreign trade was financed from the mother-country. But the US was, however, completely autonomous in the making of policy decisions about the use of her surplus. As it turned out, autonomy in this field meant a marked preference for gold, the extent of which should not be underestimated, when we think that in 1914 the States had 25% of world total gold money and in 1910 she had 31% of total world official gold reserves (see Tables 13 and 16).

We are now in a position to appreciate how deeply the problem of United States gold absorption embarrassed the British monetary authorities. The Bank of England had to control the London gold market with an average gold reserve of only about £30 million; moreover, it could not count on support from the British commercial banks, as the latter were in the enviable position of 'power without responsibility'. The Bank was doubtless not unaware that the London discount market derived a large part of its total profits from financing American foreign trade.

The basic importance of India as the main stabilising element should now be clear. Britain was able to depend on an economy which had a large export bias and a thorough dependence on Britain for imports, and which was underdeveloped enough to generate a surplus that could be invested in London. Thus, the City of London could maintain its leading position both in short-term international finance and in long-term investment, and could remain, until 1914, the main source of international liquidity.

London's international role, however, also depended on the structure of the British financial system. The joint-stock banks placed at the City's disposal an enormous amount of 'raw material' which the latter could process to finance proportionately less and less British trade and more and more world trade. But the raw material was British, i.e. the deposits were generated in Britain. Increasingly pressed by American financial vagaries and by the independent countries' high preference for gold, the London money market could only remain in balance by substantially altering its interest rates. London rates were altered to attract money from abroad, i.e. genuine foreign money, but above all to bring British-owned money back to London. So British commercial banks had to be persuaded to keep more foreign and less home bills in their portfolios—which is tantamount to saying that, in the end, British home trade absorbed American oscillations.

The precise nature of the mechanism that regulated the international monetary system of our two decades has long been a source of hot dispute, especially as regards Britain's ability to shift the adjustment burden to other countries. It should by now be clear that the United States was the largest disrupting factor and India the largest stabilising factor; Britain's role, however, must not be overlooked. It is valuable in this context to observe the behaviour of the British economy, compared to the world economy, in the cycles that occurred during the period under review. In her work on pre-1914 cycles,[22] Ilse Mintz has pointed out that, over the whole period, the British economy expanded only when the rest of the world expanded—which is not surprising when we recall the degree of British dependence on foreign trade. But we also learn that, very often, the British economy went much earlier than the rest of the world into a contraction of trade. This had occurred only since 1900. In the previous decade, British cycles had been perfectly synchronous with world cycles. But from 1900 to 1913, Ilse Mintz notes that the British economy preceded the world economy into contraction in 13 quarters, while it was synchronous in only four quarters. In my opinion, the explanation lies in the fact that the British economy was unique in possessing a financial system that allowed funds to be freely shifted between home and foreign placements, according to where the highest profits could be made. As Bagehot had written as early as 1873, 'English capital goes securely and instantly where it is most required, and where it yields most, as water runs to find its level.'[23] The huge advances in international exchange networks in the 15 years before 1914 required a huge amount of finance, and London was the only place where local financial institutions could freely choose between placing their funds at home or abroad. In most cases, their choices caused no imme-

[22] I. Mintz, *Trade Balances During Business Cycles: US and Britain since 1880*, Princeton 1959.
[23] *Lombard Street, op. cit.*, p. 13.

diate repercussions on the gold market, but credit conditions in England were certainly affected, thereby giving rise to a changeover from expansion to contraction earlier than that experienced by the rest of the world.

World expansion led to increased pressure on the gold market; as money supply expanded in the gold standard countries, so gold reserves were required by law to keep pace with it. The countries whose expansion caused a trade deficit (i.e. the industrial countries) therefore had to accumulate gold when they should have been losing it. To prevent the Ricardian mechanism from working, the monetary authorities of those countries mobilised their lines of first defence, falling back on the foreign exchange deposits they had accumulated in the vaults of the major financial countries. Thus only a trickle of gold flowed from the 'deficit' countries to the 'surplus' ones. The gold recycling mechanism, which worked well as far as colonial territories were concerned, was only partially effective where independent primary exporters such as the United States were involved.

The vital function performed by India must be emphasised. Expansionary phases coincided in Britain with export surpluses; this has been explained by claiming that the increase in foreign investment, which also took place during expansion, induced an increased demand for British exports by the countries invested in.[24] Ilse Mintz has, however, noted that the growth of British exports in the expansionary phases was much more due to an increase in their value than in their volume. Britain, as we know, redirected her exports more and more towards the markets of her Empire, where any increase in the price of her exports could only induce a rise in their value, as foreign competition was absent. Thus pressure on British gold reserves was at least partially reduced. Further relief came from the automatic 'recycling' of the Empire's surplus to London.[25]

Now that we have seen how important these funds were, we can understand why the Bank of England and the joint-stock banks competed so fiercely over them. We must also consider another protagonist of *fin de siècle* monetary history: France. France had become the centre of her own monetary area, but, unlike Germany,

---

[24] Such was Alfred Marshall's interpretation: see his *Official Papers, op. cit.*, p. 285.
[25] It is tempting to see these years as the cradle of British stop-go policies.

she had not established a first line of defence around her gold reserves. France, like England, based the defence of her monetary stability, in the event of international gold rushes, on her position as a creditor and (unlike Britain) on a massive gold reserve. Thus, being the only country except Britain with a commercial deficit who did not defend her reserve by means of foreign currency sales, France was also the only country to make her gold reserves available on the London gold market. This assertion may be challenged by quoting several traditional gold devices employed by the Bank of France to keep gold in France. But it is nonetheless true that, in spite of those controls, gold flowed from Paris into London, when Bank rate rose sufficiently high. This was particularly true of the first of the two decades under discussion. Naturally, when Paris lost gold to London, France's monetary vassals would lose gold to Paris.

The quarter-century of international monetary history which is here analysed should really be divided into two sub-periods, with the Boer War as a watershed. The Boer War, we may now state on the strength of unanimous historical opinion, broke forever the great peace of the Victorian Age. Nearly thirty years of peace had led, in the developed world, to a definite bias of the international monetary system in favour of fiduciary liquidity. As international security waned, monetary rearmament got under way: perhaps before, but certainly not later than, its military equivalent—which meant a frenzied quest for gold, by great nations and small. In Britain the old debate about the sufficiency of the reserve flared up again; the wrangle acquired a distinctly bitter flavour when it was noticed that, on the occasion of the Boer crisis, the 1907 crisis, the Agadir crisis and the Balkan War crisis, the British commercial banks were quick to respond to Bank rate rises by reshuffling their portfolios, but little gold was attracted to London. Gold production had kept growing from 1900 to 1907 but after that it levelled off, although at a high level. Thus, given the unceasing demand for gold for industrial use, central banks could only lay their hands on the metal by discouraging private demand for it; which, as we have seen, is exactly what they did. The gold rush also meant a decline in the central banks' foreign currency holdings, which is even more noticeable when we discount the foreign exchange holdings of Russian, Indian and Japan, which were almost completely politically motivated.

In the years following the Boer War, the international monetary system once more showed a distinct tendency towards becoming a pure gold standard—a system which would degenerate into pure 'cash and carry' with the growing expectation of a major European war.

When confidence ebbs it is always the banker who suffers most. Britain was the world's banker, so she had to face the severest problems. The situation was somewhat eased by Indian and Japanese deposits, but the basic deterioration of the financial climate could not be checked. British monetary authorities had to use stop-gap measures such as the transformation of the Indian reserve into British government securities at the time of the Boer War. On the occasion of the American crisis of 1907, the Bank of England was forced by the turn of world events to raise its discount rate to 7%— a level it had not reached since 1873. And there Bank rate remained for two full months: there was simply no alternative. At the same time rates on short-term loans to the New York Stock Exchange shot up to 125%; and the Bank of England's reserves, from a maximum of 140 million dollars on September 8, 1907, dropped as low as 86 million on November 6.[26] The 7% Bank rate certainly coincided with an inflow of gold into Britain. But most of the flow came to London primarily because it was the only free gold market and people knew they could recover their gold later. As Hartley Withers commented, it could not be ascertained how much of the gold that flowed via London to New York was specifically owed to New York and how much was simply drained from other centres by London's dominating political ability.[27] Withers, who was on the spot, considered it possible that Bank rate, that perennial weapon of London finance, only continued to work because the States decided to bear the burden of readjustment by drastically decreasing imports and increasing exports. The crisis, in other words, was solved by recourse to current rather than capital account. Withers' intuition is borne out by the data on US trade which is given below.

It was precisely because of America's ability to generate a huge trade surplus just when the US money market wanted gold, that the Bank of England had to meet a huge increase in gold demand. The Bank therefore once more utilised Indian funds; and, in addi-

---

[26] See W. Mitchell, *op. cit.*
[27] H. Withers, *op. cit.*, p. 102.

tion, it asked the Bank of France for gold—not via Bank rate, but through direct *ad hoc* negotiation.[28]

U.S. Visible Trade (millions of dollars)

Month	Imports	Exports	Balance
Sept. 1907	103·4	135·4	32·0
Oct.	111·8	180·4	68·6
Nov.	110·9	204·5	93·6
Dec.	92·3	207·1	114·8
Jan. 1908	85·0	206·2	121·2

Source: W. Mitchell, *Business Cycles*, Berkeley 1911.

[28] On this subject see R. S. Sayers, *Bank of England Operations, op. cit.*, p. 102ff, and H. Withers, *op. cit.*, p. 221. For confirmation of these works, see also Blackett's memorandum.

SEVEN

*The Crisis of 1914 and the breakdown of the
International Gold Standard*

In the first chapter of this book I have gone to some lengths to show how the still current mythology about the pre-1914 gold standard has been created by post-war eulogists of that system, who set out to write its hagiography rather than its history. I have attempted to demonstrate, from contemporary accounts of pre-1914 monetary history, that such mythology is almost without substance.

It should also be evident how increasingly difficult it became for the British monetary authorities to maintain control over the system as the two and a half decades wore on. We have studied the elements favouring their efforts, together with the more potent elements working against them.

Another factor I have tried to bring out is the system's increasing inability to remain in equilibrium—an inability that gathered greater momentum as time went by. All attempts to rebalance had the unpleasant feature of being themselves unbalancing in the long run. The decade preceding 1914 was therefore a period in which the inherent de-stabilising aspects of stop-gap remedies manufactured a potential powder-keg. The ingredients became ever more explosive; and between the Boer War and July 1914, it took progressively less friction to strike sparks. So when the sparks themselves were large ones, the whole financial world was ignited; such was the case with the Boer War, the American crisis of 1907, the Balkan War.

The International Gold Standard was therefore very shaky by the summer of 1914; it had been so weakened by recurrent crises that the mere risk of a European war was sufficient to destroy it—the

Standard fell to pieces *before* war had been declared between any great powers. The London financial market, in particular, collapsed long before Great Britain declared war on the Central Powers. By the time Britain did go to war, the City had already been rescued by emergency governmental intervention.

It would have been far more extraordinary if the contrary had happened; if international financial operators had been caught napping by so massive an event as the Great War. In fact, they did not even wait to see Janus' temple officially open. They had long since caused, by their activities, the end of stable peace-time finance, thereby compelling governments (in some cases willingly, in others, principally Britain, highly reluctantly) to inaugurate war finance.

That the 1914 crisis definitely brought down the International Gold Standard has never been disputed. That the tree felled by the crisis was already rotten, I have tried to show in this book, besides examining the nature of the rot.

However, as to the immediate determinants of the 1914 crisis and the way in which it developed and was resolved, debate has raged ever since 1914. In the course of the intervening decades, distinguished writers have taken widely differing stands. Interpretation has hitherto been hampered by the dearth of official documents on the crisis. But the opening of the British Treasury and Prime Minister's Office Archives in the mid sixties has made accessible a large quantity of documents. These provide in my opinion sufficient evidence to warrant a fresh history of the crisis—reassessing its protagonists and their degrees of responsibility in order to provide a more accurate account of the sequence of events. I intend to devote the remainder of this chapter to such an account. First, however, let us briefly review the available literature on the subject.

The most recent reconstruction of the crisis is by Professor Sayers.[1]

The events of the last days of July and the first days of August 1914 warrant the use of the words Crisis . . . for there was a complete and prolonged breakdown of the financial markets: the foreign exchanges, the Stock Exchange, and the discount market . . . (p. 63). The trouble began, as one would expect, in purely international business, spreading thence to the Stock Exchange, the banks and the discount houses. The superstructure of inter-

[1] R. S. Sayers, *Gilletts in the London Money Market, 1867–1967*, Oxford 1968.

national credit was based on a comparatively small quantity of gold, and only a fraction of the gold could be quickly mobilised for actual payments. The continuance of the flow of international payments depended therefore on a substantial maintenance of the volume of international credit . . . and, there being no international monetary fund or other *deus ex machina* to step into a breach, this meant that the ordinary non-governmental lenders must go on lending if payments were to continue . . . (Ibid). The probability—and in the first days it was no worse than a probability—of widespread war in Europe was sufficient to disrupt the delicate structure, and, on Monday 27 July, the trouble in London really started. There had already been heavy selling in continental Stock Exchanges, and the prospect of non-payment of remittances due to London became serious; in these circumstances, the news of Austria's ultimatum to Serbia was sufficient to spark off actions in the City which, though precautionary by intention, proved destructive in the event. The accepting houses refused to commit themselves to new business and foreign banks in London called in Stock Exchange loans; the foreign exchanges swung violently in favour of London. On the Tuesday [28th], war having broken out between Austria and Serbia, the risk of general European war looked much worse. London houses were trying to call in loans made in continental markets, foreign exchange dealings became very difficult and (so it is supposed) some London banks began to call in Stock Exchange loans (p. 65).

So according to Sayers, it was the merchant and foreign banks who were the immediate determinants of the panic, which then spread to other financial institutions. In Sayers' opinion the process seems to have been automatic and almost inevitable, under the circumstances. Professor E. V. Morgan[2] came to the same conclusion in his much more detailed analysis of the crisis, on which Sayers' account is essentially based. An equal conviction was expressed by Sir Ralph Hawtrey,[3] who explicitly attributed the primary responsibility for the crisis to London and its position as:

an international short-term creditor, in virtue of the London acceptance business . . . (p. 123). The approach of war caused a

[2] E. V. Morgan, *British Financial Policy, 1914–1925*, London 1953.
[3] R. G. Hawtrey, *A Century of Bank Rate*, London 1938.

sudden fear that the delicate exchange mechanism [on which the remittances of the drawers of Bills on London to London accepting houses, who had to pay for those bills at maturity, depended] might be interrupted. There was a rush to acquire funds in London, and on the 28th of July . . . the demand for sterling exchange, especially from the United States, attained such a magnitude that the foreign exchange market broke down (Ibid).

The interruption of the exchanges starved merchant banks of liquidity, and endangered their ability to meet their obligations. Consequently the bills they had accepted, kept in the portfolios of joint-stock banks and discount houses, suddenly became illiquid; and the joint-stock banks began to recall their loans to the discount houses, thus forcing them to go to the Bank to have bills discounted. July 31st saw crisis grow into panic. The urgent need for sterling had led to a flood of sales on the Stock Exchange at a time when the jobbers, bewildered by the imminence of war, had no idea how far to mark down prices, and were unwilling to buy anything on terms. On the Friday morning it was hastily decided that the Stock Exchange should be closed. (P. 124.) Hawtrey adds that joint-stock banks feared their depositors would panic and attempt to convert their deposits into gold.

A different version of the opening of the crisis was provided by J. M. Keynes,[4] like Hawtrey a contemporary observer. According to him, the trouble began in the Stock Exchange; but although it is true that foreigners tried to unload bonds and shares they could not realise on the Continent (Continental exchanges having already closed down), this was not really what sparked off the crisis. The real culprits were the joint-stock bankers. Keynes noted that, at the end of July 1914, British stockbrokers were owed large sums by foreign creditors, on whose behalf they had bought stocks. Since a fortnightly settlement (actually 19 days) fell due exactly at that time, London stockbrokers expected to receive the money owed them from abroad, which they could use to repay their short-term debts to joint-stock banks. But the closure of foreign stock exchanges and the postponement of settlement by the Paris Bourse made the London brokers' credits irretrievable, so that several dealers were compelled to 'hammer themselves up'. To avoid a chain-reaction of

[4] J. M. Keynes, 'War and the Financial System, August 1914', in *The Economic Journal*, 1914.

failure, the Stock Exchange was closed on July 31. This drastic measure was also taken, according to Keynes, to prevent joint-stock banks from dumping on the market a huge quantity of stocks held as collateral of loans they had made—the prices of those stocks had fallen, and debtors could not make good their losses by repaying part of their debts, as was the usual practice.

Keynes had no hesitation in accusing the joint-stock banks of aggravating the crisis. His indictment was based on simple logic: the City was creditor to the rest of the world (to the tune of about £350 million so Keynes guessed), and the banks were creditors to the City. It was the banks who took the decision to drastically reduce their credit by recalling as much money as they could, in order to gain the liquidity they were sure their depositors (who the banks expected to panic) would demand. Owing to the German submarine menace, gold could no longer be transported; foreign debtors therefore had no way of repaying their debts to London finance houses, as all alternative sources of finance were to be found in London and had dried up as a result of the joint-stock banks' decision to curtail credit.

It was this short-sightedness on the part of joint-stock banks that Keynes held responsible for the closure of the Stock Exchange and the imposition of a moratorium on all bills accepted by London houses and all bank deposits. Keynes was well aware of the blow to London's financial prestige; in particular, the prestige of the accepting houses. He strongly doubted whether the latter would ever be able to resume the primary role they had played in international acceptance until July 1914.

As will be evident, my own reconstruction favours Keynes' macro-economic interpretation of the crisis. Unlike more recent writers, Keynes condemned in detail the joint-stock banks for transforming grave difficulties into fullscale international crisis—crisis which concluded an age. But I do not concur with Keynes' passionate and over-riding contempt of joint-stock bankers, whom he considered as the villains of the piece. He refused to consider their behaviour within the context of the British financial structure; and he did not hesitate, both in private and in public, to define the banks' behaviour as illogical and idiotic[5]—without stopping to con-

[5] See, in addition to Keynes' articles of 1914, his public and private correspondence during the crisis, reproduced in Vol. XVI of his collected writings.

sider that they might have adopted a correct micro-economic strategy. As will emerge from the remainder of this chapter, I support this micro-economic interpretation; which was, in fact, originally Keynes' own idea, confided in writing to a friend.

This more deterministic approach is, however, very different from that of Sayers. Sayers, as we have noted, explained the joint-stock banks' fears in terms of their alleged conviction that there would be a public run on them as soon as war broke out. Such fears were repeatedly and loudly voiced by bankers, but they do not square with actual developments in those crucial weeks, nor with the bankers' own behaviour in previous crises—1890, 1902, 1907. I hope to amplify this in the rest of the chapter. I shall try to show how bankers used the 1914 crisis as an occasion to damage the Inner Circle of the City beyond repair, so that they could substitute themselves in lucrative international business. This takeover had already been progressing for several years, as has earlier been demonstrated. The crisis of 1914 was seized on by the banks as a chance to complete the process.

The first six months of 1914 had seen longstanding internal tensions in the British financial system become even more strained. Joint-stock banks determinedly continued their twenty year old campaign to exclude traditional intermediaries from their functions: I have already described the battle over the acceptance business and the joint-stock banks' attack on public deposits. The final straw for the financial establishment was the setting up by the banks of a secret 'Gold Committee', chaired by Lord St. Aldwyn, whose secretary was Tritton; the Committee, as described earlier, had the task of co-ordinating the efforts of individual banks to accumulate gold reserves to rival the official Bank of England reserves. Sir Edward Holden of the Midland Bank had acted as a catalyst in the process, in the same way as he had been the protagonist of a decade of bank amalgamations. The Gold Committee's programme was international in outlook: gold reserves had after all accumulated in all leading countries, and after five years of searching debate the federal reserve system had been established in the United States. In the course of that debate, it had been convincingly argued that the 1907 crisis had been made much worse by the lack, in the United States, of a lender of last resort. Looking at the Bank of England's puny gold stock and at her inflexible note issue, British joint-stock banks had begun to believe that they had no effective lender of last resort either. Following the Baring crisis, Goschen had asked them to increase the balance they held at the Bank of England. They had obliged, only to discover that the Bank used their funds to compete with them in the discount market. The basic contradiction in the system was re-emphasised: a central bank was being made to perform public functions at a cost which it had to recoup and supplement with profit derived from private commercial banking operations—but those operations were in competition with the very intermediaries it was supposed to control. Joint-stock banks soon withdrew their support, devoting themselves instead to constructing an alternative credit network which excluded the traditional finance houses. As that network remained acephalous the banks' Gold Committee was founded to study the possibility of some form of federal government for the network.

By the early months of 1914 the Gold Committee's activities had become frankly open. It seemed that the banks were reaching a basic agreement on the joint use of the gold reserves they had piled up: this had been proved to some extent by the banks' intervention to shore up a provincial bank, without reference to the Bank of England. The impression had been also strengthened by Holden's public request for a Royal Commission to be appointed to investigate the problem of reserves.

I have made mention of the consternation, fear, and resentment aroused in the City's Inner Circle by the banks' unorthodox activities. The Treasury was also attempting to become the supreme moderator in British financial affairs. As regarded gold reserves, the Treasury staff displayed a tendency to side with the financial Establishment—to whom they were in any case much closer—for educational and social reasons, than they were to the banks.

At the end of February 1914, the Chancellor of the Exchequer requested from the Treasury's permanent under-secretary, Sir John Bradbury, a document expressing the Treasury view on the subject of gold reserves. It was the outcome of Holden's outspoken request that a Royal Commission be appointed. On March 3 the Governor of the Bank of England went to Whitehall in order to formally deprecate Holden's proposal.

The memorandum the Treasury sent to the Chancellor is kept in the Treasury Files of the Public Record Office (T 170 19); it is dated May 22, 1914. It was written by Basil Blackett, a brilliant young Treasury man and a friend of Keynes, who declared in the note he appended to the memorandum that he had 'discussed many points with Mr. R. G. Hawtrey', who was at the time also at the Treasury. The memorandum, a resumé of which was sent to Lloyd George on February 28, 1914, appears as Appendix A1.

In the memorandum Blackett set out to consider all the main points of Holden's case for increasing the reserves, and all aspects of the latter's proposal to reform the prevailing system of reserves management. He also did some guesswork on the size of banks' private reserves, helped by the Governor of the Bank of England's estimate.

He summed up the arguments advanced by the prevailing system's critics as follows:

It is said that, in comparison to the volume of banking and exchange transactions, British gold reserves are too small; that they are small compared to those of other countries, and that the latter have been increasing their reserves in recent years, while the same did not happen in Britain. It is also said that British reserves are a smaller proportion of total transactions than they used to be. It is affirmed that British trade suffers from the payment fluctuations of the official discount rate, while France with her strong reserves, manages to avoid such fluctuations. Dissatisfaction is also expressed at the way the Bank manages her reserves. Suggestions are offered on how the cost of keeping the Reserves ought to be shared; it is, in particular, suggested that the Government, as it gets the deposits of the Post Office Savings Bank, ought to contribute substantially to the Reserves.

Blackett went on to analyse these points. He noted first of all that comparing Britain's reserves to those of other countries was not a fruitful exercise, as no other country had such a highly developed banking system or used cheques so widely; only in England had notes and coins become such an insignificant proportion of the total money supply—which drastically reduced the banking system's cash requirements. In some countries such as the United States and Germany, on the other hand, there was a legal requirement to expand gold reserves when the quantity of notes and inconvertible paper was expanded. Moreover, Blackett noted that England was the only country to have enjoyed such a long period of peace and absence of social upheavals. Hoarding had therefore disappeared, since the motives that induced it had disappeared; and the habits of British bankers reflected the absence of any fears of the public asking for their deposits back.

Finally—and this was the most important argument Blackett used—Britain was the only country excluding France which was a creditor to the rest of the world; she also had the largest gold market in the world. This made it possible for gold to flow to London whenever it was required there.

Blackett went on to state that there were two types of reason why a reserve was necessary: internal demand and external demand for gold. As regarded the former, it could be met by supplying Bank of England notes or, when the worst came to the worst, by suspending Peel's Act. The latter measure had only been resorted to in extreme cases in the past; but there was no reason why it should not become more widely used in the future, nor why it should not be regulated by a law, thereby reforming the British monetary system along the same lines as most other countries (who had originally taken their inspiration from the British system). As for foreign demand for gold, Blackett acknowledged the fact that it could not be met out of official British reserves, which were not large enough. It was therefore necessary to consider what ways were open to Britain to attract gold from abroad, and how long it would take before gold arrived in London in sufficient amounts.

London received the greater part of the gold mined each year, and the Bank of England was always ready to buy it at the price of £3 17s 9d an ounce. If the Bank wanted to, it could always obtain gold by offering a price competitive with the market price; if it did not do so more frequently, this was because it would thereby shoulder the whole burden of reinforcing the reserves. Gold was normally attracted to London by increasing Bank rate, thus causing the restricting of credit internally and the attracting of capital to London. Both these effects induced the exchanges to move in favour of London, but the latter was the faster, because of the possibility it offered to arbitrageurs. Interest on British capital exported in previous decades could be invested in other countries as well as in Britain; but an increase in Bank rate caused interest to be invested in London.

Finally, Blackett remarked, although it was true that many large countries had become in recent years increasingly restive towards allowing gold to emigrate (even if only temporarily), another phenomenon had at the same time taken place: the accumulation of gold reserves by South American and other small countries. Their gold could be much more easily attracted to London—though later on in the memorandum Blackett noted that in 1907, Brazil, although she had piled up a £20 million gold reserve, preferred to see her exchange rate depreciate rather than let any of that reserve go. There was something strange in reserves, he reflected—because people were used to seeing them high, they considered their decline as a very dangerous phenomenon. Blackett added that there also existed the Indian Gold Standard Reserve, which was deposited in London and could very well be employed to defend the pound (but he noted that such a use ought not to be publicised, otherwise Indian patriots would certainly have condemned it). How quickly did the mechanism respond that Britain used to attract gold? Blackett considered that in times of peace the ease of communications allowed a rapid inflow, helped by the fact that the Bank of France, in her own interests, would come to the Bank of England's rescue—since a financial catastrophe in London would certainly induce a much graver one in Paris.

What effects would the outbreak of a European war involving Britain have on English reserves? Blackett observed that it was often said, on the precedent of the Napoleonic War, that such an event would cause Britain to suspend convertibility. But the Crimean War had not caused any such suspension. And the outbreak of a European war which caused all financial markets except New York to close, would certainly be a grave event; but it would reduce the British authorities' problems rather than increasing them. As it turned out, since Britain was a creditor country, and since the outflow of gold was interrupted by a 10% Bank rate and by the danger of ships being captured by enemy vessels, the only problem to be faced was that of an internal drain. To deal with the latter, it would be sufficient to extend the fiduciary issue—since if war broke out in late summer, there would certainly be an increase in circulation, due to mobilisation, but this would be counterbalanced by a decreased demand for gold for export.

Going on to examine the Bank of England's position as keeper of the gold reserve, Blackett noted that the 'Old Lady' had managed until the eighties to impose her will on the City by the strength she derived from her size. After that decade, because of the emergence of joint-stock banks, the Bank had experienced increasing diffi-

culties, and had become heavily dependent on joint-stock banks'
deposits. Such dependence, Blackett asserted, led joint-stock banks
to criticise the Bank's policies and to refuse her directives. At the
same time the Bank's directors looked enviously at the large dividends other banks paid to their shareholders. As a result, Blackett
concluded, joint-stock banks obtained every advantage from the
system without having to face any responsibility; and the opposite
was true for the Bank of England. In theory, the Bank was the
centre of the system. In practice, the banks set up their Gold
Committee to manage their reserves by themselves, and combined
whenever one of their colleagues was in difficulties and had to be
rescued—an operation which would previously have been effected
directly by the Bank of England. All these, Blackett declared, were
'symptoms of the shifting in the centre of gravity'.

Thus, since the Bank could not sacrifice her modest dividend by
heroic action in defence of the Reserve, the burden of a high Bank
rate was shouldered by trade and industry, while the joint-stock
banks made ever higher profits. As the Bank of England depended
on the banks, she was led to consider their claims more seriously
than she considered those from the real sector of the economy. That
was why it had not so far been possible to organise a defence
against the annual autumn gold drains which caused Bank rate to
rise very high.

As for Sir Edward Holden's proposals that the banks create a
gold reserve, this would be acceptable only if the banks were prepared to deposit the reserve with the Bank of England, and to
administer it on a joint basis with the latter. 'For the moment these
reserves are equally capable of being used to hinder the policy of
the Bank of England, and tend only to intensify the divergence
between the seat of responsibility and the seat of power'.

Blackett took a dim view of Holden's other proposal that the
banks ought to give £20 million in sovereigns plus £40 million in
accepted bills to the Issue Department of the Bank, in order to receive £60 million in Bank notes, while the Government would
give the Bank £11 million in gold, thereby paying its debt to the
Bank and at the same time building up a reserve against Post
Office Savings Deposits. If the banks had gold, why should they, in
an emergency, want Bank notes? They could pay out gold, and get
notes from the Bank in the normal way. Moreover—Blackett noted
—Holden had said nothing about who would decide when there

was an emergency and who would administer the note issue. His proposal also introduced compulsory reserves, which had proved most harmful in the American crisis of 1907. And the repayment of the Government's debt to the Bank would mean a loss of $2\frac{1}{2}\%$ interest on the sum for the Bank and a capital loss of 25% for the Government, since the latter in order to get gold, would have to issue Consols, now quoted at 75. Moreover, Post Office Savings Banks were not really banks, and needed no reserves because they could not go bankrupt. Keeping reserves was a cost inherent in the business of banking, and must be wholly borne by banks. If the Government were to share it, then the taxpayer would be paying for it, and the Government would be unduly favouring the banking industry compared to other industries.

Blackett sent his memorandum for comments to Keynes, who provided them in a letter dated June 24, 1914.[6] He said he believed it was not correct to assert that only banks would suffer from a panic. In a modern crisis, it was not realistic to expect banks to go bankrupt. The loss to the community would derive from the fact that banks, in a crisis, tend to cut out credit to their weakest clients, and those are compelled to dump their stocks on the Stock Exchange. A 10% Bank rate would certainly not cause the banks any hardship.

On the issues raised by Blackett, Keynes made three points:

(1) The present controversy did not really have to do with the size of reserves but with where, in the future, the centre of power and responsibility would lie in the London money market. Reserves were, at most, only slightly inadequate; but the problem of distribution of power was of great importance, and had to be given the highest attention by the Government.

(2) The Government must try to get into the fight, even at the cost of contributing to the Reserve, in order to gain negotiating power with the banking community; but it had to act without introducing new legislation, accepting the (not really legitimate) proposal of setting up a reserve against savings deposits.

(3) New legislation was, however, required to make the banking system more elastic. Keynes considered that banks now had so many branches that the merest wish on their part to increase their cash reserves only slightly would lead to a strong decrease in the

[5] See footnote 5, p. 131.

Bank of England's gold holdings. It was essential that banks could count on Bank notes in an emergency.

Keynes' position thus differed in important features from that taken by Blackett in his memorandum. They had arrived at a common diagnosis of the nature of the transformation undergone by the British financial system. They also agreed in seeing the banks as protagonists of the financial crisis that a European war would spark off in London. But while Blackett passionately sided with the City, considered the joint-stock banks' motives with contempt and denied the value of Government intervention, Keynes outlined with great clarity an important objective determinant of the banks' behaviour, and considered it strategically essential to establish a Government bridgehead in the banking world.

The Chancellor of the Exchequer had also requested advice on the subject from Sir George Paish, the Government's statistical expert. Sir George replied promptly by sending him a memorandum which, while less modern and penetrating than Blackett's, was more cautious and balanced.[7] The great British banks—Sir George stated—were very worried about the possibility that a great power, if hostile to England, could deprive her of her gold in a matter of days by demanding the simultaneous repayment of a mass of bills and short-term deposits. This had already been done by France in Berlin at the time of the Agadir incident; and German bankers had again experienced a capital outflow in 1912, during the Balkan War, and had reacted by deciding to pile up reserves. English bankers thought it might be wise to follow the German lead, especially in view of the huge size of bank deposits in England.

Bankers, Sir George continued, also complained about the continuous depreciation of Government securities, which had compelled them to mobilise all their hidden reserves in order not to reveal the losses they had suffered on their Gilt Edged.

Sir George then recalled that when, 10 years before, Asquith (then Chancellor) had asked his advice on the appropriateness of a Government investigation of the banks' position and the reserve problem, he had answered negatively on both points, as he had considered that, since the economy was then just emerging from recession and moving in a favourable direction, it was not appropriate to cut credit by increasing reserves. Now, however, the

[7] T 171 53, reproduced in Appendix B.

prospect was vastly different: there was expected to be a world recession, caused by every government rushing to gold. In such a situation, the British economy would have an excess of liquidity. It was therefore a good time to appoint a Royal Commission to advise on the adequacy of reserves and on how to put the huge British banking system on a solid foundation. Since banks had already piled up a sufficiency of reserves, Sir George added, the Commission's task would be confined to deciding whether that gold should be kept by the banks or should be deposited at the Bank of England. Sir George personally thought the last option was the best, as reserves would then be visible to all and would reinforce confidence. The measure would have to be implemented in practice by ordering that the banks keep 2% of their deposits at the Bank— whose Governor, he further suggested, should remain in his post for much longer than two years and should be appointed with Government approval. Banks should moreover be assured that their gold, deposited at the Bank, would be used only in emergencies, and that could be done by asking the Bank to keep her reserve/ liabilities ratio oscillating between 45% and 70% instead of the present 30%–60%. Finally, Sir George declared himself in favour of introducing a clause allowing the Bank to issue an unlimited number of notes in an emergency, after having been authorised to do so by the Chancellor. He also favoured Government participation in the reserve.

In short, Sir George Paish proposed reforms very similar to those which would actually take place in future decades. But whereas he wanted to see them introduced by new legislation, most were actually introduced by gentlemen's agreements.

The banks, however, showed no sign of wanting to surrender the cash they had piled up to the Governor. They planned to create an alternative reserve kept entirely under their control. Sir Felix Schuster, chairman of the Union of London and Smiths Bank, who was the most respected *doyen* of the joint-stock bankers, put this plan forth publicly in a speech to his bank's shareholders on July 22, 1914. His views were authoritatively underwritten by *The Times*[8] in a leading article which, starting from Schuster's speech and then advocating reform of the British monetary system, concluded that, if a possible financial crisis were to be faced effectively, 'the only

---

[8] *The Times*, July 23, 1914, p. 21.

possible effective remedy, the only secure bulwark is a gold reserve, systematically and scientifically collected, and distributed among the great banking institutions which collect it'.

On July 24, Austria sent her ultimatum to Serbia. As Blackett had foreseen, and contrary to the fears expressed by bankers and shared by Paish, sterling became progressively stronger in international markets. Since it was the vehicle-currency *par excellence*, everyone wanted it to make payments. Only in Paris, the one financial centre seriously in credit to London, did the exchanges turn against sterling so that gold had to flow from London. As Blackett had also foreseen but discounted, New York remained open and London was able to obtain gold from there in large amounts. (London had, in any case, been doing that since June; and became more aggressive in the last week of July, when 30 million dollars of gold were shipped to London—as we learn from the foreign exchange column of *The Times*.)

Throughout the world's stock exchanges, stocks were sold furiously. London was no exception; but since the exchanges turned in London's favour, it was clear that (a) British investors were selling their portfolios in all stock exchanges, and (b) foreign investors who sold their stocks in London were not exchanging the proceeds for either gold or foreign currency. They merely made their portfolios more liquid, though always in sterling. All of which reinforces the opinion of Keynes and Withers that the wave of sales in London was really caused by the Bank of England asking jobbers to 'top up' their debts, by paying money to make up for the capital losses suffered by the shares they gave banks as collateral for their loans. Jobbers were compelled to sell at whatever price they fetched, in order to get hold of the cash the banks wanted.

Meanwhile, the banks began to put pressure on the discount market, calling back loans they had made to bill brokers and thus compelling them to go to the Bank of England for assistance. In the last week of July, the Bank increased its portfolio of 'other securities' by a good £13½ million. We may infer that as much cash went into the banks' coffers.

On July 27 Serbia rejected the Austrian ultimatum. In Paris and Berlin, the stock exchanges were struck by panic, while in London the wave of sales mounted but was still absorbed by the market. In London, the crucial day was the following one, which was a settlement day. Even *The Times*, usually a supporter of joint-stock banks, reported that day that the banks had asked the discount houses to pay back their debts, forcing them to knock on the door of the Bank of England. Tuesday July 28 was the black day on which the crisis escalated.

Austria declared war on Serbia on July 29. In the hope of somehow allaying the panic that had been wrought in London by the internal causes we have already noted, *The Times* published a remarkable leader under the title 'The strength of London'. The writer stated that the events of the last few days had subjected the London money market and the Stock Exchange to heavy tension, and both markets had so far stood the pressure well. This solidity was in sharp contrast to the weakness shown by Continental markets, in several of which trading had been suspended, so that all burdens had been shifted on to London. Large amounts of stocks normally traded on the Continent had been sold in London in the last three days, and had been absorbed remarkably well, with New York's help. Foreign banks in London had made things more difficult by asking stockbrokers to repay their debts. English banks, even if they had been compelled somewhat to reduce their credits to the Stock Exchange, had shown much greater consideration towards their customers.

Thus *The Times* gave currency to the chauvinistic interpretation we have described above, with the open intention of covering up the banks' responsibility for the aggravation of the crisis. This version was not however accepted by those who had been direct witnesses of events, such as the Bank of England, the merchant banks and the Stock Exchange dealers: these had no qualms about directing their ill-feelings towards the joint-stock banks.

On the same day, Mr. Joynson-Hicks put down in the Commons a question to the Chancellor of the Exchequer, asking whether the latter had been in contact with the Bank of England to organise a meeting of bankers to control the financial situation that had come about. Joynson-Hicks exhorted him to do this as soon as possible, if he had not already done so.

In fact Lloyd George, so far as we can make out from available documents, had not yet taken any initiative. After Joynson-Hick's question, he immediately asked Sir John Bradbury to organise a visit by a Treasury party to the Bank of England; the visit took place the same day. The Treasury men were received by the Governor, Cunliffe, accompanied by some members of the Committee of Treasury, namely Lord Revelstoke, Sir Edward Hambro, Goschen and Cole. To the delegation's question, the Governor replied that:

> his opinion was confirmed by the other directors present ... that the Bank of England was in a very strong position, and that any special steps of the nature suggested would be unnecessary, and indeed harmful as tending to excite apprehensions.
>
> The Bank of England, and the Joint-stock banks (with whom the Bank of England keeps in close touch through periodic meetings) had the situation in hand. Money so far is plentiful and cheap, indeed, if it were not for the European crisis, a rate of 2% would be appropriate: the situation so far as the Banks are concerned is normal, though the same could not quite be said of the discount houses who have been putting up rates, with the result that the Bank is discounting largely today.
>
> The Governor and the directors present unanimously advised a reply to the following effect: 'I have been in consultation with the Bank of England, and I am advised that there is nothing in the financial situation at the present moment which would make such a suggestion necessary or advisable.'[9]

The opinion was also expressed that it would be better if the Governor did not go to see the Chancellor, in case alarming inferences were made.

In its opening reply to the Government, the Bank of England clearly took up a position to defend the whole financial community against Government intervention. When we recall the venomous declaration made only a few months earlier by Mr. Cole on the behaviour of commercial banks in the money market, we can only deduce from the Bank's declaration to the Treasury delegation that it was meant to prevent the establishment of a horizontal committee of representatives of all banks and other intermediaries, which would organise a defence against the crisis. In order to kill this proposal, the Bank did not refrain from painting a picture of the financial situation in London which it knew to be patently false: the only slight problem of Cuncliffe and Co. seemed to be the discount houses' decision to put up rates, and even here they could apparently keep control.

[9] T 170 14, reproduced in Appendix C.

But in reality, the crisis had already broken out in all its fierceness. The accepting houses (some of which were owned by the Bank's directors) were on the verge of bankruptcy, since the banks were not giving a penny to their foreign clients, who had for decades borrowed in London to meet their maturing bills' payments—and the bills had been accepted by London houses. Discount houses and bill brokers faced the same fate, as the banks had asked them to repay the loans that were their working capital. Stock Exchange dealers, who worked on loans from foreign banks, had been compelled to dump their stocks on the market to be able to return the money they had borrowed. By so doing they had compelled the joint-stock banks to ask their customers to 'top up' their Lombard accounts, as the value of the collateral had slumped.

In spite of the Olympian serenity of the Bank of England, the situation became exacerbated on July 30. Seven members of the Stock Exchange had 'hammered themselves up'; as a result, transactions were practically suspended for two hours. The Bank raised its rate from 3% to 4%. On July 31, the Stock Exchange governing body ordered that trading be interrupted. The same decision was taken in New York, the only other market that had remained in operation. Bank rate was raised to 8%, in the hope of receiving what gold one does not know—perhaps it was hoped to stop the 'internal drain'. Now that the tragedy had been consummated, and all the features that made London the heart of international financial life had been lost, the joint-stock banks, which had deliberately caused the panic (they were the main source of international liquidity, and had abruptly interrupted its flow), were ready to accelerate the shifting of the centre of gravity in their favour, as Blackett and Keynes had realised was happening. As we have seen, they had a plan to face the emergency they themselves had created. They submitted it to the Chancellor of the Exchequer; and on July 31 Lloyd George received a letter from Sir Felix Schuster and Edward Holden, announcing their proposal.

The scheme proposed by the banks[10] should, in their opinion, be adopted when Bank rate was raised to 8%; the aim was to provide the British monetary system with the 'superstructure of a currency more elastic than gold currency,' reinforced by the reserves the

[10] T 170 14, reproduced in Appendix D.

banks had piled up. The scheme was divided into the following points.

(1) The Government must, if need be, authorise the Bank of England to suspend the Bank Charter Act of 1844 regarding the limitation of the issue of notes against securities—as had been done in 1847, 1857 and 1866.

(2) The Bank of England must be allowed to issue notes to bankers in England and Wales, up to a maximum of £45 million, against the bankers' deposit of gold or securities (keeping the proportion of $\frac{1}{3}$ gold, $\frac{2}{3}$ securities). Securities which could be deposited would be bills accepted by the bankers and approved by the Bank, and Government stock.

(3) The first measure to be taken would be the issue of £12 million in notes to bankers, against the bankers' deposit of an equal sum in gold with the Bank of England: this ought to be done as soon as the letter suspending Bank Act was sent out.

(4) The issue of notes on the terms described above had to have the features of emergency and temporariness. Bills and securities given as collateral would be redeemed at the end of the moratorium which was to be enforced.

(5) Bankers would pay the Government a tax on all bank notes they had been issued against bills and securities, and the rate of the tax would be fixed in agreement with the Treasury.

We will examine these proposals in detail, since it is detail that reveals the banks' intentions.

The scheme proposed to ensure the supply of cash 'so urgently required by our country in the present time of crisis, in order to permit the continuation of all commercial and financial efforts.' It therefore took as its point of departure an event that had not really happened, i.e. a crisis of confidence in the banking system on the part of the public. What had in fact happened was that banks had, in the last days of July, refused to pay out gold—even in small amounts—to the not overlarge number of people who had requested it. Instead of sovereigns, those people had been offered five pound notes, which they could not use at all, and had been told by the banks to go and exchange them for gold at the Bank of England. A small crowd had therefore gathered in front of the Bank, but the population had not taken the event as a sign of difficulty or crisis. At the same time, as we have noted above, the banks were draining the Bank of England of 12 million of its gold.

Banks had thus presupposed a crisis of confidence as a certainty: as we read in their document, 'the scheme we propose for your acceptance is one which has slowly matured after lengthy discussions and has lately received the approval of the special Gold-Subcommittee of the clearing banks, under the presidency of Lord St. Aldwyn, as suitable for adoption as a recognised means of providing an emergency currency'. But as the public had not produced the panic behaviour which was expected of them, the banks had themselves had to engineer a crisis of confidence (albeit only a small one) by refusing to pay out gold and by strengthening with Bank of England gold.

They were accused of that very act by Sir John Bradbury in a brief[11] he wrote for Lloyd George as soon as the latter had read the banks' proposals.

A fall of £12m. in a week [in the Bank of England's reserves] is no doubt considerable—he wrote—and if it represented spontaneous hoarding of gold on the part of individuals it might even be alarming. But all the evidence to hand tends to show that the general public have behaved with great coolness, the withdrawals from banks (including the Post Office Savings Banks) have been moderate in amount, and the reduction of the Bank of England stock of gold represents, in the main, amounts taken by other banks, and held by them as precaution against contingencies. The reserve has in fact been mobilised, not disbanded. That the banks of the country should reinforce their cash balances to enable themselves to meet exceptional demands should such demands occur is prudent and reasonable, but suggestions have been freely made that bankers in their anxiety to retain their gold have at any rate in some instances tended to restrict the payment out of specie and offered notes instead of gold to their customers, when gold was preferred. If such action has been taken—and whether it has or not I regret to say that I have heard it advocated on grounds of policy by bankers of some experience—I cannot state too emphatically that I regard it as most mischievous and dangerous. A currency like ours, which is in the main metallic, has many advantages but it has one great danger: it is unable to defend itself against the practice of hoarding coin, if that practice

___
[11] T 170 14, reproduced in Appendix E.

assumes large dimensions; and if the banks which should be its principal guardians set the example of that practice their customers will inevitably, and indeed must necessarily, follow it. So long as a customer can obtain sovereigns, shillings, and pence for his daily requirements, from his banker, he will be content to depend on that source of supply. If difficulties are placed in the way of his obtaining them he will apprehend great difficulties in the future and will protect himself by laying in a store. The development of banking which has been one of the most remarkable features of the last half century has laid upon the joint-stock banks very serious and important duties in relation to the currency and if specie payments are to be maintained—and Heaven forbid that they should be suspended while a sovereign remains to pay—it is essential that they, no less than the Old Lady of Threadneedle Street, herself, should make it a point of honour to maintain them ... In times like the present it is of primary importance that nothing should be done to create distrust of, or even make unpopular, the Bank of England note.

Bradbury concluded by saying that if banks kept on paying out gold without complaining, there would be no need to break 'our honourable tradition of 92 years of uninterrupted convertibility'.

But as Bradbury remarked in a note[12] appended to a copy of his brief that he sent to Bonham-Carter (who brought it to Asquith's attention) Lloyd George was favourable to the banks' scheme. The Cabinet Committee was equally favourable, and, what was more, according to Bradbury it was even committed to the general outlines of the scheme.

Lloyd George again asked Sir George Paish's advice on the issue. The latter replied in a letter dated August 1st, 2 a.m.[13] Sir George provided a rather blurred interpretation of the situation—he maintained that the great London finance houses risked bankruptcy since they could not retrieve their foreign credits, and could neither get credit nor sell their securities because the Stock Exchange was closed. He added that hoarding by individuals had begun on a large scale. In his opinion, a general moratorium should be decreed, if the great finance houses were to be saved from bankruptcy. And it was on their existence that the international trade of Britain

[12] See Appendix E.
[13] T 170 14, reproduced in Appendix F.

vitally depended. At the same time Bank Act should be suspended, as well as sterling convertibility, and one pound notes should be issued.

Thus the Chancellor of the Exchequer received diametrically-opposed advice from his institutional experts. He agreed with his colleagues to send the banks a reply to their proposal; the reply was dated August 2.[14] Lloyd George declared that the Government accepted the banks' offer to deposit £12 to £15 million with the Issue Department of the Bank of England, against Bank notes. The Government, he said, wanted to make clear that it did not intend, by accepting the offer, to agree with the banks' proposal to pay gold to the Bank rather than to their clients. In any case, he added, since the banks' proposal seemed to be the outcome of meetings of a Gold Subcommittee and had not been approved by all banks, it could only be taken as an *una tantum* remedy, in no way prejudicing the country's monetary system in the future.

As for the issue of banknotes against the deposit of bills and securities, Lloyd George made clear that this would be regulated as follows:

(1) It should be restricted to amounts the Treasury considered necessary to circulation.

(2) It would take place only when Bank rate was at 10% or more, and would be considered as a loan made by the Government to the Bank of England, at an interest equal to Bank rate.

(3) Bills and securities given in exchange for Bank notes had to be approved by the Bank of England.

Meanwhile, on August 1, Bank rate had been lifted to 10%, at the Treasury's express request—the level at which Bank rate had stood when the Bank Charter Act had been suspended on the three previous occasions. The Treasury had made this a condition to be fulfilled before a letter, requested by the Bank, would be sent authorising the latter to exceed the legal limit on the issue of notes should that be necessary.

On August 2, R. M. Holland, honourable secretary to the Clearing Bankers' Association, sent Lloyd George a letter[15] in which he reported the decisions taken at a meeting of Clearing Bankers—in which the directors of the Union Discount Company and the National Discount Company had also taken part—on the subject of

[14] T 170 14.
[15] T 170 14.

the emergency measures to be adopted. The resolutions approved were:

(1) That the Bank Act should be suspended in accordance with the memorandum handed to the Treasury on the evening of August 1.

(2) That Bank notes to the value of £1 and 10 shillings should be issued as soon as possible.

(3) That specie payments by the Bank of England should be suspended as soon as the issue of £1 notes was made.

(4) That the proposed moratorium should be made general for one month.

(5) That the supply of silver coin should be increased.

(6) That the August Bank Holiday should be extended for at least two more days, to enable the completion of all necessary arrangements for the convenience of the public.

The last point was reiterated the next day by an Assembly of Merchants and Bankers in the City (chaired by the Governor of the Bank of England), and a postponement of three days was proposed. The proposal had been moved by Lord Revelstoke and seconded by Sir Edward Holden; it thus reflected the unanimous will of the British financial world. Lloyd George conceded the postponement. On August 3 came the Royal Decree ordering a moratorium of one month on all bills.

The curtain thus descended on the 'first act' of the crisis. The accepting houses had been saved from bankruptcy; and the whole City had thereby been shored up, at least temporarily. The joint-stock banks, however, had never had any intention of causing the violent death of the traditional institutions. They had only wanted to threaten them with the possibility of such a death, in order to have them rescued *in extremis* and to paralyse their future action. With the agreement on a moratorium, the banks succeeded in doing just that; and, by accepting it, they also put the Government in their debt, and could now ask favours.

The 'second act' of the crisis, the most interesting and the least known, is represented by the conference held at the Treasury by Lloyd George. He was assisted by the last Chancellor of the Unionist Government, Austen Chamberlain; by the Governor of the Bank of England, Cunliffe; by Sir John Bradbury; and by several other dignitaries. Industrialists, merchants, bankers and stockbrokers also attended the Conference, which took place on the

4th, 5th and 6th of August. Taking advantage of the extension of Bank Holidays, the Chancellor consulted with the most representative leaders of the British industrial and financial *milieu*, in order to clarify his ideas on the country's economic situation, and to decide what other measures it would be necessary to adopt. He had to make up his mind about the other four points contained in the bankers' proposal.

The typed record of this Conference is one of the most fascinating documents in the whole of British financial history.[16] Absolute secrecy allowed the participants to express themselves with great frankness; as a result, the record reads like a theatrical play. And the plot—the struggle between opposite financial factions—is worthy of Brecht. We shall therefore review the course of events in detail.

Soon after the conference began, Lloyd George received a short memorandum from Keynes, in which the latter strongly argued against suspending convertibility.[17] As we have already seen, Sir John Bradbury was convinced that Lloyd George and the Cabinet Committee favoured the bankers' plan. Basil Blackett had the idea of asking Keynes to write against it. Keynes wrote his memorandum quickly and delivered it himself to London in a rather adventurous way.[18]

The memorandum faithfully reproduced the reasons given by Blackett in his May Paper, to explain how absolutely impossible it was for foreign dealers to take gold out of London, since the world was a net debtor to England. The only exception was France; but— and here Keynes followed Blackett's argument—why should the Bank of France want to embarrass England just now? Even if she did want to do so, she would not be able to take out more than 15 million: not enough to embarrass the Bank of England. Nor had England any reason to need gold for her purchases abroad. Her credits, and the income from past investment, would be more than sufficient. If convertibility were to be suspended, Keynes argued, London's role as the centre of the international monetary system would end: who would trust a currency which abandoned convertibility at the first sign of danger? If Britain suspended now, when no gold could be transported because of exorbitant insurance

---

[16] Kept in T 170 14.

[17] Keynes' Memorandum is to be found both in T 170 14 and in Vol. XVI of his *Collected Writings*.

[18] See the *Collected Writings*, op. cit., Vol. XVI.

premiums introduced for fear of German submarines, everyone would think that Britain would not hesitate to suspend on another occasion when gold was allowed to leave London. Moving on to the 'internal' side of the problem, Keynes noted that suspension of the Bank Act did not necessarily have to be accompanied by suspension of convertibility. On the contrary; one of the former's aims was to avoid the latter, by extracting gold from internal circulation. As to hoarding, Keynes very openly reiterated the accusations levelled at the banks by Bradbury in his brief: 'The recent heavy drain of gold from the Bank of England has been mainly due to a fit of hoarding on the part of the joint-stock banks. This gold will be available again as soon as these banks regain their equilibrium'.

Keynes departed from Bradbury's version when he advised that banks ought to discourage the public from requesting gold; they ought instead to pay out Bank notes, except when gold was to be genuinely used for payments abroad. In all other cases the public were to be sent to the Bank of England if they persisted in demanding gold.

Keynes thus favoured maintaining only *external* convertibility, in order to maintain London's unblemished image as the financial centre of the world; he discarded the pseudo-problems of internal convertibility, as he did not see them as plausible in the English context (here, he agreed with Blackett). He consequently took a detached view of the proposal by Bradbury to have the Treasury, rather than the Bank of England, issue small notes. It was, he believed, a measure that could be taken, but it was not essential; and, if it were taken, the notes would have to have some promise of convertibility written on them. That *was* essential, to reassure the public. But it was supremely important to avoid suspending external convertibility.

According to Basil Blackett,[19] Keynes' memorandum worked wonders where his own May Paper and Sir John Bradbury's brief of August 1 had failed to work. It convinced Lloyd George to go to the Conference ready to give in on many issues, but not on convertibility. By contrast with his previous position (which we are told was one of support for the banks' scheme, including suspending convertibility), Lloyd George had made a 180 degree turnabout.

After his memorandum had been read and its main message so

---

[19] See the *Collected Writings, op. cit.,* Vol. XVI.

well received, Keynes was called in to help at the Treasury for the duration of the conference. In his correspondence of that period, as well as in the articles he subsequently wrote on the subject, he gave, as I have said earlier, the clear impression of considering the banks' actions in causing the panic as the work of people who had lost all sense of the situation—whereas he had only two months earlier pointed out how the banks' escalation to power, and the Establishment's desperate resistance, had been responsible, and would be responsible in the future, for the upheavals shaking the British financial structure.

When Lloyd George's conference began in a room in Whitehall on August 4, the banks had already brought about the virtual ruin of the accepting houses. In order to rescue the latter, the Government had, by the moratorium, frozen about 350 million pounds' worth of bills in the banks' vaults, since the banks kept bills as assets against their short-term liabilities. Hence the bankers' request that the moratorium be made general. Meanwhile, however, banks kept on with the credit squeeze which they had arbitrarily begun in the middle of July, and which had caused the crisis.

In the first part of the conference traders and industrialists denounced this squeeze in very harsh terms: they affirmed that the country was keeping cool and there was no panic, only credit having been cut. Once it was restored, everything would be back to normal.

Sir Edward Holden, for the banks, replied that the squeeze was inevitable: banks had had $\frac{7}{8}$ of their assets frozen by the moratorium. If, at the end of the Bank Holiday, a large quantity of bank notes of small size could be available, the emergency would be alleviated.

But Lloyd George wanted first of all to establish the exact substance of the banks' scheme to deal with the emergency. He asked the industrialists and traders to withdraw, and conferred privately with the bankers. The scheme, as compared to the version given above, had undergone some change. The first point—that the moratorium should become general—remained the same. Immediately after this point, however, a proposal had been inserted whereby the bankers, in the case of a general moratorium being declared, agreed to make available funds payable in cash at their tills for the convenience of employers, so that they could pay wages and salaries. Such funds were not to exceed the employers' credit ceilings as they stood on the day of the moratorium. Bankers also offered to make cash available to all their clients, to an amount not exceeding 10% of each client's credit balance as it was on the day of the moratorium; this would apply to current as well as to deposit accounts.

As for cheques and other paper presented for payment at the Clearing House, the bankers proposed they should be dealt with normally, but reserved the right to decide against any case where it was thought that clients wanted to shift their accounts from one bank to another. They proposed that the Bank of England should advance cash to the banks against Clearing House certificates, in amounts proportional to the advances taken by each bank. This facility would be additional to the traditional methods of obtaining advances from the Bank, and should remain in force for a month. Finally, the banks asked that their clients should not be informed about the possibility of cashing cheques until the day after the re-opening of the Clearing House.

When the bankers had finished spelling out the details of their proposal, Lloyd George informed them that on the first day of re-opening the banks would be made available 25 million pounds in notes, 7.5 million of which would be one pound notes. He asked the bankers to suggest how the cash should be split among them; but he hastened to add that the Government was not going to suspend convertibility.

The bankers, through Holden and St. Aldwyn, insisted on the essential importance of this measure. They said there would not be enough cash when the banks re-opened. Lloyd George objected that industrialists had stated there was no sign of a panic. Holden, however, repeated his fear that when the banks opened again, everybody would try to secure cash, and there would then be no alternative but to give them the banks' reserves or the Bank of England's gold. But the one pound notes would be available, re-torted Lloyd George. Holden then wanted to know what bankers would be asked to give in exchange for those. Securities, answered the Chancellor. But the transaction could not be concluded in time, objected Holden. St. Aldwyn suggested that bankers could give Clearing House certificates in exchange for notes. Those certificates would be presented to the Treasury, and the Treasury would pro-vide the notes. Lloyd George replied that this was a new proposal, and he would have to study it with his advisers. Meanwhile, would the bankers withdraw to elect a permanent Committee which would negotiate with the Government on present and future problems? They did so; and while they were absent the Governor of the Bank of England arrived, and asked whether the new scheme was a substitute for the banks' earlier proposal to deposit their gold at the Bank of England. Lloyd George said he thought that the two schemes could co-exist.

Holden and the rest of the bankers' Committee were re-admitted. Holden began to complain that the bankers' gold was evaporating, and that after they had paid out wages on Saturday, very little of it would be left. Lloyd George reassured him. He was certain all confidence would return as soon as the country heard that industry, the banks and the Government had all conferred and reached agreement.

The Chancellor then announced to the Committee (composed of Holden, Schuster, Esdale, St. Aldwyn, Bell and Tritton) that it was the Government's intention to reduce Bank rate to 6%. He also asked the bankers to suggest to him the text of a declaration making the moratorium general, which he would read to the traders and industrialists who were waiting outside. He also proposed to hold a press conference for financial reporters: he would not tell them all that had been decided, but at least something, and he would exhort them to write articles emphasising the atmosphere of complete agreement in which the banks, the Bank of England and the Government were taking decisions to keep the country's credit intact. Finally, he proposed to continue discussions with bankers on the emergency scheme the next day.

The representatives of trade and industry were then re-admitted and the banks' proposal was read out to them: general moratorium, suspension of Bank Act, suspension of convertibility. The real sector's representatives reacted very strongly, asserting that they were absolutely against suspending convertibility. Naturally, Lloyd George was only too ready to come to their support. Holden, for the bankers, again said suspension would be necessary, at least until the new bank notes arrived at the tills of every bank. Lloyd George replied with the view of traders and industrialists: that there was no need to suspend, if the Government managed to print the new notes on time. The bankers then tried to shift responsibility onto the Bank of England; one stated that it was general opinion that the Bank could not help the bankers because it feared a run on its

Reserve. It was up to the Governor whether he wanted to have people go to him for gold and be unable to obtain it. Cunliffe, so tersely drawn into the fight, indignantly refuted the bankers' allegation. If the Bank were open, he stated, he could pay his way in gold. It would be a real pity, he added, if convertibility were to be suspended now. A Royal Decree ought not to include such a clause.

Warm applause from the traders and industrialists saluted Cunliffe's words. Lloyd George, now certain of the mood of the assembly, hastened to request from traders and industrialists an explicit declaration on the suspension of convertibility. He suggested that they meet to elect a Committee, who would draw up the declaration.

But there would be no need for that, said Lord Mersey, who had chaired the meeting of representatives of the real sector. After the Governor's declaration, everyone had become convinced that if the Bank of England did not feel the need to take so drastic a measure as suspension, then such a request would certainly not come from traders and industrialists, who thought it was absolutely undesirable. Mersey's words also met with great applause.

It was then left to Lloyd George to formally ask traders and industrialists whether it was true, since it was not necessary to have both the suspension of convertibility and the issue of small bank notes, that they wanted the latter but refused the former. He received enthusiastic agreement.

The first round of consultations thus came to an end. We may place two interpretations on it: we may take it as a congerie of events ordered by chance to result in a victory for the Chancellor; alternatively, we may think that the sequence of events was arranged by the Chancellor, so that the interplay of diverse interests would help him to make his view prevail. I favour the latter interpretation: the representatives of the real sector were meeting in a different room from that in which Lloyd George was conferring with bankers; it is therefore not hard to imagine that they would be appropriately briefed by Bradbury, Blackett and other Treasury men.

In any case, the first round of consultations brought out the leitmotifs of recent British financial history: the rivalry between the bankers and the Bank of England, and the traditional alliance in an emergency between the Inner City and the Government against the bankers.

The latter saw their emergency scheme dissected and reformulated in a very different way: by means of well-directed *coups de théatre*, Lloyd George had managed to remove suspension of convertibility from the scene, and to extract from the bankers a declaration to continue dealing with their clients according to normal practice.

The bankers were left only one front on which to carry on their battle: the regulations concerning the issue of the new notes. On that field, over the next two days, they engaged the Government and the financial establishment in fierce combat; and they did not refrain, as we shall see, from blows beneath the belt.

Discussion began the next morning, at 9.30 in Whitehall, on the issue of new notes. Austen Chamberlain was the main protagonist during a good part of the meeting: Lloyd George had asked him to take the chair, as he himself had to go to a Cabinet meeting at 11 o'clock that morning.

The first problem to come up for discussion was whether one pound notes should be issued by the Treasury or by the Bank of England. The Treasury thought they should issue them and that they must not be immediately convertible. When this opinion was made known to the bankers, Holden and Schuster immediately declared that, in such a case, the public would try to get rid of the notes; and they would therefore be sold at a discount. They also found it remarkable that the banks had been forced to keep convertibility whereas now the Government was planning to suspend it, at least partially, by issuing inconvertible notes.

Chamberlain intervened to point out that the aim of reserves was that they should be used in an emergency. If the Government and the banks showed reluctance to use gold from the very start, then the public would lose confidence and demand gold. The more gold that was available to them, he said, the less they would want to get hold of it, and vice versa.

Regulations were then considered concerning securities to be exchanged for notes by the banks. Here the biggest problem arose. Banks had proposed to pay for the notes with Clearing House certificates of deposit, but the Government tried to convince them to give a combined and separate guarantee on the notes they would take. The bankers had no intention of agreeing on a joint guarantee; they could only go as far as offering individual ones. Stalemate being complete on that point, discussion was suspended.

Next, the text of a declaration Lloyd George would read that same day in the Commons to restore maximum confidence, was considered. He had to announce the general moratorium and the issue of one pound notes. A heated discussion flared up on what exact convertibility clause should appear on the notes—whether the phrase should be 'convertible into gold', or 'convertible into Bank of England notes' or 'convertible in the same way as a Bank of England note'.

Cunliffe took the opportunity to say that banks had, for all practical purposes, declared Bank of England notes inconvertible, since they were refusing to exchange them for gold. One pound notes, he added, would have to be issued only because of the banks' behaviour over Bank notes. As five pound notes were now being exchanged at a discount, he thought it was not very helpful to mention that the new notes would be convertible in the same way as Bank notes.

Chamberlain suggested that the new notes carry the inscription 'convertible into gold at the Bank of England.' Sir John Bradbury made a last stand on the advisability of making new notes inconvertible, in the case of convertibility being suspended; but Chamberlain sharply retorted that the latter event would certainly shortly follow on the former.

Next, there came the issue of how general the general moratorium should be. All agreed that foreign debtors should be excluded, as well as British government liabilities. Someone proposed to exclude the debts of the government of India and of the colonial governments; this brought about a strong protest on the part of the Governor, as Indian money was about the only liquid funds he envisaged coming to the Bank during the moratorium. But the only ally he found was Koch, the representative of the Stock Exchange dealers, who objected to the exclusion of foreign and colonial governments who had lent many millions to Stock Exchange dealers. The rest of the company, however, were of the opposite opinion; and it was they who prevailed.

Now the real fight began. Giving all sorts of excuses, the bankers refused to authorise the Chancellor to declare in Parliament that they would be ready at the end of the Bank Holiday to satisfy the cash requirements of their clients for the needs of daily life, the payment of wages and salaries, and the normal treatment of cheques. They had not been able to prevent Lloyd George from declaring these points to traders and industrialists, but now they wanted to retrieve what had been extracted from them before it was solemnly declared in Parliament.

At first sight, the declaration Lloyd George and his advisers had drawn up did not differ in content from the bankers' own proposal. A closer look at both revealed, however, that the Chancellor and his staff wanted to pin the banks down to a straight declaration of 'business as usual' while the latter had formulated a devious text with many verbal and syntactic escape clauses to be used, if they felt like it, to suspend payments.

Obviously the banks had dug in on this issue, and had no intention of retreating. The typed record goes on for pages and pages of inconclusive discussion, showing how complete the stalemate was.

What bankers seemed to fear most was that the Bank of England might be given a good chance to take their clients away from them, now that it appeared to be totally supported by the Government. If the public were left free to draw from their current accounts by cheque, so their argument ran, they would take the opportunity to transfer their accounts to the Bank of England, which now looked safer than the banks. Also, they did not want the Chancellor to reveal to the public that the banks had agreed to pay up to 10% of a client's credit in cash: they would prefer to keep a discretionary silence on that point.

Lloyd George decided to give in to the second request, and drew up a more general version of his statement, in which no percentages were mentioned and banks could pay either in gold or in legal tender notes (meaning the new one pound notes).

The concession was, however, not sufficient to get the banks to agree on the point concerning cheques. It was thus decided to leave that hanging for the time being and go on to discuss the way banks would pay for the new one pound notes. The banks announced they had changed their mind. They now offered a first mortgage on their assets for the amounts of notes each of them would take— such was the right conceded to owners of debentures, and it would only bind the banks individually. They asked, moreover, that the mortgages should not be registered in the Statute Book. The Government was not amused by the banks' offer. Matters were further complicated when Bradbury announced that the Treasury were of the opinion that, since the notes issued to banks had to be considered a loan by the Government to the banks, the latter were supposed to pay an interest rate equal to Bank rate on the amounts they would take.

Since this was too much for the banks to decide on immediately, Lloyd George advised them to withdraw to consult privately on the issue. After some time, Chamberlain was sent to ask them what decision they had arrived at. He returned to announce that banks had no intention of accepting a joint mortgage and in any case insisted on not having it entered in the Statute Books. Banks did not trust each other enough to give a joint guarantee; they did not want the public to know they had mortgaged their assets, as they might lose some accounts to the Bank of England.

But Lloyd George and his advisers were not going to give in. Cunliffe, Bradbury and the Lord Chief Justice, Lord Reading, had made statements accusing the banks of sharp practice: while the agreement would give them complete Government support, the Government was given no guarantee. Lloyd George therefore again sent Chamberlain, accompanied by Lord Reading, to explain the Government's point of view to the bankers. Meanwhile, he took advantage of the stalemate to see a deputation of Scottish and Irish bankers.

Here a rather interesting interlude took place: Sir George Anderson, the Scottish banks' spokesman, and Sir John Purcell, spokesman of the Irish banks, were treated, both by the Chancellor and by the other participants, as if they represented foreign financial institutions; and as such they themselves behaved. The English bankers had so far given no information about what had been decided up to then; so they now had to give the Scottish and Irish bankers a summary of events and proposals made. On the question of having notes issued by the Treasury, Anderson had no doubt: the notes would have to be issued by the Treasury if they were supposed to be valid in Scotland. If the Bank of England issued them, he stated, nobody in Scotland would touch them, because the Bank of England had nothing to do with Scotland. The Treasury, on the other hand, represented the Empire; hence its financial legitimacy in Scotland. He thought in any case that the new notes could not arrive in Scotland in time, and asked that convertibility be suspended in Scotland until they arrived. Purcell echoed the last proposal, which was certainly not at all welcome to the Chancellor and his advisers. Were suspension to be announced, even if it were limited to Scotland and Ireland, the effect on world opinion would be disastrous. Lloyd George consequently discarded the proposal altogether; and, after some dealing, Anderson and Purcell agreed to accept that Bank of Scotland and Bank of Ireland notes be declared legal tender in Scotland and Ireland respectively, until the new Treasury notes arrived. As for the mechanism for issuing the latter, Lloyd George begged the Scotsman and the Irishman to stay in the room, as the modes of issue had still to be determined in consultation with the English bankers. The latter then came in again; St. Aldwyn, on their behalf, informed the Chancellor that they considered a 3% interest rate on notes to be appropriate. Should an interest equal to Bank rate (i.e. 6%) be adopted, the public—especially traders—would suffer, since banks would have to ask more than 6% on their loans. As to the total amounts of notes to be issued, St. Aldwyn reported that the banks thought it should be around 20% of bank deposits, i.e. about £220 million. Banks, he said, had not yet agreed on how to split the total among themselves.

Lloyd George was clearly amazed at the enormity of the sum of notes requested by the banks. He realised that at a 3% interest charge, the banks all had the chance to make a huge profit on the transaction. The Government could not agree. As a complete impasse resulted, he advised bankers to withdraw and return to him only if they agreed to his proposal that all banks should receive an equal amount of notes at a certain interest rate; after which those banks which wanted more would have to pay an interest rate which would be fixed at the Government's discretion.

The English bankers having withdrawn, agreement was reached with the Scottish and Irish Bank representatives. The English bankers then returned, to announce that they had no intention of budging. Lloyd George could do no more than send them away till the next morning.

He had now little more than one day left to reach agreement on an emergency plan to satisfy most of the financial world. As complete deadlock seemed to have been reached, he decided, as Goschen had done in 1890, to ask the House of Rothschild to arbitrate the dispute. He therefore sent a message to Lord Rothschild begging him to come to Whitehall the next morning. As we shall see, the ruse was successful once again.

On August 6, consultation did not seem to begin too favourably. Cunliffe agreed to declare publicly to the bankers that he would send back clients who might want to take their accounts to him. He had realised that this was the fear behind the banks' hesitation to restore the payment of cheques (to Lloyd George's great surprise: he said he thought bankers only feared one another). At the same time, however, Cunliffe asked the Chancellor to request the banks to charge the same rate on their loans that they would pay on Treasury notes. Otherwise banks would profit from the operation, while the Bank of England was compelled to lend at Bank rate.

Lloyd George expressed his agreement with Cunliffe. All his advisers, he said, had come to the same conclusion, that banks could not be put in a situation where they made extra profits out of the emergency. The time had now come, he added, to tell the bankers what the Government had decided. There was no time left for further haggling. The first proposal the Government would make was to issue Treasury notes to banks up to 10% of each bank's current accounts. Lord Reading had requested that a ceiling be imposed; some of the advisers, however, thought it would be unwise to impose any ceiling. Chamberlain expressed the opinion that 20% might be a better figure. Cunliffe stated that the very event Reading seemed to fear—that banks might use the notes to solve problems that had nothing to do with the emergency—was the main reason why the notes would be issued. A bank failure, he said, whatever its causes would now be lethal to the whole system.

The Government also intended to ask banks to mortgage their assets to guarantee the restitution of the notes they would receive. They intended to charge an interest rate on the notes; and all advisers except Koch agreed that it ought to be as high as Bank rate. Koch suggested that a rate one per cent lower than Bank rate would be appropriate, to make up for the risk incurred by the banks on loans. Both the Chancellor and Chamberlain seemed to see Koch's point, but Cunliffe would hear nothing of it. He thought that, in the case of bankers being favoured, the Bank of England would suffer. The banks, he said, were being bailed out by the Government. A miserable 1% would be nothing to them, especially if it was only to be charged for a few months. It was eventually agreed that the Chancellor would ask the banks to make no profit from the transaction; and that only if they insisted would he offer them a $\frac{1}{2}$% profit.

The government's fourth proposal was that banks should themselves decide how to split the total of notes that would be issued. Before discussing this, however, Cunliffe asked the Chancellor to listen to a declaration he was to make. The Bank of England's gold was now down to 10 million, and there was no doubt at all that banks were making themselves overstrong, and were hoarding gold in view of possible needs. He wanted Lloyd George to make it understood to bankers that they, the bankers, would find themselves in an extraordinarily difficult position if the Bank of England had to suspend convertibility while the banks had millions of sovereigns in their vaults; the Chancellor should make it very clear that he would make life extremely difficult for bankers if the country was compelled to abandon convertibility while they hoarded gold.

Lloyd George asked him what had happened to the bankers' proposal to deposit 10–15 million of their gold at the Bank of England. No more had been heard of that, said Cunliffe, nor was it necessary in the new circumstances. He only wanted banks to be issued with a severe admonition. So was it the banks who were the greatest culprits, asked Lloyd George. Cunliffe said that it was. Chamberlain intervened to point out that he had reminded the banks that they would have to use their reserves, and that it would be folly to pile up gold now. Revelstoke, realistically, observed there was nothing the Government could do to force the banks to obey their orders. Cunliffe retorted that their gold could be sequestrated; Lloyd George suggested he could tell them the Government would suspend convertibility. But, observed Revelstoke, was that not precisely what they wanted in the first place? Cunliffe disagreed; he considered that Tritton had been horrified at the thought. Yes, said Lloyd George; but they had since changed their minds.

Now the bankers were called in. St. Aldwyn repeated their demand that an issue of notes equal to 20% of each bank's current accounts be made, against a first claim on their assets. The Chancellor told them that Cunliffe would now make an important statement. The Governor declared he would refrain from accepting new accounts from clients who wanted to shift from the joint-stock banks to his bank; in fact, he added, he had already sent quite a few away. His statement was welcomed by the bankers, who expressed their gratitude to him.

Although the road now seemed open to fruitful negotiation, the bankers took very badly the Government's proposals about the interest charges on new notes and the legal mortgage on their assets. Before they withdrew to decide, Lloyd George issued them with the admonition Cunliffe had requested. The Committee advising the Government, he said, had the distinct impression that the banks had showed a disposition to accumulate gold in order to reinforce their position. If that went too far, the Government could be obliged to suspend convertibility. Nobody wanted that to happen. All the measures that the Government were considering would be taken on the understanding that the banks would help the Government. The crisis had to be overcome without suspending convertibility—which could be done only if the banks helped by setting an example to the public. The Government would help the banks only if they paid heed to the Government's warning.

It could scarcely be expected that the banks would take Lloyd George's severe warning in good part. In fact, when they came back, St. Aldwyn stated on their behalf that the banks rejected the accusation that they were hoarding gold. He also asked the Chancellor to reconsider the Government's proposal about interest charges, as bankers feared their clients would dislike it intensely if it were kept as it was. Banks would have to charge higher rates on loans, but would also have to pay higher rates to their depositors. The banks therefore asked the Government to charge only 4% on the notes issued. The interest charged now on loans was 5% and it would go higher if banks had to pay 6% on the notes.

Lloyd George sought Cunliffe's opinion. The latter said he did not see how the Government could authorise the banks to lend at less than 6%, when the Bank of England was compelled by the suspension of Bank Act to lend at 6%. The Government would be discriminating in favour of the banks and against his bank, he added. Holden retorted that if the Government compelled the banks to charge a rate as high as Bank rate, traders and industrialists would rebel against the Government and accuse it of profiting from their misery. It would be a situation, added Esdale, that would play havoc with all British banking conventions.

St. Aldwyn, Chamberlain and Lloyd George conferred briefly and decided that the bankers should withdraw. Now Lord Rothschild entered the stage. He began by telling the Chancellor and his advisers that they were issuing the new notes to favour the community, not the banks. If the banks were handicapped by the Government, it would be the community that would suffer. He himself was perfectly disinterested; the argument had nothing to do with him. He had come only because he was asked. Above all, Rothschild concluded, the public must not receive the impression that the Government were profiting from their misery.

Cunliffe was not moved by those words. The Government, he said, compelled him to charge 6% on all the millions of pounds he was lending to those people whom the banks would not accommodate; and at the same time they were going to lend at a lower rate to the very people, the bankers, who were pushing their clients to the Bank. One way out would be to reduce Bank rate to 5% so that the Bank of England's clients would not be discriminated against; there would be no external consequences, as gold could not flow out. Several advisers were ready to point out to him that the bankers intended to pay on the other new notes an interest of $1\frac{1}{2}$% less than Bank rate, whatever level the latter stood at. Thus Cunliffe's proposal did not coincide with the bankers' plan.

What really was the Governor's fear? Was he afraid that if banks, when they received the notes, were to offer loans at $1\frac{1}{2}$% less than Bank rate, the people who had borrowed from the Bank at 6% would use those loans to repay the Bank the money they had borrowed? That was precisely his worry. He said that it would be an extremely distasteful action. Rothschild agreed that it would indeed be unpleasant. He proposed that the new notes be given to the banks at the lower rate, if they undertook not to use them to lend to clients who would repay their debts with the Bank of England. That, intervened Lloyd George, would amount to lowering Bank rate to $4\frac{1}{2}$%. Even more than that, some advisers added; Bank rate would cease to exist. It would be the banks who now fixed Bank rate, Cunliffe objected. Sir John Bradbury joined in to support him in even more vivid terms. Equally vividly, Lord Rothschild replied that if banks were to be charged Bank rate, they would not collaborate with the Government, as they would think they were being unjustly taxed. 'They cannot do anything,' exclaimed Cunliffe. 'They can play you a nasty trick,' retorted Rothschild, 'they are very powerful.' He believed banks should be told they would be charged less than Bank rate, if they did not use the money to lend to the bill brokers who borrowed from the Bank of England.

Lloyd George objected that, if the banks began to lend at $4\frac{1}{2}$%, the Bank of England would lose all its clients. Rothschild was, however, firm in his opinion. Did he not believe—asked Lloyd George—that a promise to lower Bank rate might be enough to satisfy the bankers? Rothschild thought this was very hard to answer. He said the rumour might be spread that the Government were profiting from the country's needs, which would be very harmful. All other advisers were against Rothschild's opinion. Chamberlain suggested that if Bank rate went down to 5%, the banks would have no reason to consider themselves ill-treated. He also stressed it was most important for the public to believe that all measures had been taken in an atmosphere of great harmony, and without hesitation. He advised Lloyd George to tell the banks that Bank rate would be reduced to 5%.

This would have been a real breach of common law. But Lloyd George was even ready, in the circumstances, to go so far. He said he would make the declaration, only adding that Bank rate would be reduced on Friday if things went well, in order to leave the Government some flexibility.

The bankers returned. The Chancellor told them that a rate of interest equal to Bank rate would be charged on the new notes; otherwise, the Bank of England would be deprived of her right to fix Bank rate. But, he added, the banks had convinced the Government that it would be preferable to fix the rate at which they lent to their clients. He proceeded to tell them that it would be possible, if all went well, to reduce Bank rate to 5% on Friday.

The bankers made a last effort to get their way on interest rate as well. St. Aldwyn proposed that an impartial person be called in to arbitrate the dispute between them and the Bank of England. But Lloyd George told him that the decision taken had not been the Bank of England's own. The latter's representatives had been asked to explain their viewpoint; but there were in the room several impartial persons who had all forcefully expressed the opinion that the Government make the declaration he had just read out. He added that an agreement had to be reached without delay, and on the Government's own terms.

The bankers insisted; they contended that their field of activity did not coincide with the Bank of England's own. In any case, they promised not to compete with it. They invoked the spectre of an industrial slump. They even went so far as to pretend not to have understood the Government's terms. They tried to obtain a guarantee that Bank rate would not rise again. The Stock Exchange representative, Koch, rallied to their support, warning the Government about the difficulties their measures would cause for trade and industry. But all was in vain. Lloyd George and his staff had de-

cided to retreat no further. Lloyd George assured the bankers that
all he needed was a temporary agreement. The situation could be
examined again in the future. The public would know about the
banks' guarantee, but they would not know the interest rate the
banks would pay on notes.

Eventually the banks were persuaded to agree.

Lord Rothschild's merit in all this tiresome negotiation is easy to
understand. First, he used his authority to remind the advisers of
the bankers' huge power. Second, he backed with his eloquent
silence the Chancellor's proposal, which the banks were finally
persuaded to approve.

To whose advantage was the agreement? Certainly banks were
defeated from the tactical point of view: they wanted suspension of
convertibility and they did not get it; they wanted a favourable
interest rate on Treasury notes and they did not get that either.
Moreover, they formally agreed with the Government to carry on
transactions in a climate of normality and to call off the tough
squeeze to which they had subjected the economy until then. The
moratorium was, as they had asked, made general, but the banks
were not allowed to run it at their discretion. Finally, the banks
were severely reprimanded by the Chancellor for their behaviour
towards the Bank of England.

As for the banks' long-term strategy—the exploration of the
traditional financial intermediaries' residual functions—the negotia-
tions went very well for them. The credit squeeze they had enforced
in the last weeks of July caused merchant banks and bill brokers to
risk insolvency, and the latter were saved from bankruptcy only by
Government intervention. But the Government moratorium on
bills, while it saved them, also caused the paralysis of their
financial transactions. The banks on the other hand were still very
liquid, having drained the market and the Bank of England of
cash, and were therefore in a position to inherit the functions of
the traditional intermediaries.

The threat the moratorium represented to the finance houses'
existence was well realised by Keynes. On the issue, he wrote a
second memorandum to Lloyd George, which is dated August 5.[20]
He pointed out that normal international trade transactions would
resume only if bills could again be discounted. But discounting
could not be resumed because the merchant banks could not find

[20] Now published in his *Collected Writings*, Vol. XVI.

credit and, as a result, could not accept bills—which could only then be discounted by banks and discount houses. The situation, he added, could be saved in two ways. Either the Government should guarantee the merchant banks' past transactions, so that they could enter into new business, or the Government could limit its action to guaranteeing the merchant banks' new business.

Keynes thought the first alternative was unlikely to bring new life to the discount market. He said that even if the Government guaranteed their past transactions, merchant banks would not have enough resources to cover possible losses on new acceptances. The Government should therefore back their new acceptances as well, if it wanted to revive the discount market. Merchant banks should thus form a syndicate with joint liability, whose acceptances the Government would guarantee up to 9% of their value. Keynes further suggested that the moratorium be given different deadlines for different places. Even if his proposal had been implemented *in toto*, Keynes knew it would not be enough to bring the British financial structure back to the status quo. He concluded his memorandum by declaring that in the future, a larger share of accepting business should be done by banks, rather than by accepting houses.

The stifling of the discount market resulting from the moratorium was felt by traders and industrialists as well. It was not long before they sent Lloyd George and Chamberlain their *cahiers de doleances*, proposing schemes to get out of the stalemate.

So on August 12, Lloyd George called a new conference in Whitehall, to try to solve the problem of restoring short-term finance to trade and industry. He asked representatives of accepting houses, joint-stock banks, traders and industrialists, to attend. Sir George Paish, Basil Blackett and Austen Chamberlain were also present, as well as Cabinet members such as Lord Reading, Lord Mersey, Reginald McKenna, Sir John Simon, Herbert Samuel, Walter Runciman and the Marquess of Crewe.

It was easy to reach agreement with the accepting houses. Bankruptcy was the only alternative; any other solution was therefore good for them. Lloyd George had already suggested a scheme which seems to have been prepared by the Trade and Industry Associations, but bears a strong resemblance to Keynes' own proposal.

The idea was to form a syndicate of accepting houses, with joint liability, which would accept liability for bills that would initially be given to the Bank of England. The syndicate would be given the opportunity to postpone payment by obtaining loans from the Bank of England, at a rate 2% over Bank rate. Naturally, the Bank of England would only be able to make the loans by using fiduciary paper, especially the one pound notes issued by the Treasury.

This scheme favoured the Bank of England, giving it enormous influence over the discount market, and at the same time solving its problem of how to find money to finance the new activity. The joint-stock banks were favoured as well, since the bills in their portfolios would become liquid again, while the moratorium remained valid on their deposits.

The conference was therefore summoned to decide how the Bank of England and the joint-stock banks were to split the accepting houses' spoils among themselves. As we see from the scheme, the Bank was to be the one that gained most—which the joint-stock banks found difficult to swallow.

The accepting houses were able to put up no kind of resistance other than a refusal to accept joint liability on bills. They wanted liability to be individual, as each house was in a different financial situation. They also tried to preserve their right to require the drawers of bills to pay up some day, which meant preventing the financial networks they had established with their overseas clients from being inherited by the banks and the Bank of England.

All participants at the conference were convinced that there was a very good chance the joint-stock banks would end up as the main heirs of the acceptance business. Keynes thought so; so did Lloyd George, who went as far as declaring this to the attendants of a further conference, held on October 24.

As a result, the accepting houses resorted to passive resistance, which meant that they collaborated as little as possible in the implementation of the scheme they had approved, by limiting new acceptances to a minimum. By the scheme, they had been freed only from the pressure of maturities; they were still fully responsible for their acceptances. The joint-stock banks and the Bank of England were conversely freed from all liability. In fact, as Lord Mersey noted in the course of the conference—asking for his formal dissent to be registered—according to the scheme, banks could give their bills to the Bank of England to get money without having to accept them, as had been necessary before the emergency measures.

Several writers, when commenting on the crisis, have expressed the opinion that Lloyd George constantly discriminated in favour of the joint-stock banks. I do not think, after having read the documents, that such a position is tenable. It was not Lloyd George who supported the banks. The latter's position was so strong that they could not fail to solve the crisis in their favour: it is all a matter of exactly how much they gained. And it can safely be said that Lloyd George succeeded in confining their gains, by defending the City from their attack.

The banks were strong enough to call all his bluffs. As with all weak Governments, he had only the extreme measure of imposing those controls over the financial systems that were theoretically available. In the conference of August 24, he did not miss the opportunity to threaten the banks with the possibility of imposing such controls. All sorts of very trustworthy persons, among them Chamberlain, had proved to Lloyd George with documents that the banks were still making themselves strong, and had not relaxed the squeeze as much as Government measures allowed.[21]

The banks were asked to give reasons for their behaviour at the conference. Their representatives gave all sorts of specious and unsatisfactory motives, all revealing the fear of inter-bank competition and of competition between banks and other financial institutions. But the Chancellor was not at all impressed by their plea of not guilty. Before he sent the banks away, he gave them the following solemn warning:

If we find ... something has to be done in addition to that

[21] Moreover, the English banks had tried to make the Scottish banks the sole scapegoats. A circular, signed by Sir George Anderson and sent out to all branch managers of Scottish banks, stated: 'you will clearly understand that no new advances of any kind, however satisfactory the security offered may be, must be made either by way of loan or overdraft'. This document reached Lloyd George, who asked Anderson to give an explanation. Anderson flatly stated that the circular was exactly like the one sent out by the English banks. But, the Governor of the Bank of England declared that he had seen the English banks' circular and that it was in no way similar to that sent out by Sir George. The latter was indignant, but could do nothing to justify himself. Perhaps his circular was less ambiguous than the one published by the English banks, but in view of the protest over the banks' behaviour in those weeks, of which we have records of all kinds—declarations, letters written to the Chancellor and to Chamberlain, results of private enquiries conducted by Government officials—it is difficult to believe that the spirit of the documents radically differed.

[i.e. the banks' transactions] to finance the business of the country, then I shall have to take very serious steps. We are now working under conditions that nobody has ever seen the like of before and we have to feel our way very cautiously. You may find in the course of the month that some proposition has to be put before you that neither you nor I at the present moment are contemplating; but we shall have to face it. Unless you can see your way perhaps to take very much greater risks than you are taking now, I am convinced of this—it looks to me at the present moment as if the State would have to come in and undertake very much greater risks; but that involves very much greater control. You see, we cannot take all the risks off your shoulders, without having much greater control that we have now. Still, perhaps we are anticipating. I would infinitely prefer it should be done by the banks themselves because you know your business, and it is a very serious thing for the State to step in. I would say that even if I did it in the end it would be a very regrettable necessity; because here you are, you know your business, you know your customers, and have your trained men in every City and Town in the Kingdom who know every man they are doing business with, and if the State steps in it will be only when it is absolutely necessary to save the life of the Nation. I should not contemplate it otherwise; but, still, do not forget that what we have to do is to save this Country and that has to be done whatever steps may be necessary for the State to take ... Do not forget this, that we have just taken as much responsibility as we can take without control, and if we are going a step beyond that, I think it is far better that we should understand each other, it means that we shall then have to do something in the nature of Control, and of course that we do not want to do—not because we do not want to do it, but because I think it is a bad thing unless we are forced to do it. It would be really altering the whole character of the business of this country.

Lloyd George knew perfectly well the banks would be little deterred by his threats. He had therefore to negotiate from a position of weakness. But we must admit that he made the most of his scant assets—an achievement all the more creditable when we consider that, before the beginning of the crisis, he was altogether innocent of economics.

APPENDIXES

APPENDIX A

T 170 19: GOLD RESERVES (B. P. BLACKETT)

Note

This memorandum is the outcome of a request made by the Chancellor of the Exchequer at the end of February 1914 for a statement of the views of the Treasury on the subject of the Gold Reserves of the United Kingdom. Sir Ed. Holden's demand for a Royal Commission on the subject had led the Governor of the Bank to ask for an interview with the Chancellor for the purpose—as appeared when the interview took place on March 3—of deprecating Sir E. Holden's proposal.

Owing to the short time available all I could do was to put together some hasty notes on the subject, which were given to the Chancellor of the Exchequer by Sir John Bradbury, together with some notes hastily prepared by himself and a note by the late Mr. W. Blain of the Treasury, on the special question of the claim that the Government Savings Banks ought to have a special Gold Reserve of their own.

I have used all the material thus available very freely in this memorandum, and have also discussed many points in it with Mr. R. G. Hawtrey. But for the views expressed throughout, the responsibility rests with me alone.

B.P.B.
22.5.1914

GOLD RESERVES

I. *The Bank Charter Act, 1844 and the Cheque System*

1. The gold reserves of the United Kingdom are very largely conditioned by the Bank Charter Act of 1844, and by the cor-

responding Bank Acts of 1845 relating to Scotland and Ireland. Prior to 1844 there was no statutory provision for the maintenance of any central reserve of gold in this country. The main purpose of the Act of 1844 was not, in fact, to provide a central reserve, but the creation of such a reserve was its most successful achievement and, although most of the hopes which were entertained by the authors of that Act have been falsified, the successful accumulation and retention of a central Gold reserve at the Bank of England, which was an incidental result, have been enough to maintain the Act on the Statute Book unrepealed and unmodified for 70 years.

2. On this point paragraph 104 of the Report of the Royal Commission on Indian Currency and Finance, 1914 (Cd. 7236) may be quoted: 'In this country the intention of the framers of the Bank Charter Act of 1844 was to prevent the abuses attendant on the issue of notes without the backing of a metallic reserve by securing the retention in reserve of coin against every single note issued over and above the maximum amount which was allowed to be covered by securities ... Its result has been to reduce notes to a very insignificant position in the British Currency system. The complete inelasticity imposed by the Act of 1844 upon the currency of notes ... has only been tolerated because of the discovery in the cheque system of an alternative means of obtaining an elastic paper currency which could not be obtained through the note issue under the Act. The main paper currency of the United Kingdom now consists of cheques, and the Gold Reserve of the Bank of England, though nominally supporting a comparatively small note issue, is really the ultimate support of a gigantic currency of cheques and other credit instruments of which the notes of the Bank of England form only a small portion'.

3. In normal times indeed the notes of the Bank of England are nothing more than gold certificates, for in such times the notes in reserve in the banking department are seldom of less value than £18,450,000, the amount nominally issued against securities.

4. The panic of 1847, only three years after the passing of the Bank Charter Act made it clear that the belief that the Act would prevent commercial and monetary crises was unfounded. The suspension of the limit on the fiduciary issue during the crisis did not, however, lead to any modification of the Act. Its operation was still too new and knowledge of financial theory too limited to permit of a clear perception of what was amiss. So enlightened an economist

as Stanley Jevons actually propounded the theory that commercial crises recurred every decade or so under the influence of sun-spots according to some law analogous to the connection between the moon and the tides. The theory secured a wide acceptance, and the recurrence of panics in 1857 and again in 1866 seemed to lend it the support of experience.

5. But before the panic of 1857 a great discovery was made. This was that the most potent instrument for conserving and replenishing the Gold Reserve of the country was to be found in the rate of discount.

6. The country had thus by a series of accidents provided itself with a not unsuccessful banking and currency system. More or less incidentally the Act of 1844 had established a central Gold Reserve, and an instrument had been found in the shape of the discount rate for regulating that reserve. In the cheque system the country had a paper currency far superior to the legal tender notes which had been regulated into relative insignificance by the Act of 1844, and finally, in the extra-statutory power assumed by the Government in a crisis to suspend the Act, a means of creating an emergency currency had been invented by which to overcome the worst terrors of such a period.

7. Thus though the Bank Charter Act was again suspended in 1857 and 1866, and in 1857 for the first time and last time the fiduciary notes were actually issued in excess of the legal maximum, bankers and merchants have remained ever since fairly well satisfied with the system of gold reserves which experience had built up and sanctioned, and apart from Mr. Goschen's unsuccessful attempts in 1891 to introduce £1 notes after the Baring Crisis of 1890, no serious effort has been made to remodel that system.

II. Agitation for Increased Gold Reserves

8. For the last 30 years, however, the question whether the amount of our Gold Reserves is adequate has been continually canvassed, and it seems to be almost a commonplace among bankers to-day that those reserves are now inadequate and ought to be increased. It is possible, no doubt, that the persistent efforts of Sir E. Holden (the Chairman of the London City and Midland Bank) to

rouse his fellow-bankers to a sense of this inadequacy, and the support which has been given to this view by the more vocal portion of the banking community represents less unanimity than appears on the surface, and that the comparative inaction which has so far attended these efforts is due to the effective inertia of the unconvinced, and not solely to the difficulties which stand in the way of any scheme of distributing the burden of increase.

9. Sir E. Holden has, however, had some success. A strong committee of bankers, under the chairmanship of Lord St. Aldwyn, has been studying the whole subject with a view to formulating proposals, and it is believed that most of the big London banks have in recent years accumulated special Gold Reserves of their own apart from the central reserve at the Bank of England. Whether these special reserves are important in the aggregate or not is difficult to determine, because (as also the proceedings of the Committee) they are kept secret. Only the London County and Westminster Bank publish figures of their average daily cash in hand and at the Bank of England (the London City and Midland Bank have promised some fuller particulars from December 1914) but even these figures, which in nearly every case lump together till money, special reserve, and cash at the Bank of England, do not help much for the purpose now in question. That the special reserves are not absolutely negligible is certain, but whether they are important additions to the available gold resources of the country it is not known. (The present Governor of the Bank of England says that they are not, and he ought to know.) In any case so long as they are kept secret and in the sole control of the banks which have created them, they contribute nothing to the real strength of the central reserve, and are important only if they are a preliminary to the strengthening of the central reserve upon some prescribed scheme.

10. However this may be, the activity of Sir E. Holden and his demand for a Royal Commission on the subject make it worth while considering with some care whether or not the present reserves of this country are adequate.

The case put forward by advocates of an increase of the Gold Reserves may be grouped as follows:

(i) Comparisons with foreign countries.

It is urged

(a) that in proportion to the volume of our banking and exchange transactions our Gold Reserves are smaller than those of foreign countries.

(b) that the Gold Reserves of foreign countries have of late years been increased to an extent out of all proportion to the very small additions made in this country.

(ii) Comparisons with former periods.

It is urged that, regard being had to the enormous growth of our banking and exchange transactions, our gold reserves are relatively very much smaller than in the past.

(iii) Complaints of the fluctuations of Bank rate.

It is said that British commerce suffers from the frequency of the changes in the Bank rate, and the steadiness of the Bank of France's discount rate is contrasted to the disadvantage of our own, it being contended that the size of France's Gold Reserves is the cause of her steady Bank rate.

(iv) The agitation also touches on other points, including complaints of the management and methods of the Bank of England, in its regulation of the Gold Reserves;

(v) And suggestions are offered as to the distribution of the burden of the cost of making additions to the reserves, a not uncommon cry being that the Government as holding the deposits of the savings banks, should make a substantial contribution.

It will be convenient to begin with a discussion of the first two heads, comparisons with foreign countries and with former times.

(i) COMPARISON WITH FOREIGN COUNTRIES

11. There is no need to produce statistics to prove that our Gold Reserves are small in comparison with those of foreign countries. The proofs are indeed so convincing that people are apt to accept them unquestioningly as proving the truth not merely of the propositions that our reserves are smaller in proportion to the turnover than those of foreign countries and that such proportion is even smaller to-day than 20 years ago, but also of the conclusion which these propositions are intended to establish, namely, that our Gold Reserves are smaller than they ought to be. It is, however, quite fallacious to accept them as proving the inadequacy of our

Gold Reserves. This conclusion would follow only if it can be shown that conditions here and elsewhere have been and are sufficiently similar to justify these mathematical comparisons.

12. How far, then are such comparisons justified? As already shown the great bulk of the internal exchange transactions of this country so far at any rate as aggregate totals are concerned, is carried on very largely by means of cheques, and only to a very small extent by means of legal tender, whether coin or notes, except perhaps the United States of America, where conditions are otherwise very dissimilar, the cheque system has not obtained a vogue in any way comparable with its vogue in this country in any of the foreign States with whose Gold Reserves comparison is usually made. In most foreign countries legal tender currency forms the main basis of internal exchange, and a considerably larger gold reserve is required to maintain the convertibility of a currency of legal tender notes in normal times than is necessary as a support for the cheques system. (This statement may seem a little dogmatic, but it is really not questionable, and in a memorandum of this sort a certain amount of dogmatic assertion is inevitable if reasonable limits are to be respected.) In other words, if we confine attention to internal exchange alone and regard the Gold Reserves as the working balance necessary to maintain the convertibility of the circulating medium, so far as it does not consist of full-value coin, the working balance of gold required in the United Kingdom is smaller than the working balance needed in countries with a large legal tender currency in circulation. The prevalence of the cheque system here, therefore, justifies relatively smaller Gold Reserves, and makes mere arithmetical comparisons of the aggregate amounts held here and elsewhere quite valueless.

13. It is equally impossible to draw conclusions as to the adequacy of our Gold Reserves from statistics of comparative increases in this country and in others during recent years. Each extension of the cheque system economises gold and justifies a reduction in the ratio between the working balance and the total transactions, and a very great increase in the latter may involve no actual increase, or only a very small one, in the size of the Gold Reserve. On the other hand, where the currency consists mainly of legal tender notes, an expansion in the volume of transactions involves a proportionate increase in the amount of gold in reserve. This may be the direct result of statutory enactments relating to legal tender etc.

as, e.g. in Germany or the US, or it may be a necessary measure of prudence as, e.g. in France.

14. Again, the insular position of our country and our comparative freedom from fear of foreign invasion, and the fact that for many generations a state of war has been unknown within the British Isles have all encouraged the banking habit to an unprecedented degree, so that to all appearance the hoarding habit is entirely eradicated. All over the continent of Europe the reverse is the case; in almost every European country there are people living who have experience of war within their countries' borders; and every crisis in the foreign relations of one state with another is immediately reflected in the books of the banks as the result of hoarding on an indefinite scale. Prudent banking cannot neglect to make special provisions against difficulty at such times in the shape of a relatively large Gold Reserve, whereas in this country the very prevalence of the cheque system is a symptom of the absence of any such tendency on a large scale, and hoarding as such is a danger which does not enter into the calculations of any banker.

15. Now the effect of hoarding in a country where legal tender notes are mainly used is that, instead of being deposited at banks large sums are retained by individuals in the form of such legal tender notes, and in order to provide for keeping such notes convertible, banks of issue are compelled either by statute or by their own rules or habits to increase their holdings of gold in reserve proportionately. A general dearth of liquid resources and a danger of a currency famine ensues. At such a moment it is of great importance that the central banking institution of a country should be willing to support any concern which is intrinsically sound by granting liberal credit during temporary stress, and this naturally involves a heavy strain on the reserves of the bank, which is reflected, not necessarily so much in an actual decrease in the amount of gold, as in a fall in the ratio between gold in reserve and notes in circulation.

16. It is permissible to believe that undue importance is attached to the dangers of such a situation, seeing that the hoarded notes when they are eventually released will not to any considerable extent be presented for encashment in specie, but will simply be redeposited with the banks from which they have been withdrawn or withheld and the excessive amounts of notes in the hands of the public are thus only nominally in active circulation, and do not really

constitute any large addition to the probable demands on the
Central Gold Reserves or involve much risk of inflations or of a
depreciation of the currency. So long as they are hoarded indeed
there is no inflation. The danger arises when the hoards are let
loose, and some precaution is undoubtedly needed to provide
against this danger and to secure the rapid withdrawal of notes at
this moment, and a prior increase in the Gold Reserve is, no doubt,
effective for this end. Even so, it is still open to question whether
the precautions taken are not excessive.

17. But, however this may be, the fear of hoarding is undoubtedly
one of the reasons which accounts for the relatively large Gold
Reserves of countries other than Great Britain and wherever the
ratio of banking reserves to liabilities is dependent in any way on
statutory regulation, the banks have no option but to provide
against hoarding conditions by keeping large Gold Reserves.

18. Finally, our position as a lending nation gives us a power of
attracting gold from abroad whenever we require it such as no
other country, with the possible exception of France, can command.
This is a further justification for the relative smallness of our Gold
Reserves, while the enormous increase in our investments abroad in
recent years justifies the relative smallness of the additions we have
made to those reserves during that period. Moreover, the fact that
London is the greatest market for gold in the world and the clearing house of the world's trade, and as a money market is rivalled,
if at all, only by Paris, enables London very quickly to replenish
her Gold Reserves. It is true that the freedom of her market for
gold makes London more liable to demands for gold for export
than e.g. Paris but this is far more than counterbalanced by the
advantage which the free gold market ensures in obtaining and
retaining gold.

19. It may be urged at this point that these last arguments are of
little force in justifying the great disparity between the holdings of
gold in England and France respectively, seeing that as a creditor
nation and in importance as a money market France is at any rate
not far behind this country. It must be conceded at once that the
disparity is very striking and the case of France, therefore, perhaps
deserves some special attention. The legal tender note system prevails in France, and on this ground some disparity in the size of
the gold reserves here and in France is explicable. French people
again have not quite grown out of the hoarding habit. But on the

other hand, the ratio of gold reserves to notes in circulation is not in France subject to any legislative restriction, and the directorate of the Bank of France has practically a free hand in the matter, its notes being issued against the general assets of the Bank in such proportion as the directors think it fit and the limit on total circulation which is fixed by statute from time to time being always placed at a figure which is considerably in excess of any probable demand. If the hoarding habit is not as dangerous as is generally believed, according to the view put forward in this memorandum, why should the Bank of France keep a very high Gold Reserve for fear of hoarding? Is it not clear that, compared with the Gold Reserves of France, our own Gold Reserves are inadequate?

20. I think that, however much stress is laid on the value of the cheque system in economising gold and whatever allowance be made for the special reserve needed for maintaining the circulation as unlimited legal tender of the French five franc piece—this coin is in practice equivalent to an inconvertible note printed on silver—it is undoubtedly true that the disparity between the two Gold Reserves is partly attributable to the deliberate policy of the Bank of France, and that, if the policy was adopted here, the British Gold Reserves would need to be very considerably increased.

21. No doubt the size of the French Gold Reserves has a commercial value in steadying the Bank rate (a point to be discussed later) and a national value against the contingency of a European war. But it is far from impossible that a smaller reserve would secure these ends with equal success, and that the economic waste involved in keeping so large an amount of barren metal is too heavy a price to pay for these advantages.

22. It is undeniable that the Gold Reserves are often excessive in some other countries where the proportion of cash to liabilities or of gold to notes (when legal tender notes are largely used) is regulated by statute. The most striking case is that of the United States where in spite of a colossal gold reserve and although cheques have a considerable vogue, the country went through a terrible financial crisis in 1907 due to shortage of legal tender. It is not suggested that the crisis was caused by the size of the Gold Reserves, but that it could have been successfully met with very much smaller reserves had the banking and currency system been a rational one, the moral being that the system is at least as important as the size of the Gold Reserves. The statutory regulations under which the American

banks work thus make comparison between the Gold Reserves of the United States of America and this country quite valueless.

(ii) COMPARISON WITH FORMER PERIODS

23. What has been said in regard to comparisons with foreign countries is enough to show the uselessness for proving inadequacy of comparisons between the relative increase of Gold Reserves and commercial and banking activities in this country during the last few decades. It will suffice here to give one illustration of the operation of the cheque system in husbanding the Central gold reserve of the Bank of England, and, though this illustration belongs to a much earlier period, it is representative of less striking but equally active changes which are continually working in the same direction. About the year 1854 the London Clearing House was re-modelled, with the result that all the daily settlements between the big banks, which had previously been effected by means of Bank of England notes, were thenceforth made by cheques drawn on the accounts of the banks at the Bank of England. By this means something short of a million pounds worth of banknotes were released and the immediate effect of the change was equivalent to the addition of an equal amount to the real reserve of the Bank against special demands.

III. *Are our Gold Reserves Inadequate?*

24. Instead of proceeding to deal on argumentative lines with the remaining parts of the case of the advocates of increased Gold Reserves, which contain complaints of the operation of Bank rate and of the methods and capacity of the Bank of England in conserving the Gold Reserves, it is perhaps preferable to approach the question of the adequacy of the Gold Reserves from a more detached standpoint. In order to determine the question, it is necessary to consider

(a) The possible causes which may deplete the Gold Reserves and

(b) The means available for meeting such depletion and the time required for making these means effective.

(a) THE POSSIBLE CAUSES WHICH MAY DEPLETE THE GOLD RESERVES

25. The Gold Reserves may be depleted either by increased demands for legal tender currency for internal use or by demands for gold for exports. In either case the demands may be either normal or abnormal.

Internal demands for gold

26. Well-ascertained seasonal demands for gold for internal purposes such as occur at holiday times etc. do not, strictly speaking, deplete the real reserve against emergencies. They are however of importance if an abnormal demand happens to coincide with a seasonal demand.

27. Apart from seasonal demands, a normal demand for additional legal tender arises whenever there is an expansion of trade, additional cash being required for payment of wages etc. In this country, owing to the inelasticity of the fiduciary note issue, such a demand for additional legal tender can only be satisfied by an outflow of gold from the central reserves, or by attraction of gold from abroad. In practice the latter means of supplying a demand operates only through the channel of the central reserves.

28. An abnormal internal demand for additional legal tender arises only at a time of financial crisis and collapsing credit. A general and enduring collapse of credit (which would mean a revival of hoarding as is scarcely thinkable) would involve a demand for legal tender so enormous as to make any conceivable Gold Reserve altogether inadequate. A reserve in such circumstances would be a mere drop in the ocean, and recourse to a fiduciary issue, i.e. an effective suspension of the Bank Charter Act, would be inevitable, and would probably require to be followed up by the issue of a forced currency of legal tender notes. The whole credit system of the country is based on the assumption that credit itself will not completely collapse, and it is useless to think of reconsidering this premiss.

29. A temporary collapse of credit due to over-trading or over-speculation is the contingency against which the Gold Reserves are really required, and the question of the adequacy of those reserves, so far as internal demands are concerned, is simply whether they are sufficient to make such an emergency rare and to prevent it from developing into a complete collapse when it arrives. As a

matter of history there has been only one occasion (1857) since the passing of the Bank Charter Act of 1844 on which the Government's undertaking to suspend the Act, or the knowledge that this emergency method of relieving the situation was available as a last resort, has not been enough to restore sufficient confidence and prevent an actual breach of the law as it stands. In other words on only one occasion has the Bank of England's Gold Reserve proved actually insufficient to meet demands on it at times of maximum stress. Even in 1857 the fiduciary notes issued in excess of the legal limit did not exceed one million pounds in value on any one date, and the period of actual excess issues lasted less than a fortnight.

30. In the past then our Gold Reserves have never proved entirely inadequate. At the present date our position as a creditor of other nations is so strong that a temporary collapse of credit at home, so far from leading to an efflux of gold, would give rise to a calling in of foreign loans and a consequent influx of gold from abroad. It is therefore highly probable that any such abnormal internal demand will be met without absolutely exhausting the existing Gold Reserves on the existing statutory basis. Even if the worst happened and our means of securing gold from abroad proved to be too slow in effecting this purpose—and as will be shown presently this is contrary to all reasonable probability—such a demand can be met by a temporary excess issue of legal tender notes against security, a temporary suspension of the Bank Charter Act as in 1857, and no likelihood exists as of a suspension of cash payments.

31. As the law now stands suspension of the Bank Charter Act assumes the appearance of an heroic extra-statutory expedient dictated by an appalling and overwhelming danger. It may be well that the adoption of this expedient should be protected against abuse by such Restrictions—this must be discussed later—but apart from the historical one, there is no particular reason why suspension of the Bank Charter Act in emergencies is not regulated by statute in advance, in which case it would be regarded as a normal and natural means of meeting a situation which, though abnormal in the sense that it is happily rare, is, on the other hand, normal in the sense that its recurrence from time to time surprises nobody. Most foreign countries which have copied or adopted the British example have not imitated this particular feature of our system, but have made statutory provision in advance for the application of special remedies in similar crises.

Demand for Gold for Export

32. Normal demands for gold for export occur every Autumn, and the resulting hiatus has to be filled in the same way as that caused by normal internal demands. In either case our unrivalled power of attracting gold from abroad is unquestionably sufficient, and the real point of any complaints as to the inadequacy of our reserves is not that they are actually inadequate, but the idea that the means adopted for strengthening and preserving them, viz. the raising of the Bank rate, could be more evenly and more sparingly applied if the reserves were larger.

33. Abnormal demands for gold for export result from financial crises in other countries. Here, as in the case of internal demands, whatever the amount of our Gold Reserves, we must in the long run rely on the power to attract gold from elsewhere. No one questions that we have power ultimately to attract an ample supply, and the important question is whether time is available. This question will be more conveniently discussed under the next head.

(b) THE MEANS AVAILABLE FOR MAKING GOOD A DEPLETION ON THE
GOLD RESERVES AND THE TIME REQUIRED FOR MAKING THESE MEANS
EFFECTIVE

34. Gold required to make good a depletion in the reserves must be obtained either direct from the mines or from existing stocks in other countries. London, as the great free market for gold, is the centre to which most of the world's gold production is shipped. Many mines, including those of India, West Africa, and, most important, South Africa, send their raw gold to London to be refined, so that this gold necessarily passes through the London market. On arrival here, the gold is sold to the highest bidder. Any that remains finds its way to the Bank of England at the fixed price of £3 17s. 9d. an ounce. If, therefore, the Bank of England is specially anxious to increase its Gold Reserve it can always compete in the market with other buyers for the new gold. This involves offering more than £3 17s. 9d. an ounce for it. Bankers and merchants constantly grumble because the Bank does not adopt this course more frequently, but the Bank's reluctance to do so is natural as is the desire of the bankers and merchants that it should be done, for the result is to throw the whole cost of strengthening the reserves on the Bank of England and to avoid any raising of the rate of discount

or disturbance to the money market and to trade. It is equivalent, in fact, to the sale by the Bank of England of exchange on the foreign country to which the gold would have gone at a rate of exchange somewhat less favourable than the ruling rate of the day. The main use of this expedient is in cases where the foreign demand for gold is very temporary and can be thwarted by this means, but in the nature of things this expedient can be applied successfully only to a very limited extent, and is therefore of small importance.

35. The normal method by which gold is obtained is the raising of the Bank rate. A rise in the rate of discount operates (i) to check the demand for credit in this country, and thereby the demand for legal tender, and (ii) to increase the remuneration of capital employed in London and so to attract surplus funds from employment elsewhere. Each of these results has a tendency to move the foreign exchanges in London's favour. The second of them works very quickly if only because of the profitable arbitrage business which a high rate in London and a lower rate elsewhere makes possible pending the adjustment of the exchange rates. The exchanges accordingly begin to move towards the point at which it becomes advantageous to make remittances to London by means of gold. Once the import specie point is actually reached, gold begins to come in (mainly in the form of sovereigns or to a lesser extent other gold coins) from the central reserves of other countries, and before that point is reached, it usually becomes unprofitable for other countries to purchase for export the new gold coming to London from South Africa etc. and the Bank of England is thus enabled to secure a large share of the weekly arrivals.

It is true that most foreign countries place such restrictions on the outflow of gold that the specie point may be exceeded without gold flowing to London, i.e. they prefer to let their internal currency go at a discount. And to a certain extent they may even continue to compete for the new gold in London regardless of the rate of exchange and the heavy cost to themselves. But as shown later, their interests will usually prevent them from taking such action if London's need is urgent.

36. The annual interest on the enormous sums invested by this country abroad is largely paid for in normal times by the export to this country of local products of those countries where the money is invested, but even so there remains a very large surplus still owing, which would have to be remitted to this country in cash if it were

not for the fresh investments of British capital which are made abroad year by year to assist and stimulate the development of other lands. Thus by merely checking the rate of fresh investment abroad, the people of this country can, at some sacrifice no doubt, but without serious inconvenience, at once draw to an extent that may be regarded as for present purposes absolutely sufficient on the gold resources of such places. The regulation of the rate of discount provides, therefore, an extremely effective lever for attracting gold to replenish a depleted reserve here.

37. Furthermore one of the most noticeable phenomena of the current history of the present century has been the rapid rate at which Gold Reserves have been accumulated by countries which formerly had little or no gold. The Argentine, Brazil, India, the Straits Settlements, have all built up special funds to secure the stability of the exchange value of their local currencies while Chile and other countries are on the point of following suit. Twenty years ago a temporary withdrawal of British financial support from one of such countries was reflected almost entirely in a sudden drop in the exchange, so that the only adjustment possible occurred without the passing of metal or at least of any appreciable quantity of metal. To-day the exchanges in these countries move only within or around the comparatively narrow limits of the two specie points, and adjustment can always be effected by the passing of gold out of local reserve. Indeed this is the object for which the reserves exist. By their means India, Brazil etc. have gained the enormous advantage of a stable exchange, while the United Kingdom has been enabled to invest ever increasing amounts in the development of these countries with full confidence that the funds so invested will not, as in former days, be locked up in times of need at home, but that a sufficient amount of liquid assets convertible without ruinous sacrifice into sterling money will be available in the country at a pinch.

38. Here then in the conversion funds of the South American Republics, and the Gold Standard Reserves of India, the Straits Settlements etc. are new stores of gold which exist for the direct purpose of being available at times of need for export to the older monetary centres of the world. The successful efforts made by these countries are often held up to the admiration of the people of the United Kingdom as an example of what we ought to have been doing for our own Gold Reserves. But (apart from the fact that the

special demands of those countries have naturally been reflected in a reduction of the surplus available for building up Gold Reserves here), it is quite evident that the creation of these new reserves has greatly strengthened the position of London's reserves. For good and sufficient reasons in their own interest, these countries have, in fact, relieved London's Gold Reserves of part of their former burden, and *pro tanto*, these new reserves take the place of corresponding additions to our reserves and furnish a strong presumption that our present reserves are adequate, seeing that they have increased, if but slightly, above the figures of twenty years ago when none of these new external reserves existed at all.

39. Our means of attracting gold have been shown to be enormously powerful. It remains to consider whether there is any reasonable doubt that they can be made effective within the interval required to prevent a drain of gold whether for internal or external purposes from resulting in a collapse.

In the case of normal demands, there is little doubt that ample time will always be available. The point for consideration is whether the means used to replenish the reserves will operate quickly enough to meet either an exceptionally strong normal demand which threatens to become abnormal, or to stem the tide of an abnormal demand when it comes.

40. The interval within which gold can be attracted from abroad depends ultimately on physical conditions, such as the time required to ship gold from Berlin, Rio, New York, Cape Town to London. Thus the increased rapidity of transit and improved communications generally provide an additional justification of the slow growth of our reserves in the last few decades. In times of peace, an internal crisis, due to over-investment or over-trading, ought to be capable of being dealt with very quickly. Gold arrives in considerable parcels from South Africa weekly, and the whole of this could be secured by the Bank of England. In addition, although it is part of the hypothesis that prudence has been insufficiently exercised, commitments abroad can always be rapidly reduced, and gold made to flow in from the reserves of other countries. It is difficult, therefore, to believe that replenishment from these two sources will not be rapid enough to keep the gold in the issue department of the Bank from falling below the legal limit.

41. It is, no doubt, possible that the rate of new gold production may fall suddenly, and probable that it will not continue at the

high figures of the last decade. The ultimate effects of such changes are too controversial to discuss here, even if space permitted. It is enough to assume the existing conditions, so long as they exist, naturally permit of gradual adjustment, while a sudden stoppage of the mines, though it might conceivably hasten the arrival of a crisis, could hardly coincide with the moment of crisis, and arrangements would have been made for speeding up the attraction of gold from elsewhere, if it were known that no gold was forthcoming from South Africa. In any case, the actual rate at which gold is produced is not in itself vastly important from the point of view of Gold Reserves.

42. Again, foreign countries are too much interested in the stability of the London money market to regard a threatened collapse with equanimity. At the time of the Baring crisis in 1890 the Bank of France actually lent the Bank of England three million sovereigns. In the American crisis of 1907 (which is now the classic instance of demand for gold for export) the Bank of England did not respond to tentative suggestions made by the Bank of France that similar assistance should be offered. But this country secured a considerable amount of gold from Paris, and this could not have happened without the good will of the Bank of France, which can apply very effective checks on the export of gold when it desires to do so. Now an internal crisis, with London as the storm centre, would be world-wide in its effects, but the surest way in which other countries such as France could protect themselves would be by supporting London, just as London by maintaining a free market for gold is always supporting the Gold Reserves of all other countries.

43. The action of France in 1890 and in 1907 was not purely philanthropic, and it is only by co-operation, whether between rival bankers in London or rival nations all over the world, that the modern system of credit can be sustained at all. When, therefore, it is urged that it is derogatory to this country's dignity, and, indeed, dangerous in view of possible unfriendliness, that we should be dependent on French assistance, it may be answered that this is the natural state of things wherever a crisis occurs. Moreover, French assistance, even in 1890, was probably not essential to prevent a complete collapse, as is shown by the contrast of 1866, when London had great difficulty in making a 10% Bank rate effective in securing gold, although the Paris rate was only 6%. What French

assistance in 1890 did was to enable the crisis to be promptly mastered, to the great relief of Paris. The same conditions are bound to hold good at the next internal crisis, so long, at least, as peace prevails, since even a temporary collapse of London as a free market for gold would dislocate the machinery of all the money markets of the world.

44. It is perhaps permissible to mention, while considering the question of the interval required for the attraction of gold from other countries' reserves to become effective, that, in her own interest, India, as also other countries, keeps much of her Gold Reserve in London, entirely separate from the Bank of England's Gold Reserves, just because, when a crisis occurs, whether in India reacting on London, or in London reacting on India, the gold will be needed in London. Physical questions of transit are, therefore, entirely eliminated in these cases. This is no doubt an argument which must be cautiously advanced, for political reasons, particularly in regard to India, but while the justification for the location of India's Gold Standard Reserve in London is that it is to India's advantage to keep it there, the presence of that gold in London instead of in India might in given circumstances be of immense value in this country.

45. Abnormal demands for gold for export differ little from abnormal internal demands from the point of view of the interval available. The position of London should, on the whole, be slightly stronger when the demand is for export. The problem is in the first instance to prevent the development of an internal crisis whereas an abnormal demand at home implies the actual presence of critical conditions amongst us. It may be said generally that it is on the whole always easier to prevent or check the drain of gold abroad than to prevent or check the drain of gold into internal channels. Moreover when the demand is for export, the raising of the Bank rate can be made so to influence foreign exchanges that gold may flow from, say, Buenos Ayres to New York as well as to London, whereas an internal demand can only be satisfied by shipment to London.

46. Here also the creation of the new Gold Reserves already mentioned and the enlargement of the Gold Reserves of some of the older European countries are obviously of assistance to London, the stronger position abroad reducing the weight of London's burden, so that from this point of view so far from being a reason for in-

creasing our reserves the efforts of other countries might be held to justify their reduction.

IV. *Effect of War on our Gold Reserves*

47. Something should be perhaps said at this point as to the possible position as regards the Gold Reserves in the case of a first-class European war in which this country was a participant. It is often said that suspension of cash payments would be an inevitable result, unless our Gold Reserves are greatly strengthened. The expectation of a suspension of cash payments is probably derived from knowledge of the fact that during and after the Napoleonic wars cash payments were so suspended for a long period. But the Crimean war did not involve suspension and there is no strong ground for believing that such a result is inevitable to-day. The first effect of a war is naturally to increase, not to decrease, the amount of the Gold Reserves of the country engaged in war, gold being attracted by the high rate of discount and as a result of preparations for a big Government loan to finance the war.

48. It is of course impossible clearly to forecast what would be the effect of a general European war in which most of the continental countries as well as Great Britain were engaged, leaving only New York (assuming the neutrality of the United States) among the big money markets of the world available from which gold could be attracted to the seats of war. A general collapse of credit is far from inconceivable in such circumstances: but in that case no Gold Reserves, not even that of the Bank of France, would suffice to prevent immediate suspension of cash payments. It is however not less probable that our position as a creditor nation would suffice to make emergency measures unnecessary and that at worst an extension of the fiduciary issue of notes would be sufficient to meet our needs. In the absence of actual invasion of the country, the natural check on the export of gold that would result both from the height of the discount rate and the risk of capture run by ships containing specie would make the problem mainly one of meeting excess internal demands. Mobilisation would naturally involve some considerable increase in internal legal tender requirements, especially at first, and if it came during the holiday season of the late summer. But even in the latter case the reduced autumn demand for export

would help to counterbalance this special case of outflow. So long therefore as credit held, the abnormal demands should not be unmanageable. It is therefore quite reasonable to hope that the country would get through the first and, from the money market point of view, the most dangerous stages of the war without exhausting the Gold Reserves.

49. Finally, the disadvantages of a forced currency in so rich a country as this are often exaggerated. In normal times the acceptability of 'banker's money' rests on the belief that debts due in gold can be satisfied in gold to the full extent of actual requirements for gold. It is only one step further for people to be compelled by law to accept legal tender notes at a time when it is known that though gold is not immediately forthcoming, such notes rest on sufficient valuable assets capable of being turned into gold at some future time when normal conditions are restored. Gold, after all, is not absolutely indispensable, and even a forced paper currency would provide the country with a very fairly workable temporary medium of exchange: for in the last resort it is not a coin with an intrinsic value equal to its face value that people need, even for foreign commerce, but a token which gives a command over commodities such as is now given by gold. The real danger is that the currency will be depreciated and that the Treasury would not be strong enough to insist on the measures needed to prevent this and restore specie payments after the war.

50. A big European war in which Great Britain stood aside might possibly prove in the end no less troublesome to our Gold Reserves, owing to the strong demand for export of gold entailed, and the actual size of those reserves is perhaps more important in such a case than if we were actually at war. In the latter case the question is rather whether any reserve, however large, would be large enough, and little would be gained by increasing our existing reserves if they are sufficient for all other contingencies but this. The former case would be a special form of abnormal demand for export of gold. If, however, the arguments already set out to prove that our reserves are adequate in time of peace to meet all demands for export are sound, there does not appear to be any ground for holding that this special form of demand would be too much for them.

51. The conclusion seems to be that, regarded as a preparation for war, our Gold Reserves are either adequate in amount or else

are incapable of being raised to a figure which would make them any more adequate.

V. The Bank Rate

52. We can now turn back to the argument of advocates of increased Gold Reserves which finds fault with the frequent fluctuations of the Bank rate and urges that larger reserves would serve to steady it. In regard to the discount rate there is some slight conflict of interests between the banker and the merchant. The banker would perhaps sleep more comfortably in his bed if (at someone else's cost) the level of the Gold Reserves were permanently raised; but he has little desire to effect a diminution in the range and frequency of the Bank rate's fluctuations. On the whole he prefers a fairly high average Bank rate, and he certainly is not prepared to go to expense in increasing the Gold Reserves for the sake of reducing the average rate. What he really wants is a higher average of Gold Reserves which will give him a greater sense of security, and to let everything else go on as much as at present.

53. The merchant, on the other hand, believes himself to have a real interest in obtaining a more stable Bank rate. He is moved to rapturous envy by the straightness of the line in the statistical charts which indicates the French Bank rate when he compares it with the jagged line showing that of the Bank of England. At the same time the merchant, no doubt, thinks that with larger gold reserves he will get a lower average Bank rate as well as a more stable one, again judging from French conditions during the last decade; and he would be willing with some cheerfulness to endure a slight increase in the average discount rate for a year or two, if it were definitely due to concerted action to raise the level of the reserves, and nothing was done meanwhile to throw doubt on his belief that the final result would be to give him for the future a stable rate, averaging on the whole rather less than at present.

54. When all these hopes and expectations are examined more closely, it becomes very doubtful whether there is much substance in them. It is curiously difficult for mankind generally when dealing with or thinking about a reserve of any kind to remember that it is a reserve. Once a reserve is set aside, any attempt to use it is likely to be stigmatised as 'tampering with the reserve'. This is

more than ever true in regard to gold reserves. Brazil, at the moment, supplies a good illustration. Having accumulated a sum of about 20 million pounds in gold in the Caixa de Conversao to secure stability of exchange, Brazil was so loth to use it that not long ago the exchange was allowed to fall considerably below specie point and the country was made to endure great inconvenience due to a dearth of legal tender, mainly to prevent the gold from being depleted; and since the gold has been issued more freely for the precise object for which it was intended, people interested in Brazilian securities have been alarmed by sensational paragraphs in the financial press drawing attention to the dangerous depletion of Brazil's reserve of gold.

55. Now both the banker and the merchant, when they talk of increasing the Gold Reserves of this country, mean by that phrase a permanent raising of the average to a higher level. Once the higher level has become habitual to them, both bankers and the City generally will at once become nervous whenever the reserves show signs of falling below the new level, and steps will be taken to conserve them. The comparative steadiness of the French rate is only in part due to the size of the Gold Reserves; it is possible only because Paris is not a free market for gold and the Bank of France has other means than a raising of the discount rate by which to check the export of specie. The application of these means must involve nearly as serious a curtailment of credit as does a rise in the discount rate in London. While, therefore, greater steadiness of the Bank rate would certainly assist the British merchant in making necessary calculations as to the margins of profit, he envies French conditions only because he fails to see the other side of the picture, and he would strongly resent the increased and, as he would say, arbitrary restrictions on credit which would necessarily have to be applied to take the place of the automatic action of a raised Bank rate.

56. Moreover, it is very frequently the case that the discount rate is high because profits are high and the merchant can afford to pay the rate for bona fide business purposes. 'It is better to stop a runaway horse by heading him up a hill than by running him into a stone wall'. The merchant, at any rate, would greatly prefer to be allowed to decide for himself whether he would pay the rate demanded or restrict his business rather than be compelled by his bank to adopt the latter alternative. His present grievance against the discount rate is really a grievance against an economic law. He

thinks it hard that the Bank should step in and take away a bit of his profit just when he thought he had done really well, but the Bank's action is dictated not by covetousness but by prudence and recognition of the fact that high profits are tempting people out of their depth, and that inflation will result unless the Bank intervenes. It may, therefore, be regarded as certain that, however large a total the average level of the reserve be raised, the Bank rate would have to be moved up and down fairly frequently to maintain the average, and the average Bank rate would not be lessened, and that a successful approximation to French stability in the matter of discount rates is not compatible with the retention of London's position as a free market for gold.

57. All that the merchant could really hope for from the increased reserves would be that the changes in the discount rate might be a little more gradual, the range remaining as at present. This result would be a consequence of the more comfortable night's sleep which bankers would have gained from the increase. But very much the same result could be obtained without any increase in the permanent level of the reserves, if the preparations were made a little earlier each year against the autumn drain, and the Bank rate raised in anticipation of the demand before its effects become seriously felt, so as to avoid a sudden and steep rise in the rate when depletion actually takes place. This means nothing more than a temporary strengthening of the reserves against seasonal demands with a view to allowing them to be depleted more readily, and involves none of the cost attaching to a permanent raising of the level. The difficulty in the way of this course of action at present is probably the uncertainty of the Bank of England whether it could carry the other banks and the market with it and make a higher rate effective at an earlier period than according to present practice. This question leads naturally to the next point, the complaints sometimes heard as to the Bank of England's management of the machinery which controls the Gold Reserves.

VI. The Bank of England's Position as Guardian of the Gold Reserve

58. The Bank Charter Act of 1844 had the effect of increasing the importance of the Bank of England as the central banking

institution of the country and in giving it a practical monopoly of note issue in England and Wales strengthened its position as guardian of the only important Gold Reserve in the British Isles. As other banks grew in importance the Bank of England became more and more what it is to-day, the bankers' bank. The few branches which it possessed in the provinces in earlier years have lost in importance and some of them have been closed, the Portsmouth Branch being the latest among them to be extinguished.

59. Up till the 1880s, the Bank's sway in the London money market was held undisputed, and it was able effectively to exercise the sole responsibility for watching over the country's Gold Reserves. The other big banks held, and hold, their reserves either in the form of Bank of England notes or, more largely, in the form of cash deposited at the Bank of England. The growth of the London Clearing House and the extension of the Clearing House system to the provinces tended in the same direction, because it became an essential condition of membership of the London Clearing House that a balance should be held at the Bank of England by means of which debits and credits at the daily clearance could be adjusted. For a long time, therefore, the Bank of England, intimately related to the chief banks in London and throughout them to the country banks, and sufficiently their master to compel their attention to its wishes, had no difficulty in making the Bank rate effective, and the open market rate of discount responded unquestioningly to any move in the Bank rate or any other indication of the wishes of the autocratic Old Lady of Threadneedle Street.

60. From the '80s onwards this supremacy has been more and more challenged. The large London banks, which have not only absorbed the majority of the older private and provincial banks, but have constantly tended to amalgamate between themselves, as for example the London and County with the London and Westminster Bank, now somewhat overshadow the central Bank.[1] To-

---

[1] Cf. Mr. Cole's evidence on behalf of the Bank of England before the Royal Commission on Indian Finance and Currency, questions 3348, 3352 and 3372–3 (Cd. 7069 of 1913) in which objection was taken to the practice of the India Office in lending out its London Balance in the City, on the ground that loans are made regardless of the interests or wishes of the Bank of England in the matter of the Gold Reserve. This objection has been largely met by the undertaking recently entered into by the India Office to keep a minimum proportion of its balance (one fifth or one sixth according

day the total of the deposits of other banks with the Bank of England probably approaches the aggregate or even exceeds the total of that Bank's Gold Reserve. The Bank of England is compelled therefore to show more deference to the wishes of the great banks and must rely on their ready co-operation to make the Bank rate effective. Mutual assistance and consultation between the big banks and the Bank of England have become more imperatively necessary, and the centre of gravity has shifted to some extent from the Bank parlour to the Committee of the Clearing House as representing an alliance of all the most important banks.

61. This gradual change has moreover led to a certain amount of friction. The directorates of the big banks, perhaps not unnaturally, are inclined to be very critical of the Court of Directors of the Bank of England, and are no longer willing to credit that Court with the possession of all the financial wisdom of the City, urging that specialisation and the hurry of modern commercial life make it difficult to keep the Bank Court thoroughly representative and up to date. The big banks tend therefore to resent anything like dictation from the Bank of England. Meanwhile the Bank of England's directors and shareholders look with natural jealousy on the large dividends paid by other banks as compared with the 9 or 10% which is all that they themselves can earn so long as they pay due regard to the responsibilities of the Bank's position as the Bank of the Government and the guardian of the country's credit responsibilities which fortune thrust upon them in days when they had no rivals.

62. In these circumstances the power of the Bank of England to make the Bank rate effective is much less than it was up to some 30 years ago. Yet the responsibility remains and ostensibly no change has occurred. Several significant features show the reality of change. The secret Committee of Bankers under Lord St. Aldwyn's chairmanship to consider the whole question of the Gold Reserve, the Special Gold reserves which the big banks are said to be creating for themselves and the fact that syndicates of banks come into existence when special measures are required for supporting a firm

---

to amount) with the Bank of England free of interest. This arrangement is doubtless satisfactory for the Bank and for this country, but it is open to objection from India's point of view, especially as no such restrictions are placed on the activities in the matter of lending of foreign Governments, many of which lend out balances in a similar way.

which has got into temporary difficulties, whereas in old days the Bank of England would have taken on such a task alone, are all symptoms of the shifting in the centre of gravity. But so far no practical steps have been taken to readjust the situation on a considered basis.

63. It would, no doubt, be a mistake to over-estimate the dangers and difficulties of the situation, but there is perhaps ground for thinking that the merchant's interests do suffer to a small extent thereby. It is fairly clear that the large banks have got off cheaply hitherto in regard to the cost of maintaining the Gold Reserves. The Bank of England cannot be expected to endanger its modest dividends by heroic measures, and the merchant, who cannot escape paying whatever rate of discount the Bank of England, the big banks and the money market between them make effective, will provide his share of the burden without special provision. The big banks, on the other hand, while reaping a large share of the profits, are under no definite obligation to assist in paying their share of the cost of maintaining the reserves. Self-interest and the obvious need for co-operation may prevent them from flagrant abuse of their power and good fortune, and full credit must be given for the absence of any complaint against them. But when in small things their interests conflict with those of the merchant, there can be little doubt that the Bank of England is likely to pay somewhat more attention to them and somewhat less attention to the general interests of the merchant than would otherwise be the case. As already suggested, this may be the reason why efforts have not been made to secure a more gradual raising of the rate in preparation for the autumn drain, and the habit of window-dressing for balance sheet purposes, which would be purely childish if it did not also involve some slight but real inconvenience to the merchant owing to the temporary tightening of the market which results, may be instanced as a further symptom of the undue preponderance of these banks in the scale.

64. It is not impossible that the agitation for increased reserves is largely the result of a recognition of these unsatisfactory features in the present situation, and that, while mistaken as to the need for such increase, the movement may lead to a clearer perception of the seat of the trouble, and so to the application of an effective remedy. Sir E. Holden has actually included in his programme several proposals which would assist to this end, such as statutory

definition of the obligations of big banks in the matter of Gold Reserves and publication by all banks, both British and foreign, which accept deposits in this country, of fuller accounts, showing, in particular, the real amount of the cash reserve. As already stated, only the London County and Westminster Bank now publishes figures of its average daily cash holdings, though the London City and Midland Bank, of which Sir E. Holden is chairman, has promised some further figures in December 1914, with the object of inducing other banks to follow suit; but, even where window-dressing does not vitiate the available figures, they do not help very much. The creation of special Gold Reserves by these banks might prove really valuable if it were made a step towards the handling of them over to the Bank of England on agreed terms and subject to some well-considered scheme of central control in which the big banks would, for the first time, secure a recognised voice. But for the moment these reserves are equally capable of being used to hinder the policy of the Bank of England, and tend only to intensify the divergence between the seat of responsibility and the seat of power.

65. It is not proposed here to develop this subject further or to attempt to work out a scheme for restoring a perfectly effective central control. There is no reason to suppose that the big banks are anxious to usurp the functions and with them the responsibilities of the Bank of England: they are too well aware of their existing advantages. Quite possibly, therefore, some very slight modification of existing conditions will suffice, if once the big banks recognise, as they seem to be doing, the necessity for regularising and defining their practical participation in the responsibility. The essential point is that the control should be single and central, and that the responsible authority should have adequate powers of effective action.

VII. Emergency Measures

66. If this question, which seems ripe for settlement quite apart from any question of an increase in the aggregate reserves, should involve the intervention of Government or require legislation, the further question of a revision of the Bank Charter Act will probably rise again. As shown above, suspension of the Act is the recognised

safety valve in an emergency, but instead of being automatic, it requires a Deus ex Machina to open it. Many people hold that this condition of things is right and desirable. It is certainly difficult to substitute a good automatic safety valve. The simple German method of a tax on excess fiduciary issue of notes beyond a given maximum has the disadvantage of being too rigid. The rate of tax is fixed, but the rate of discount at which an emergency currency becomes desirable is one which varies widely according to circumstances: 6% might be famine rate in one crisis while 10% might not be excessive for a time in another. This difficulty could, no doubt, be got over by leaving the rate of tax to be settled ad hoc by the Chancellor of the Exchequer on each occasion. But this might not be acceptable to the City, and its only advantage over present methods is that, though the Deus ex Machina would still be called in, he would not be influenced (for good or ill) by the knowledge that a subsequent statute of indemnity must be obtained from Parliament.

67. The late Lord Goschen's scheme for the £1 notes had many points in its favour, but was wrecked on the rock of popular prejudice in favour of gold coins. It would have secured some economy of gold by centralising the store of gold in the country and thus made available for emergencies some part of the gold now in the pockets of the people where it is of small value when a demand arises for export. Possibly the country would accept some such solution if it were confined by statute to emergencies, but this involves the disadvantage that the emergency currency would not be, as it ought to be, indistinguishable from the currency in use in normal times.

68. Sir E. Holden has suggested (speech on March 5, 1914, at the annual meeting of the London City and Midland Bank) that the joint-stock banks (and presumably all banks receiving deposits in this country) should be compelled to keep 6% of their liabilities in gold, showing the figures in their balance sheets and that an amendment to the Act of 1844 should empower them, in the case of a breakdown of credit, to send into the Issue Department of the Bank of England 20 million sovereigns and 40 million worth of bills of exchange and take out in exchange 60 million pounds of bank notes. He further suggested that the Government should by way of a Gold Reserve against the savings banks deposits, pay off their debt of

11 million pounds to the Bank of England, gold being accumulated in its place.

69. Apart from the question, to be discussed later, how far, if at all, the Government should contribute to the cost of keeping Gold Reserves, the latter suggestion would extinguish the Bank's Charter (unless fresh legislation was passed) and would cost the Bank $2\frac{1}{2}\%$ on the whole 11 million pounds, and would cause the Government to lose the difference between the redemption of Consols at 75 instead of at par, without in itself strengthening the Gold Reserves in any way. For the danger to be faced is not the presentation of part of the fiduciary issue of notes for encashment in gold, but a shortage of legal tender currency. Some scheme for an emergency issue of notes must obviously be framed before the 11 million pounds gold thus provided could be of any conceivable use to any one, and, whatever scheme were chosen, there is no real connection between the 11 million pounds of Government debt to the Bank and the problem at issue.

70. The first part of Sir E. Holden's scheme seems to contain one idea which is on the right lines, viz., the power which is suggested should be given to the Bank of England to issue notes against bills of exchange. Modern doctrine on the subject of note issues, as illustrated in the Federal Reserves Act of the US in 1913, is becoming more and more firmly favourable to the view that bills of exchange are the most suitable cover for notes. Apart from this idea, the scheme does not appear to be very useful. So long as the banks, other than the Bank of England, have gold remaining in their special reserves, why should resort be had to an emergency currency? All that is needed is for them to use their gold, either directly or by exchanging it for Bank of England notes in ordinary course. There is clearly a tendency here to forget that reserves are meant to be used, as appears still more strongly when Sir E. Holden adds that 'the remaining portion of the banks' gold' (after the 20 million pounds had gone to the Bank of England) 'would be retained in the vaults of the various banks'.

71. Apart therefore from the suggested use of bills of exchange, Sir E. Holden's scheme does nothing to solve the problem of the machinery to be used in an emergency. It contains no suggestion as to the authority with whom should rest the decision to issue emergency notes or the criterion for determining when the moment for such issue has arrived, nor is the question of the utilisation of the

profits of such issue discussed. Finally, it suffers from the very serious disadvantage of introducing into this country the system of statutory reserves against banking liabilities which proved so disastrous in the United States in 1907, and is objectionable always because a reserve loses all value if it cannot be freely used.

72. It is much easier to criticise other people's suggestions than to frame a satisfactory scheme of one's own, and I shall not do more here than state my own belief that a good scheme for an emergency currency thought out in advance and authorised by Parliament in advance would be an improvement on the existing arrangement and should not be incapable of being devised. On general grounds extra-statutory action is always undesirable, and the fact that the emergency is one which must generally be sudden when it arises, and may well occur during a state of war, seems to afford good ground for preparing and arming ourselves against it at leisure and during peace.[2]

VIII. The Incidence of the Cost of Maintaining Gold Reserves and the Question of a Government Contribution

73. It remains to consider certain questions as to the incidence of the cost of maintaining the Gold Reserves which are always raised when any proposal is made for their increase, and in particular the suggestion that the Government ought to contribute. No more need be added here to what has already been said incidentally on the

---

[2] So long as £5 notes remain the lowest normal denomination of notes the emergency currency should probably conform to the normal unless the inconvenience of a £5 note and the obvious desirability of a £1 note when change is scarce force the adoption of the latter. It seems clear that a tax equal to the rate of discount at the time at which the crisis becomes so acute as to demand the emergency measure must be imposed and continue so long as the emergency currency circulates. If there were real objections to leaving the sole responsibility with the Chancellor of the Exchequer, possibly an ex-officio committee, consisting of e.g. the Governor of the Bank, the Lord Mayor of London, and the Permanent Secretary to the Treasury for the time being, might be established by the Amending Act containing provisions for a written statement of reasons for decision and a written record of advice tendered to be laid before Parliament. The main difficulties would arise in framing regulations as to the time-limit, if any, during which excess notes should be legal tender, and the maximum amount, if any, to which such excess notes should be restricted.

question of the incidence of the cost as between bankers generally and the Bank of England, but there are one or two further questions into which it may be well to go a little more deeply.

74. For what purpose is a Gold Reserve required? Ultimately the answer is, it is required to prevent the banker from going bankrupt. It is a condition of the banker's existence as a banker that he must at all times be able immediately to meet his liabilities in legal tender money to the full extent of any demand that may be made on him, and the Gold Reserves exist solely in order to provide him with a working balance against all possible demands, whether normal or abnormal. So far as normal demands are concerned, no one will dispute that the full cost of maintaining the Gold Reserves should fall on the banking community, taking it as a whole, and ignoring for the moment any distinction between the Bank of England and other banks. It is of course the case that the banker can pass on the cost to his customers, just as a wholesale dealer passes on the cost of maintaining stocks in reserve to his customers. But in the sense that the keeping of reserves diminishes gross profits, the banker must clearly pay the whole cost of keeping reserves against normal demands.

75. But is the same argument wholly valid in the case of abnormal demands? The answer is surely in the affirmative. Perhaps the easiest way of arrival at that answer is to show the impossibility of any alternative. There seems to be only one, that the tax-payer should bear or share the cost of keeping a reserve against other than normal demands. The question here is not for the moment concerned with the Government's position as holding savings banks deposits. The claim that the Government should share the cost in that capacity rests on the assumption that the Government is a banker, whereas the question now asked is whether the tax-payer should assist the banker in bearing the cost.

76. Now it may be conceded at once that the regulation of banking and currency is one of the primary duties of the State and that the Government should look after the interests of the banking community as well as those of other industries. It is true again that the Government, by giving a practical monopoly to the Bank of England for Government business, instead of putting that business out to a comparative tender, make the tax-payer contribute something out of his pocket to the maintenance of the Bank and thus to its power to maintain the Reserves. Mr. Cole, ex-Governor of the

Bank, mentioned in a speech on the subject of Gold Reserves about two years ago the higher average of Government balances in recent years (which is largely due to chance) as a contribution by the Government to the cost of increasing the reserves, but the contribution is so indirect, being accidental rather than intentional, that it is impossible to found any argument upon it. Again the Government recognise that it is their duty, within somewhat indefinite limits, to manage their balances, with some regard to money market conditions and the Bank's control of the Gold Reserves, but this is done, so far as it is done, in much the same way as any big customer consults and defers to the wishes of his bank when his own interests are but slightly affected by meeting his bank's convenience.

77. None of these facts or arguments afford any ground for saddling the taxpayer with any charge in relief of the banker's burdens in respect of the Gold Reserves. Banking is a commercial enterprise in this country conducted for private profit. If the taxpayer were to contribute to the expense of the Gold Reserves he would be giving a bounty to a particular industry, that of banking, and though some of the benefit might accrue to industry generally so far as the whole profit was not absorbed by the banker, no modern-day Government is likely to view with favour a proposal to subsidise the banker and the capitalist out of the taxpayer's pocket.

78. The function of the Government is rather to secure that the banker shall conduct his business on lines that will not threaten disaster to the country and to compel him to keep an adequate reserve and to observe other necessary precautions, if he cannot be induced to do this without compulsion. The necessity for any such governmental action would usually arise from the desire to protect the many sound bankers from unfair or unscrupulous competition by the few. In the matter of Gold Reserves it seems very doubtful whether any such protective action is called for unless it is the enforcement of more frequent and more detailed statements by the banks of their cash position. If further specific action is eventually needed, it will probably be in order to carry out in practice some scheme for modernising the central control of the reserve on which the considered opinion of the banking and mercantile community has reached some sort of unanimity. This can hardly be said to be the case yet, though the Report of Lord St. Aldwyn's Committee may assist in this direction, unless the Committee is led astray by the endeavour to make out a case for Government's

assistance, by laying stress on the Government's activities in regard to savings banks.

79. The claim that the Government should keep a special Gold Reserve or make a special contribution to the Central Gold Reserve in order to provide against the liabilities of savings banks depositors is a specious one, and the strength of the claim has undoubtedly been somewhat increased by the introduction of the system of withdrawal on demand. It should be noted, however, at once that the claim whatever its value is for a contribution not from the taxpayer but from the Savings Banks Fund, and the cost of contributing would logically fall on that Fund alone. If as a result its power of paying its way were permanently impaired, the proper way of meeting the loss would be a reduction in the rate of interest payable to depositors.

80. The arguments used in support of the claim are mainly (a) that the Government should as a banker share the burdens which other bankers have necessarily to carry and (b) that there are special risks of panic among the class of persons to which the savings banks depositor belongs. There is this amount of truth in the second argument that, if ever hoarding on a large scale were to reappear in this country, it would undoubtedly be most likely to occur among the class of savings banks depositors. But no Gold Reserve less than practically the whole of the aggregate amount of deposits would suffice to pay the depositors in such circumstances, and even then the reaction of such a run on credit generally would be enough to bring down the whole credit system of this country. For dealing with a small run the savings banks are better off than commercial banks, because ample notice is required for all but very small withdrawals, and their life and death do not, as with commercial banks, depend on being able to meet all liabilities on demand. The whole credit of commercial banks depends on belief in their ability to do this; the savings banks depend not on prompt payment but on the knowledge of the security of the Government.

81. There is nothing in the history of savings banks which would support the demand for a special Gold Reserve. Adequate arrangements are made for till money and such runs as have occurred have always been easily met by the sale of securities. Inconvenient as heavy withdrawals are to the Government's finances, they do not cause any drain on the Gold Reserves. In fact when they do occur it is usually because depositors want the money to spend owing to the

encroachment on their savings caused by unemployment and trade depression, and just at this time the banks are always likely to be embarrassed not by shortage but by congestion of their reserves. Withdrawals of money to be immediately spent or deposited with other banks leave the Gold Reserve question untouched.

82. The truth is that there is almost no community of interests between the savings banks and commercial banking, and it is a mistake to call the Government a banker in its capacity as holding savings banks' deposits. The reason why hoarding is slightly less improbable among savings banks depositors than elsewhere is precisely that such people are comparatively unacquainted with banking. Money is usually placed in a savings bank in order to be kept there, and the liabilities of the Savings Banks Fund are completely covered by Government securities, whether in the form of stocks or of a direct charge on the consolidated fund. Money is placed in a commercial bank in order to be drawn out, and the very essence of commercial banking is that only a small part of the assets is immediately realisable at any given moment or in any way so well secured as are the assets of the savings banks. The kind of crisis against which a banking reserve is necessary arises directly out of the operations of commercial banks, and there is nothing in those of the savings banks that could conduce to such a crisis. People do not rely on the savings banks for securing legal tender money at a moment when credit money is not in favour, nor did the savings banks make their profit out of the arrangements for the supply of credit which render the crises possible. This is what commercial banks do, and on the principle, therefore, that the reserves should be kept up at the cost of those who reap the profit, it is the commercial banks and not the savings banks which should pay for the precautions necessary to secure the realisation of such profit.

APPENDIX B

T 171 53

Memorandum on British Gold Reserves sent to the Chancellor by Sir George Paish (January or February 1914)

Banking reform has now become a live question in the City. It has been under discussion for many years, and more especially since the Boer War when the Bank of England rate for a time ceased to be effective in attracting gold, and when bankers consequently became seriously uneasy as to their situation. Another influence fanning the agitation for reform has been the growing commercial and banking power of Germany, and the growth of uneasiness lest the gold reserves of London should be raided just before or at the beginning of a conflict between the two countries. In view of the enormous financial power now possessed by the great banks of the world it has become possible to accumulate bills of exchange or other demand obligations upon any monetary centre in such amounts that their sudden presentation for payment would cause grave financial consequences, and might seriously hamper a nation in raising money to conduct a great war. The anxieties of bankers in this respect have been emphasised rather than diminished by the object lesson afforded by the withdrawal of French balances from Berlin and from Vienna during the Moroccan episode. The withdrawal of French money caused great inconvenience to the German people, and had a conflict resulted the withdrawal would have entailed a monetary stringency so great and a financial crisis so severe as to have interfered with the power of the German Government to raise loans for war purposes. The experience gained by German bankers in 1911 and again in 1912 when war broke out in the Balkans, has induced them to strengthen greatly their gold reserves in the last 12 months. (The banking panic in the United States in 1907, the drain of gold from London to New York, and the nearness of the London market to a suspension of the Bank Act also impressed

upon bankers the wisdom of holding larger reserves of gold against
such emergencies.)

A fourth influence has been the enormous expansion in the size
of the banks of this country, and the extent of their liabilities. Distrust of any important English bank would now entail consequences
infinitely greater than it would have done even a few years ago. The
really gigantic proportions of English banking in these days will be
evident to you from the following statement of the growth of the
deposit and current accounts of the London City and Midland
Bank:

1881	about £2 million
1886	2·6
1891	8·1
1896	15·7
1901	44·7
1906	52·2
1911	77·7
1913	93·8

The deposits of Lloyds and of the London County and Westminster are nearly as great, while several other banks have deposits
of from 40 to 70 million. Moreover, the banks each have branch
offices running up to something like 800 per bank. Hence, a run
upon any bank in these days could not fail to have appalling consequences unless the measures for dealing with the situation and
allaying anxiety were of the completest character.

Another factor not without influence although spoken about only
in very confidential manner, is the depreciation in the prices of gilt-
edged securities which prior to the recent recovery caused the banks
to write off practically the whole of their hidden reserves, and
renders them nervous as to the effect upon their position of any
serious losses that might come from trade reaction. Bankers are
naturally indisposed to write off losses out of their published reserves fearing their disclosure might weaken the confidence of the
public. The failure of the Birbeck Bank and the necessity for
bankers to come to the assistance of the Yorkshire Pennybank to
prevent widespread distrust also stimulated them to take measures
for increasing the stability of their institutions.

These various events and influences have caused individual
bankers to strengthen their reserves already. A few years ago
practically the whole of the gold held against banking deposits in

the country was in the Bank of England, the Joint-Stock banks merely keeping coin and notes for till money. It is true that the latter kept balances in the Bank of England, but these were no more than sufficient to provide the sum they required daily to meet their differences in the Clearing House. Hence, in a very real sense there were no gold reserves in the country except those held by the Bank of England and by the Scottish and Irish banks against their notes, issued or in circulation. In consequence of the power of the Bank of England to issue a certain amount of notes in excess of its stock of gold it did keep a moderate amount of gold against its deposit liabilities, and this was the only sum, possessed by the country, available to meet any demand from abroad upon this country for gold other than the new gold arriving from the mines or elsewhere from week to week.

The stock of gold in the Bank of England has been substantially increased since the end of that year, and in the present moment it is £41,300,000, while the notes in circulation amount to £28,200,000. Therefore, at the present moment when the Bank is regarded as exceptionally strong it has an excess of only £13,000,000 of gold over its notes in circulation. Until the recent uneasiness of the Joint-Stock banks caused them to accumulate gold reserves of their own, an excess of £13,000,000 of gold in the Bank of England, over and above its notes in circulation, was regarded as a very strong position, and as warranting a low Bank rate. If this £13,000,000 of gold in excess of the note circulation disappeared, and the gold held became level with the notes in circulation, a great feeling of uneasiness arose, and the Bank of England rate of discount was put up to 5, 6 or even 7% in order to stop the efflux and to attract gold from abroad. In these days, when financial transactions are on a Brobdignagian scale in contrast with the Lilliputian business of twenty or even ten years ago, a margin of £10 million to £15 million of gold in excess of the minimum sum required to meet the Bank of England's notes in circulation is quite inadequate, having regard to the power which other nations now possess to draw gold from London should they be in urgent need of it, and the necessity of our bankers to maintain confidence among the multitude of their depositors. Hence, in recent years, the Joint-Stock banks have themselves accumulated gold reserves of something like £20 million and at the present moment the total reserves of gold held by all our banks, the Bank of England and the Joint-Stock banks, are much larger than formerly. Probably the amount of gold held by our bankers today is 8% of their liabilities, whereas a short time ago it was not more than 6%. This includes the whole of the gold held by the banks of the country as security for the notes in circulation— English, Scottish and Irish—the whole of the till money and the whole of the real reserves. In brief, whereas ten years ago our bankers regarded themselves as quite strong if there were £10 million or £12 million of gold in the Bank of England in excess of the notes in circulation, and were content with gold reserves in all the banks of about 6% of their total liabilities including both notes and deposits, they are believed to possess at the present moment about £33,000,000 of gold in the Bank of England, and in their private vaults in excess of the notes in circulation, and to hold in the aggregate about 8% of their deposits in gold.

Notwithstanding the increased strength that these additional gold reserves have given them, there is still much to be done to render the situation of our bankers as watertight as it ought to be having regard to their enormous influence and power. Opinion is, moreover, divided as to the steps that should now be taken. Some bankers—notably Sir Edward Holden—urge that a Royal Commission should be appointed for the purpose of thoroughly investigating the gold question in this country. Sir Edward maintains that the Joint-Stock banks in order to give better security to their depositors, and also to make their shareholders more secure, should keep a certain proportion of their liabilities in gold in their own possession, in their own vaults, and under their own absolute control. Others, however, maintain that, as hitherto, the whole of the gold reserves of the country should be placed in the Bank of England, and that the latter should continue to be responsible for maintaining them with the co-operation and assistance of the Joint-Stock banks. Mr Vassar Smith of Lloyds Bank deprecates a Royal Commission holding that the banks can be relied upon to take, and will take, a proper course to maintain safety. He says: 'At any rate I would advise a little patience, the subject under discussion is intricate, many sided, and requires most careful thought'.

I should here mention that the subject of gold reserves is now being investigated by a committee of representative bankers, and that Sir Edward Holden in his recent speech, a copy of which I enclose, appealed to the great public to support the policy he has strenuously advocated in that committee. (Doubtless the Governor of the Bank of England will be able to inform you as to the probable conclusions of the Committee and its recommendations.)

Sir Edward Holden not only desires a Royal Commission to investigate the gold situation as it affects the Joint-Stock banks, but also as it concerns the Post-Office Savings Bank, the branches of foreign banks in London and the provision of an emergency currency. Sir Edward wishes very much to induce the Government to hold a substantial amount of gold against its Post-Office deposits, and also to redeem its book debt of £11,000,000 to the Bank of England which forms part of the security for the Bank of England's fiduciary note issue. The amount of notes the Bank has power to issue against securities is in all £18,450,000 of which £11,015,100 is secured by the Government's book debt, and £7,434,900 by 'other' securities.

A few years ago I had the honour to submit to Mr. Asquith, then Chancellor of the Exchequer, a comprehensive report on the banking situation in which I deprecated at that time Government action to investigate the position of the banks and to increase the gold reserves. My reasons for so doing were briefly that events were then moving in a favourable direction, and that it was essential to do nothing to place any restriction on bankers' loans as there was every prospect of a great expansion in the commerce and trade of the country. Indeed, it was evident that we were likely to witness as great an expansion of trade that the world would need all the gold it could obtain, and that efforts on the part of this country to increase exceptionally its stock of gold would tend to check and to interfere with the trade improvement. The objection that I then had to an enquiry on these grounds have now disappeared. It is evident that the world's trade has received a check mainly in consequence of the Moroccan and Balkan troubles and of the subsequent accumulation of gold by Germany, by France, by Russia and by our own Joint-Stock banks in consequence of the anxieties which arose over those two questions. It is evident that our Joint-Stock banks have accumulated within the last two years the greater part of the £20,000,000 of gold they are now supposed to hold, while the Bank of Germany in the past 12 months has accumulated £20,000,000, the Bank of France £15,000,000, the Bank of Russia £14,000,000 and the Bank of England £5,000,000. Undoubtedly this competition for gold by Berlin, Paris, St. Petersburg and London is in a large measure responsible for the acute banking stringency throughout

the world in the past 12 months, and for the trade reaction that has
resulted therefrom. However, be the causes what they may, the fact
remains that trade is now tending to decline all over the world,
and it is evident that great quantities of gold will accumulate in the
international markets pending a trade revival. Such a time is
specially favourable to the appointment of a Royal Commission to
inquire into our gold reserves, and to make proposals for placing
our currency and banking systems on foundations strong enough to
support our Goliath banks with their myriad of branches, and to
cause bankers to hold a stock of gold sufficient not only to maintain the confidence of their repositors, but to protect the country
against the effects of any gold drain on foreign account whether the
engineered arising from unavoidable and natural causes.

The advantages of appointing a Royal Commission at the present
time are increased by the fact that our banks have accumulated
already the additional gold essential to the maintenance of our
banking strength both from a national and an international point of
view. All the Commission would need to do in this respect would
be to decide whether the additional stock of gold should be held in
the Bank of England or in the Joint-Stock banks. In other words,
the Commission would judge between the various views I have
already referred to.

This being the situation the Commission's findings would have
no adverse effects upon trade. Indeed, the report of the Commission
might have a reassuring and beneficial influence as it would finally
settle a question which has excited some uneasiness. Moreover,
during the investigation the stock of gold in this country may reach
quite unprecedented dimensions owing to the contraction in the
demand for currency in all countries through the setback to trade
and the fall in the price of commodities concurrently with the continued great output of new gold from the world's mines. Thus,
conditions at the present moment are the reverse of those at the
time I made my report to Mr. Asquith.

In the foregoing I have endeavoured to give you a summary of
the situation without in any way presenting my own opinion other
than to indicate that the existing economic situation is favourable
to the appointment of a Royal Commission.

My own views of the questions now under discussion are that a
Royal Commission might usefully be set up to enquire, first, into
the relations of the Bank of England and the Joint-Stock banks

with a view to ascertaining whether it is desirable for the increased gold reserves to be held by the Bank of England or by the Joint-Stock banks. I believe that the investigations of the Commission would show the desirability of holding the whole of the gold reserves in the Bank of England where they would be visible, and there they would be handled by an impartial body for the general good both in internal and external emergencies, and the advisability of all the banks of the country contributing their quota to the stock of gold held. If all the Joint-Stock and private banks were called upon to keep two per cent of their deposits in the Bank of England above the balances now kept at the Bank of England by the Clearing banks for clearing purposes, the situation would be rectified. As the status and power of the Bank of England would be greatly enhanced by such an arrangement it would be desirable for the Commission to investigate the question of the desirability or otherwise of appointing a Governor of the Bank of England for a much longer period of years than at present. Under the existing arrangement one of the directors of the Bank of England probably with little knowledge of banking is appointed Deputy Governor for two years, and then Governor for another two years. By the time he has obtained a good knowledge of the Money market his term of office expires. This system has hitherto given fairly good results; but one has to bear in mind that in these days financial transactions are much greater and more complicated than they used to be; that new and great Money markets are arising controlled by men who had a life-long training in international banking. In the event of a change in the Bank's constitution, and the appointment of Governors for longer terms than hitherto, the question needs to be discussed as to whether or not the appointment of the Governor should not be submitted for the approval of the Government of the day, as the power of the Bank in matters economic and financial would be so vast that very great care would need to be exercised in securing men for the post whose fitness and qualifications were universally recognised. I have no doubt that the directors of the Bank of England would always submit the name of a person whose qualifications were beyond question. Of course, I wish you to understand clearly that I think the management of the Bank of England in the past has been exceedingly good, and that the Bank merits the confidence of the public for the manner in which it has carried out its duties often at great sacrifice to itself. Nevertheless the official appointment of the Bank as sole custodian of the gold reserves of the country should impose a measure of responsibility on the Government also. The Joint-Stock banks will doubtless be unwilling to hand over the gold they have accumulated to the Bank of England unless the latter gives some pledge that the additional gold will not be used except in periods of emergency. This difficulty can, however, be easily overcome by a declaration from the Bank of England as to the policy it would pursue if it were entrusted with the additional gold by the Joint-Stock banks. For instance, it might indicate in a general way that whereas in the past it regarded a reserve of 60% of its liabilities as a maximum and 30% as a minimum it would in future alter its maximum to 75% and its minimum to 45%, respectively, except in times of emergency when it would call together representatives of the Joint-Stock banks and of the Government to discuss the situation and to decide upon the measures that should be jointly taken to meet the exceptional conditions.

Another matter needing investigation is the Government's debt of £11,000,000 to the Bank of England and the Government's contribution to the increased gold reserves of the country. Personally I do not see the use of redeeming the Government's debt to the Bank and of replacing it with gold. The notes issued against the debt are never likely to be tendered for payment, and in my judgment there is no use in holding gold when securities are equally good. For home circulation a considerable amount of notes is always necessary, and these notes are provided in part by the fiduciary issue against securities amounting in the aggregate to £18,000,000. There is, however, some justice in the demand of bankers that the Government should contribute to the gold fund. Not infrequently the public deposits in the Bank of England are reduced to £6,000,000, a very low figure taking into account the Government's liability to the Savings Banks. The Savings Banks deposits now amount to over £200,000,000 and the Government holds practically no balance to pay deposits if there were an exceptional demand for them. Having regard to the importance of maintaining a strong Money market especially in periods of political danger, and the desire of all bankers to do everything that is possible to guard against any financial injury which a foreign country might try to inflict upon the London money market in order to diminish the Government's power to raise war loans, it certainly seems reasonable for the

Government to contribute its quota to the gold reserves, I suggest that the Government should keep about 2% of the Savings Bank deposits in the Bank of England, a proportion which would be equal to about £4,000,000 and would raise the total new gold fund to £24,000,000.

Lastly, there is the proposal that the Bank of England should in periods of emergency and with the sanction of the Chancellor of the Exchequer be given power to issue an unlimited amount of notes in order that it may be able to meet any run upon the banks and thus to maintain confidence. The law at present contains no provision for the issue of emergency currency, and consequently on three occasions the Bank Act has been suspended with the sanction of the Chancellor of the Exchequer. The sounder course would be to provide for the issue of emergency currency to be issued only with the sanction of the Chancellor of the Exchequer.

A subsidiary reform that needs to be discussed and introduced is the publication of fuller particulars of bankers' balance-sheets with the provision that all bankers receiving deposits from the public and issuing their own cheques should be under statutory obligation to publish annually a statement of their assets and liabilities. This would, of course, include all foreign bankers trading in this country. With regard to the latter it seems desirable to have two balance-sheets, one showing the liabilities incurred in this country and the assets held against them, and the other showing the total liabilities and assets of the foreign banks. At present, foreign banks with branches in this country are not called upon to publish balance-sheets in this country although most of them supply reports in a foreign language on application.

I shall be happy to supply fuller information if you require it, but this is the best I have been able to do in the time.

With all good wishes.
Yours sincerely
To the Right Honourable David Lloyd George, MP

APPENDIX C

T 170 14 (SIR J. BRADBURY)

Visit to Bank as to Mr. Joynson-Hicks' Question

On Wednesday July 29, by direction of the Chancellor of the Exchequer, Mr. Montagu, Sir John Bradbury, and Mr. Ramsay visited the Bank of England to discuss the financial situation in the City, with particular reference to the question of which Mr. Joynson-Hicks had given notice for that afternoon, viz. Hansard 1316:

> I beg to ask the Chancellor of the Exchequer a question, of which I have given him private notice, namely: Whether he has communicated with the Bank of England with the view to their convening a meeting of bankers to take steps to deal with the present financial position; and, if not, whether he will consider the advisability of so doing without further delay.

They were received by the Governor who, after some preliminary talk, invited Lord Revelstoke, Sir Everard Hambro, Mr. Goschen, and Mr. Cole to join the discussion.

The opinion of the Governor, confirmed by the other directors present, was that the Bank of England was in a very strong position, and that any special steps of the nature suggested would be unnecessary, and indeed harmful as tending to excite apprehension.

The Bank of England and the Joint-Stock Banks (with whom the Bank of England keeps in close touch through periodic meetings) had the situation in hand. Money so far is plentiful and cheap, indeed, if it were not for the European crisis, a rate of 2% would be appropriate: the situation so far as the banks are concerned is normal, though the same could not quite be said of the Discount Houses who have been putting up rates, with the result that the Bank is discounting largely today.

The Governor and the Directors present unanimously advised a reply to the following effect:

I have been in consultation with the Bank of England and I am advised that there is nothing in the financial situation at the present moment which would make such a suggestion necessary or advisable.

The opinion was also expressed that it were better that the Governor should not go to visit the Chancellor of the Exchequer, lest alarming inferences be drawn.

APPENDIX D

T 170 14

Letter of F. Schuster and E. H. Holden, July 31, 1914

The proposal is that a Chancellor's letter should be applied for at once in accordance with the terms of previous letters.

That the bankers shall, as soon as the letter is obtained, deposit in the Issue Department of the Bank of England from 13 to 15 million of gold and shall be at liberty to deposit a further amount of 16 to 30 million of securities and/or bills of exchange approved by the Bank of England as collateral security for a corresponding issue of notes.

T 170 14

Clearing Bank's letter, officially making the proposal
(August 2nd)

Sir,
We desire on behalf of the Banks belonging to the London Clearing House to lay before you the following scheme for securing the supply of currency so urgently required by this country during the present time of crisis to permit of the carrying on of all industrial commercial and financial business.

The scheme which we propose for your acceptance is one which has slowly matured after lengthy discussions and has lately received the approval of the special Gold Subcommittee of the Clearing Banks under the presidency of Lord St. Aldwyn as suitable for adoption as a recognised means of providing an emergency currency.

The primary reason for the adoption of this scheme was that the Clearing Banks felt that, if they were to take upon themselves the responsibility of setting aside special reserves of gold, it was essential that means should be found for using such gold in an emergency as the basis of a superstructure of a currency more elastic than gold coin. The intention was that the criterion of an emergency should be the raising of the Bank Rate to 8%. This emergency is upon us unexpectedly at this moment and we thereupon invite the immediate acceptance of our scheme. The details of the scheme are as follows:

(1) The Government should authorise the Bank of England in case of need to suspend the Bank Charter Act of 1844 in regard to the limit placed upon the issue of notes against securities, as has been done on three previous occasions in 1847, 1857, 1866.

(2) Authority should be granted to the Bank of England to issue notes to Bankers in England and Wales up to a maximum of £45,000,000 against the deposit by such Bankers of (a) gold, (b) securities in the proportion of one-third in gold and two-thirds in securities. The securities to be deposited would consist either of Bills of Exchange endorsed by the Bankers and approved by the Bank of England or of securities of or guaranteed by the British Government, or both.

(3) The first step should be the deposit of not less than £12 million in gold immediately upon the issue of the letter from the Treasury authorising the suspension of the Bank Charter Act; and the issue thereupon to the Bankers by the Bank of England of an equal amount of notes against such gold. The Bankers would further obtain the right to claim the issue of notes equal to twice the amount of the gold so deposited on bringing to the Bank of England subsequently, as circumstances might require, securities or bills of exchange as cover for such additional notes.

(4) The issue of notes on these conditions would be of the nature of an emergency and temporary issue, and it would be a binding condition of the issue that the securities and bills of exchange so deposited must be redeemed at a date not later than the date upon which any moratorium that might be enacted or any extension of such moratorium was expressed to determine, provided that if on the termination of the moratorium market conditions were unfavourable an application might be made to the Treasury for a further extension of time for the redemption of such securities and bills of exchange, but no such extension should be permitted without the sanction of the Treasury.

(5) It is proposed that a tax should be paid by the Bankers on all

notes issued against bills or securities so deposited by them, the amount of such tax to be settled in agreement with the Treasury.

The advantages which we claim for this scheme may be shortly stated as follows:

1. An emergency currency will be provided sufficient for all needs.

2. An addition of from £12 million to £15 million of gold will be made to the gold in the Issue Department of the Bank of England.

3. Such addition will, in the opinion of the Bankers, by promoting confidence, have a steadying effect upon the public mind.

4. There will be no danger of an inflation of the currency because excess notes issued will flow back to the Banks when no longer required by the public, and the Bankers will, apart from other incentives to redeem the notes, be desirous of relieving themselves of the burden of the tax. As soon as easy conditions returned to the money market, the excess notes would be forced to return to the Banks, and the Bankers would carry them back by instalments to the Bank of England and redeem their gold and securities.

5. In the opinion of most of the Bankers, it is one main recommendation of the Gold Committee's matured scheme that so far from seeking to increase the fiduciary issues of notes it seeks to diminish such issues, but at the present juncture it is not desired to lay stress on this point which is only mentioned to make clear the attitude of the Bankers.

We desire to make it plainly understood that the Bankers do not desire to make any profit for themselves from the notes issued under their scheme, and it is for this reason that they propose that they should pay a tax on the notes issued against securities and bills of exchange, the proceeds of which would go first to pay the expenses of the Bank of England in making the issues and the balance to the Public Purse.

The Bankers in urging with all the force at their command this emergency issue are extremely desirous of acting in complete accord with the Governor and the Court of the Bank of England and are equally desirous of showing a complete community of interests for competitive purposes if such action were possible, far less to drain gold from the Bank of England.

Lastly they place upon record their conviction that if further issues of currency are not immediately available other and more serious steps will have to be considered by His Majesty's Government.

T 170 14

Reply by Lloyd George to the Bankers' Scheme

Gentlemen,

We have given very careful consideration to the letter signed by you under today's date on behalf of the London Clearing Banks in which it is proposed that those banks should undertake to pay into the Issue Department of the Bank of England a sum of £12 million to £15 million in gold immediately in exchange for notes, upon the understanding that they should be enabled to obtain if and when required a further issue of notes against approved securities (including Bills of Exchange) up to an amount not exceeding twice the amount of the gold so deposited.

We understand that this proposal is the outcome of deliberations of a Committee of Bankers and was intended in its inception as a scheme of general application to times of emergency, but that as it has not yet been submitted to general public criticism, your present object is to secure its adoption merely as an expedient for dealing with the present crisis without prejudice to the question whether or not an arrangement of this kind could with advantage be adopted as part of the standing currency system of the country.

On this understanding and in view of the weight which must necessarily attach to any suggestion arising out of your great practical experience and of the importance at the present juncture of securing the cordial co-operation of the Joint-Stock Banks in the measures necessary to preserve the Gold Standard, we agree to accept your offer subject to the conditions specified below.

We must not, however, be understood as accepting the view which appears to be implied in your proposals that so large a proportion of the gold now in the hands of the Banks can be better employed by being deposited with the Bank of England rather than being used in normal course to satisfy the ordinary requirements of your own customers. Indeed in consenting to the course proposed we have not failed to keep in view the fact that the gold proposed to be deposited at the Bank of England will remain through the machinery of the Issue Department of that bank available for its primary purpose, viz. to pass freely into general circulation if and as soon as the state of currency requires it.

The conditions to which we have referred are:

(1) that the primary deposit of £12 million to £15 million in gold shall be made in exchange for notes in the ordinary way.

(2) that the issue of notes against securities shall within the agreed maximum be strictly limited to such amounts as the depositing banks may satisfy the Treasury to be from time to time required to satisfy legitimate demands for currency.

(3) that the issue of notes against securities shall in accordance with the conditions laid down on each of the three former occasions on which such issues have been authorised, only be made during periods in which the Bank of England rate of discount is equal to or exceeds 10% and that the amount of notes for the time being outstanding against securities deposited by each Bank which is a party to the arrangement shall be treated as an advance by the Government to the Bank bearing interest at the rate of the Bank of England discount rate for the time being with a minimum of 10%.

(4) that the securities to be accepted—which need not necessarily be British Government securities, as also Bills of Exchange—should be subject to approval as regards both character and amount by the Bank of England acting on behalf of His Majesty's Government.

As regards the withdrawal from circulation of the notes outstanding against securities when normal conditions are restored we do not think it necessary to make any stipulations since when the rate of discount falls below 10% ordinary monetary influences will suffice to secure the return of the notes.

APPENDIX E

T 170 14

Letter by Sir John Bradbury to Bonham-Carter (undated)

I enclose a note of the sort of thing I think the Prime Minister ought to say on the subject of the currency, more particularly in regard to the action of the Joint-Stock Banks (I am afraid it is not well expressed but it is now 3 a.m. and I have had a very wearing day).

I also enclose a copy of the brief I have written for the Chancellor of the Exchequer explaining the action proposed to be taken together with the draft of a letter which it is proposed that the Clearing Banks should send him advocating their scheme and of the reply which I think should be sent to it. The Cabinet Committee is committed to the general outline of the scheme but we are in no way precluded from making the modifications which I propose and these in my opinion would render it practically unobjectionable. But I doubt very much whether the banks will accept it as modified and as the Prime Minister knows the Chancellor of the Exchequer is attracted by it in its original form.

Note

The currency situation is on the whole entirely reassuring. The position of the Bank of England at the commencement of the crisis was exceptionally strong, while any tendency which might have established itself for gold to flow abroad was immediately checked by the precautionary raising of the Bank Rate on Thursday last from 3 to 4% and I have little doubt that when the foreign exchanges, which have been completely demoralised, re-establish themselves, the high rate of 10% now established will in the absence of untoward circumstances at home bring us all the gold we require.

But if gold is encouraged as heretofore to flow to the London market, it is of primary importance to maintain the position of that market as the great free market of the world. We shall receive gold when we need it so long and only so long as we are prepared to pay gold when it is required and our first preoccupation must be to maintain our gold standard and the convertibility of our currency. In the United Kingdom unlike any other country there is a vast amount of gold estimated at not less than 70 million in active circulation. The great banks forming the London Clearing House hold some £15 million apart from till money; the Bank of England, after paying out nearly 12 million last week for home demands still holds 28 million. A fall of 12 million in a week is no doubt considerable, and if it represented spontaneous hoarding on the part of individuals it might even be alarming. But all the evidence to hand tends to show that the general public have behaved with great coolness, the withdrawals from banks (including the Post Office Savings Banks) have been moderate in amount and the reduction of the Bank of England Stock of gold represents, in the main, amounts taken by other banks and held by them as precaution against contingencies. The Reserve has in fact been mobilised not disbanded. That the banks of the country should reinforce their cash balances to enable themselves to meet exceptional demands should such demands occur is prudent and reasonable, but suggestions have been freely made that bankers in their anxiety to retain their gold have at any rate in some instances tended to restrict the payment out of specie and offered notes instead of gold to their customers when gold was preferred.

If such action has been taken—and whether it has or not I regret to say that I have heard it advocated on grounds of policy by bankers of some experience—I cannot state too emphatically that I regard it as most mischievous and dangerous. A currency like ours which is in the main metallic has many advantages but it has one great danger: it is unable to defend itself against the practice of hoarding coin, if that practice assumes large dimensions and if the banks which should be its principal guardians set the example of that practice their customers will inevitably, and indeed must necessarily, follow it. So long as a customer can obtain sovereigns, shillings and pence for his daily requirements from his bankers he will be content to depend on that source of supply. If difficulties are placed in the way of his obtaining the cash he will apprehend greater difficulties in future and will protect himself by laying in a store. The development of banking which has been one of the most remarkable features of the last half century has laid upon the Joint-stock banks very serious and important duties in relation to the currency and if specie payments are to be maintained—and heaven forbid that they should be suspended while a sovereign remains to pay— it is essential that they, no less than the old lady of Threadneedle Street herself, should make it a point of honour to maintain them.

The position of the great Joint-stock banks is so strong that they have undertaken to pay immediately into the Bank of England a sum of £12 million in gold to strengthen the Central Reserve—an offer which His Majesty's Government has gratefully accepted— but we have accepted it on the assumption that they are strong enough in the periphery (which it is their main duty to defend) to reinforce the centre and we rely upon them to see that the periphery is firmly held. I had far rather than not a sovereign of the £12 to £15 million they have promised would ever reach the Bank of England than the notes of that institution should be forced upon a single of their depositors who asks for gold.

In times like the present it is of primary importance that nothing should be done to create distrust of or even make unpopular, the Bank of England note. The grant of facilities for issuing notes against securities in excess of the legal limit is an expedient which experience has shown to be of great value in times of financial stress and it is possible—I may say probable—that that expedient will shortly have to be resorted to. It can only be resorted to without jeopardy to the gold standard if the public are willing to treat the notes so issued as being as 'good as gold' and to retain them in circulation. If the public will economise the use of gold by employing notes for all cash transactions for which they are suitable and by drawing from the banks only so much gold as is necessary from time to time to meet their immediate requirements and if the banks on their part will supply gold freely whenever it is demanded I am absolutely confident that there is nothing in the present situation which will necessitate a breach in our honourable tradition of 92 years of uninterrupted specie payments.

APPENDIX F

T 170 14

*Letter from Sir George Paish to Lloyd George, dated
2 a.m. Saturday morning, August 1, 1914*

Dear Mr. Chancellor,

The credit system upon which the business of this country is formed has completely broken down and it is of supreme importance that steps should be taken to repair the mischief without delay, otherwise it may be impossible to finance the great expenditures which the country may be forced to incur in this crisis.

In my judgment the mischief is not beyond repair provided that our great institutions are wisely administered in a period of great national danger. Obviously we cannot hope to finance a great war if at its very commencement our greatest houses are forced into bankruptcy and firms of world wide reputation are unable to meet their engagements.

At the present moment firms engaged in conducting our foreign trade are unable to meet their obligations as they cannot get the credit on which the whole of their operations are based. They are called upon to meet their obligations without being able to bring money from foreign countries to meet their engagements. Furthermore, the closing of the London Stock Exchange and of the world's bourses prevents them from selling securities in order to meet their engagements. The distrust thus created has practically stopped the discount of all bills except the relatively small number which the Bank of England is able and willing to discount with its present resources.

Beyond this situation a feeling of alarm has sprung up in the minds of many people and the hoarding of gold has commenced on a relatively large scale.

It is urgently necessary first that our great houses should be saved from disaster and that the public should be reassured as to the ability to get money under all circumstances.

Furthermore, it is of supreme importance that everything should be done to maintain the credit of this country in all parts of the world in order that food and materials may be moved from the farms to this country. The existing system of credit by means of which foodstuffs, cotton, wool, and other raw products are brought from all countries to England is our own creation and the most vital part of its machinery is in this country. It is this machinery that has now completely broken down.

The steps called for

First, our accepting houses which place money at the service of the whole world in order to move food and material must be instructed and assisted to renew their operations.

Second, Bills accepted must be discounted by our bankers as usual. Hence our great accepting houses must be saved from the bankruptcy which threatens them.

This can be done only by the announcement of a moratorium enabling them to postpone payment of their existing obligations until funds are received. This moratorium should however be of a general character as business firms of all kinds and descriptions are threatened with bankruptcy in consequence of their inability to obtain remittances from abroad—direct and indirect.

Concurrently with the issue of a moratorium it is essential to take three other steps, first the suspension of the Bank Act, second the suspension of specie payments, and third the issue of small notes of £1.

The suspension of Bank Act should be unattended by any stipulation as to the amount which each Bank may borrow from the Bank of England. The British public needs to know that it can obtain in Bank of England notes (which would be legal tender) the whole of the money deposited with the Banks. If there is any restriction whatever the measure of reassurance will be liable to fail. In proportion as it succeeds the smaller will be the withdrawals and the fewer will be the Bank notes that will need to be issued.

The suspension of specie payments will place in the hands of the Bank of England a large sum of gold which will became available for meeting any foreign payments for food and material that may be necessary.

The issue of smaller notes will bring back from circulation a large amount of gold which would also be available for making any foreign payments which may be necessary. If these steps are inadequate as they may be it may become necessary for the Government to guarantee the Bank of England for any losses it may incur from the discount of bills drawn against produce sent to this country. The object of this step is to induce accepting houses to continue to accept and thus to place money at the service of all countries in order to enable food and raw material to be sent from any part of the world to Great Britain and to enable British goods to be sent out in payment.

It is obvious that, unless the machinery of production and of distribution is kept in full working order, we shall neither be able to buy food and material from abroad nor sell our own goods in return. Our income would thus be destroyed and we should not be able to finance the great loans which the country may be called upon to raise for its own defence and to provide the money which its allies and friends will need to ensure a successful issue in the struggle which seems to be so near and so threatening.

Yours sincerely
To the Right Honourable David Lloyd George, MP

T 170 14

Letter of Sir George Paish to Lloyd George, dated Sunday August 2, 1914

Dear Mr. Chancellor,
The plan of the bankers to meet the emergency that has arisen is a good one *provided confidence is maintained*. If confidence is not maintained nothing will be of any good short of the suspension of the Bank of England Act (which would give the Bank power to issue an unlimited amount of Bank Notes) and the suspension of specie payments.

To maintain public confidence the mere addition of another £15 million of gold to the stock in the Bank of England attended by an increase of £45 million of notes is in itself likely to be ... inadequate. This becomes apparent when one realises that bank deposits amount to nearly £1,150,000,000 and that the total amount of gold now in the Bank of England is under £40 million and that including the additional £15 million it will be less than £55 million. Thus depositors have merely to ask for 5% of their deposits in gold and the whole of the gold in the Bank of England disappears. If confidence is not maintained a large part of the gold in the Bank of England would probably disappear in a few days, and specie payments would then have to be suspended. The position would then be worse than it is now when the Bank possesses the gold and it can be made available for urgent expenditures abroad.

In these circumstances would it be possible for you or the Prime Minister or even the King to note with pride the patriotism, confidence and calmness of the British people in the face of a situation so unprecedented and to point out to the nation that the welfare of all depends upon each following his avocation in the usual way and upon the maintenance of confidence not only in the future of his country but in the strength of its great institutions and that anyone who weakens our great institutions in this crisis is unintentionally injuring the nation. The maintenance of confidence means the maintenance of credit and the maintenance of credit means the maintenance of income and of power to raise whatever money the nation may need.

P.S. I misunderstood the purport of your question the other morning. This is the reply I should have given.

TABLES

TABLE 1

THE UK BALANCE OF PAYMENTS (In millions of £ stg. current)

	1871 1875	1876 1880	1881 1885	1886 1890	1891 1895	1896 1900	1901 1905	1906 1910	1911 1915
Visible Trade									
Imports FOB	316·8	336·8	351·6	342·8	371·9	422·1	482·2	566·9	655·2
Exports FOB	297·5	257·9	295·2	298·5	287·5	303·7	367·2	487·8	593·9
Balance	−19·3	−78·9	−56·4	−44·3	−84·4	−118·4	−115·0	−79·1	−61·3
Invisible Trade Payments	7·4	7·6	8·1	8·0	7·6	8·5	12·9	12·1	14·2
Receipts	32·8	29·3	28·0	27·6	26·9	27·6	25·1	49·0	58·7
Balance	25·4	21·7	19·9	19·6	19·3	19·1	12·2	36·9	45·5
Shipping Payments	5·9	6·2	6·3	6·1	6·2	7·2	10·9	13·1	14·8
Receipts	36·9	39·8	45·7	43·1	42·8	45·6	54·9	69·0	77·5
Balance	31·0	33·6	39·4	37·0	36·6	38·4	44·0	55·9	62·7
Emigrants & Tourism Balance	−11·5	−9·0	−11·2	−11·1	−10·0	−10·7	−13·0	−17·6	−22·1
Total Invisible Items Balance	44·9	46·3	48·1	45·5	45·9	46·8	43·2	75·2	85·1
Trade & Services—Balance	25·6	−32·6	−8·3	+1·2	−38·5	−71·6	−71·8	−3·9	23·8
Interest & Dividends—Balance	50·0	56·3	64·8	84·2	94·0	100·2	113·0	151·4	188·0
Total Current Account Balance	75·6	23·7	56·5	85·4	55·5	28·6	41·2	147·5	211·8

Source: *Report of the Committee on Invisible Transactions*, London 1968.

TABLE 2

IMPORTS OF MANUFACTURES INTO THE UNITED STATES (annual averages in thousands of dollars)

Product		1872–73 1873–74	1889–90 1893–94	Change
Iron & Steel				
1. From Great Britain		36,165	29,081	−7,084
2. From Europe		4,037	5,707	+1,670
Wool Textiles	1.	34,415	18,371	−16,044
	2.	14,290	18,145	+4,446
Cotton Textiles	1.	22,789	11,984	−13,795
	2.	8,783	11,108	+2,325
Flax, Jute, Hemp	1.	20,128	18,723	−1,405
	2.	855	4,215	+3,360
Silk	1.	8,801	4,368	−4,433
	2.	17,887	23,046	+5,159
Glass	1.	2,055	702	−1,353
	2.	4,720	6,678	+1,958
Ceramics and Porcelain	1.	4,233	4,235	+2
	2.	1,124	3,448	+2,324

Source: 'Annual Statements of Foreign Commerce of the U.S.', quoted by Saul, *op. cit.*

TABLE 3

EXPORTS OF MANUFACTURES AT CONSTANT PRICES
(millions of 1913 dollars)

Destination			Origin			
			Great Britain	Germany	USA	Total World
Belgium and	(a)	1899	48	33	11	157
Luxemburg	(b)	1913	37	76	11	251
France	(a)		59	31	27	166
	(b)		79	117	46	322
Germany	(a)		121		35	292
	(b)		121		84	404
Italy	(a)		17	21	6	63
	(b)		27	75	15	164
Holland	(a)		45	55	24	149
	(b)		53	96	47	236
Norway	(a)		13	15	2	31
	(b)		16	25	2	54
Sweden	(a)		16	4	2	22
	(b)		15	38	5	62
Switzerland	(a)		—	52	0	97
	(b)		17	85	1	160

Source: A. Maizels, *Industrial Growth and World Trade, op. cit.*

TABLE 4

EXPORTS OF MANUFACTURES TO EUROPE *(millions of 1913 dollars)*

From	Transport Material	Chemical Products	Metals	Machinery	Textiles & Clothing	Other Manu-factures
Germany						
a) 1899	2	18	25	22	73	71
b) 1913	16	62	84	77	86	187
Great Britain						
a)	10	20	50	32	164	41
b)	23	27	42	39	174	62

Source: A. Maizels, *op. cit.*

TABLE 5

VISIBLE TRADE OF THE UK (millions of pounds)

	North & North East Europe			Western Europe			Central & South East Europe			Southern Europe & North Africa			United States		
	1	2	3	1	2	3	1	2	3	1	2	3	1	2	3
1890	43·4	13·3	5·5	88·1	34·3	20·4	32·4	21·9	11·7	22·8	19·0	2·3	97·3	32·1	14·3
1913	86·0	38·5	11·7	104·4	61·8	25·3	90·2	47·6	21·2	30·6	33·8	2·9	141·7	29·3	30·2

1 = Imports   2 = Exports   3 = Re-exports

	UK Deficit with Europe	UK Deficit with United States
1890	68·3	50·9
1913	68·4	82·1

Source: Deane & Mitchell, *Abstract of British Historical Statistics*, Cambridge 1957.

TABLE 6

EXPORT OF MANUFACTURES (in millions of dollars at 1913 prices)

Destination			Origin		
			Great Britain	Germany	USA
Argentina	(a)	1899	33	15	9
	(b)	1913	88	59	30
Brazil	(a)		28	12	5
	(b)		47	45	18
Chile	(a)		12	7	2
	(b)		23	21	10
Columbia	(a)		4	1	2
	(b)		6	3	5
Mexico	(a)		8	5	25
	(b)		11	10	31
Japan	(a)		42	7	9
	(b)		65	28	12

Source: Maizels, *op. cit.*

MARKET SHARES IN EXPORTS OF MANUFACTURES TO LATIN AMERICA (millions of dollars at 1913 prices)

Country of Origin	Machinery, Transport, Chemicals	Textiles & Clothing	Other Manufac- tures	Total Manufactures (Percentage shares)
Great Britain	7·9	13·2	10·2	31·3
Germany	6·6	4·9	13·6	25·1
USA	7.2	1·1	7·0	15·3
Total from world	28·5	31·0	40·5	100·0

Source: Maizels, *op. cit.*

TABLE 7

EXPORTS OF MANUFACTURES TO THE BRITISH EMPIRE
(millions of dollars at 1913 prices)

Destination	Origin			
	Great Britain	Germany	United States	Total
Canada				
(a) 1899	25	4	53	85
(b) 1913	84	12	185	297
Australia				
(a)	122	9	22	165
(b)	152	20	30	232
New Zealand				
(a)	—	—	—	—
(b)	45	2	—	56
South Africa				
(a)	60	2	5	69
(b)	92	9	9	120
India				
(a)	192	16	3	227
(b)	316	33	7	394

Source: Maizels, *op. cit.*

TABLE 8

AVERAGE PRICE OF SILVER IN LONDON

Year	Pence per Ounce	Year	Pence per Ounce
1850	61	1881	51
1851	61	1882	51
1852	60	1883	50
1853	61	1884	50
1854	61	1885	48
1855	61	1886	45
1856	61	1887	44
1857	61	1888	42
1858	61	1889	41
1859	62	1890	47
1860	61	1891	45
1861	60	1892	39
1862	61	1893	35
1863	61	1894	28
1864	61	1895	29
1865	61	1896	30
1866	61	1897	21
1867	60	1898	26
1868	60	1899	27
1869	60	1900	28
1870	60	1901	27
1871	60	1902	24
1872	60	1903	24
1873	69	1904	26
1874	58	1905	27
1875	56	1906	30
1876	52	1907	30
1877	54	1908	24
1878	52	1909	23
1879	51	1910	24
1880	52		

Source: *Annual Reports of the Director of the Mint*, Govt. Printing Office, Washington.

TABLE 9

LEVELS, COMPOSITION AND LOCATION OF THE INDIAN GOLD STANDARD RESERVE (in Sterling)

	In England				In India			Total in England & India
	Securities at Market Values	Cash Lent at Short Notice	Gold held at the Bank of England	Total	Loans & Credits	Gold	Silver	
Dec. 1901	1,008,424			1,008,424		2,439,093		3,447,517
Dec. 1902	3,467,372			3,467,372	2,005	260,771		3,730,148
Dec. 1903	3,900,794			3,900,794	295,698	323,417		4,519,909
Dec. 1904	6,951,743	499,605		7,451,347	76,740	200,416		7,728,503
Dec. 1905	9,898,999			9,898,999	97,434	240,000		10,236,433
Dec. 1906	11,910,061			11,910,061	3,520,723		69,540	15,509,324
Dec. 1907	13,208,489	13,810		13,222,299	60,044	263,349	4,000,000	17,545,692
Dec. 1908	5,104,078			5,104,078	1,000,310		11,991,749	18,096,137
Dec. 1909	10,450,141	1,017,192		11,467,333	2,000,344		4,786,734	18,254,411
Dec. 1910	14,513,878	1,437,425		15,951,303			2,534,302	18,485,605
Dec. 1911	15,958,904	973,434		16,932,338			1,934,362	18,886,640
Dec. 1912	15,965,149	1,013,690	250,000	17,228,839			3,745,667	20,974,506

Source: *Royal Commission on Indian Finance and Currency*, Cmd. 7070, Appendix III, p. 97, HMSO, London 1913.

TABLE 10

BALANCE OF PAYMENTS OF INDIA (in Sterling, Excl. Government Transactions)

	1893–1894	1894–1895	1895–1896	1896–1897	1897–1898	1898–1899	1899–1900	1900–1901	1901–1902	1902–1903
Gross Merchandise										
Exports	70,965,100	72,543,300	76,174,900	69,276,300	65,024,800	75,147,600	72,650,800	71,579,300	82,976,600	85,877,900
Imports	49,304,600	46,778,300	46,211,100	47,943,100	46,177,800	45,586,900	47,141,200	50,851,900	54,346,000	52,525,300
Net Export Surplus	21,660,500	25,765,000	29,963,800	21,333,100	18,847,000	29,560,700	25,509,600	20,727,400	28,680,600	33,352,600
Export Surplus as % of Import	44	55	65	44	41	65	54	41	53	64
FINANCING OF SURPLUS:										
I British Govt. Securities	1,178,200	359,700	−1,149,800	856,100	1,705,300	45,000	414,900	−908,300	1,212,700	1,152,500
Silver, Bars and Coin	9,172,800	4,250,000	4,400,500	3,905,600	5,622,400	2,648,200	2,379,200	949,100	4,169,800	4,151,000
Gold Bars	—	—	—	—	—	1,321,900	978,700	146,500	—	898,900
Total I	10,351,000	4,609,700	3,250,700	4,761,700	7,327,700	4,015,100	3,772,800	187,300	5,382,500	6,702,400
II Imports of Council Bills	9,960,200	15,770,500	18,742,200	15,170,500	9,472,700	18,833,900	18,703,800	18,824,500	18,535,800	18,724,000
Imports of Sovereigns	427,500	−3,316,100	1,684,000	1,527,400	3,272,300	3,013,700	5,315,000	4,897,200	3,363,300	5,413,900
Total II	10,387,700	12,454,400	20,426,200	16,697,900	12,745,000	21,897,600	24,018,800	23,721,700	21,899,100	24,137,900

	1903–1904	1904–1905	1905–1906	1906–1907	1907–1908	1908–1909	1909–1910	1910–1911	1911–1912	1912–1913
Gross Merchandise										
Exports	101,973,000	105,000,400	107,806,700	117,713,300	118,240,000	102,020,000	125,253,000	139,921,300	151,896,100	164,364,800
Imports	56,548,900	64,452,200	68,720,000	72,206,700	86,600,000	90,846,700	78,040,000	86,236,000	92,383,200	107,343,900
Net Export Surplus	45,424,100	40,548,200	39,086,700	45,506,600	31,640,000	21,173,300	47,213,000	53,685,300	59,212,900	57,020,900
Export Surplus as % of Import	80	63	57	63	37	26	60	62	64	53
FINANCING OF SURPLUS:										
I British Govt. Securities	996,200	215,500	253,300	−33,300	840,000	533,300	−520,000	1,620,000	706,700	non-disposable
Silver, Bars and Coin	4,476,900	4,625,000	3,346,700	4,460,000	6,686,700	7,973,300	6,246,700	5,738,800	3,528,800	4,382,500
Gold Bars	2,428,200	3,498,300	3,413,300	4,906,700	5,133,300	2,273,300	5,240,000	7,610,900	6,712,700	7,280,800
Total I	8,401,300	8,338,800	7,613,300	9,333,400	12,660,000	10,779,900	10,966,700	14,969,700	10,948,200	—
II Imports of Council Bills	23,874,500	24,150,000	31,800,000	33,646,700	15,640,100	5,346,700	27,820,000	26,286,700	26,780,000	25,874,700
Imports of Sovereigns	8,457,500	8,577,300	2,886,900	4,953,300	6,643,300	866,700	9,213,300	8,374,900	18,465,500	17,771,600
Total II	32,332,000	32,727,300	34,686,900	38,600,000	22,073,300	6,213,400	37,033,300	34,661,600	42,245,500	43,646,300

Source: *Royal Commission on Indian Finance and Currency, Interim Report*, Cmd. 7070, HMSO, London 1913.

TABLE 11

Transactions of the Government of India in the London Money Market and Broker's Commission Expenses

	Treasury Balance Short-term Loans			Deposits with Banks			Gold Standard Reserve Short-term Loans			Deposits with Banks			Total		
	Gross Amount	Commission	Net Amount	Gross Amount	Commission	Net Amount	Gross Amount	Commission	Net Amount	Gross Amount	Commission	Net Amount	Gross Amount	Net Amount	Broker's Commission
1893–1894	10,293	515	9,778										10,293		515
1894–1895	3,373	169	3,204										3,373		169
1895–1896	9,650	482	9,168										9,650		482
1896–1897	34,435	1,722	32,713										34,435		1,722
1897–1898	20,772	1,039	19,733										20,772		1,039
1898–1899	30,562	1,528	29,034										30,562		1,528
1899–1900	51,384	2,569	48,815										51,384		2,569
1900–1901	59,114	2,955	56,159										59,114		2,955
1901–1902	79,651	3,983	75,668										79,651		3,983
1902–1903	145,306	7,266	138,040										145,306		7,266
1903–1904	140,038	7,002	133,036										140,038		7,002
1904–1905	168,398	8,420	159,978										168,398		8,420
1905–1906	218,185	10,909	207,276										218,185		10,909
1906–1907	209,656	10,361	199,295										209,656		10,361
1907–1908	137,698	6,596	131,102										137,698		6,596
1908–1909	49,669	2,432	47,237				1,270	64					50,939		2,496
1909–1910	128,163	6,336	121,837	8,236	83		8,550	428		11,640	116		156,679		6,963
1910–1911	254,685	12,819	241,866	122,236	1,222		6,380	234		44,844	448		428,145		14,723
1911–1912	249,755	6,914	242,841	134,558	1,346		500	15		34,025	340		418,838		8,615
1912–1913	280,335	5,908	274,427	98,730	987		18,745	311		21,826	218		419,636		7,424
Total	2,281,122	99,925	2,181,197	363,850	3,638		35,445	1,052		112,335	1,122		2,792,752		105,737

Source: *Royal Commission on Indian Finance and Currency, Interim Report*, App. XI, p. 318, Cmd. 7070, HMSO, London 1913.

TABLE 12

NET CREDIT BALANCE OF THE
GOVERNMENT OF INDIA ON MARCH 31
(excluding the Gold Standard Reserve and taking into
account the balance in India at the £ stg=15 Rupees
exchange rate)

	In India	In England
1893	10,181,171	2,268,385
1894	17,043,725	1,300,564
1895	15,019,659	2,503,114
1896	11,000,340	3,393,798
1897	9,249,168	2,832,354
1898	10,654,962	2,534,244
1899	11,177,669	3,145,768
1900	8,425,827	3,330,943
1901	8,767,687	4,091,926
1902	11,880,301	6,693,137
1903	12,081,388	5,767,787
1904	11,702,394	7,294,782
1905	10,597,770	10,262,581
1906	11,494,578	8,436,519
1907	10,026,932	5,606,812
1908	12,851,413	4,607,266
1909	10,235,483	7,983,898
1910	12,295,428	12,799,094
1911	13,566,922	16,696,990
1912	12,279,689	18,390,013
1913	19,543,900	8,372,900

Source: *Royal Commission on Indian Finance and Currency, Interim Report,* App. II, p. 74, Cmd. 7070, HMSO, London 1913.

TABLE 13

GOLD RESERVES HELD BY MONETARY AUTHORITIES IN SELECTED COUNTRIES (in Sterling, positions taken on Dec. 31 of the years mentioned)

	1889	1899	1910
Bank of England	17,784,000	29,002,000	31,095,000
Scottish Banks of Issue	4,591,000	6,227,000	4,918,000
Irish Banks of Issue	3,480,000	2,816,000	3,649,000
Germany { Reichsbank	12,234,000	22,939,000	32,760,000
{ War Fund	5,869,000	5,869,000	5,869,000
Austria–Hungary	5,426,000	43,982,000	54,971,000
National Bank of Serbia	345,000	286,000	992,000
Bank of France	50,471,000	74,310,000	130,050,000
Bank of Spain	6,009,000	13,485,000	16,301,000
Bank of Portugal	1,028,000	1,075,000	1,348,000
Bank of the Netherlands	5,069,000	3,730,000	10,391,000
National Bank of Belgium	2,606,000	4,329,000	5,037,000
Italy { Bank of Italy			38,670,000
{ Bank of Sicily	18,132,000	15,702,000	2,261,000
{ Bank of Naples			2,261,000
Bank of Russia	42,565,000	90,275,000	8,091,000
Bank of Finland	861,000	888,000	130,288,000
National Bank of Roumania	2,011,000	1,444,000	873,000
National Bank of Bulgaria	426,000	127,000	4,759,000
Royal Bank of Sweden	1,379,000	2,195,000	4,482,000
Imperial Ottoman Bank	740,000	1,384,000	6,171,000
National Bank of Denmark	2,754,000	3,249,000	4,085,000
National Bank of Norway	1,755,000	1,755,000	1,904,000
Swiss Banks	2,364,000	3,890,000	6,187,000
Bank of Greece	21,000	79,000	40,000
United { National Banks	17,348,000	41,860,000	46,849,000
States { State Banks	5,306,000	16,400,000	16,323,000
{ Treasury	64,459,000	82,279,000	226,131,000
Bank of Australasia	18,465,000	21,862,000	37,919,000
Canadian Banks and Treasury	1,505,000	4,651,000	22,235,000
South African Banks	1,028,000	6,740,000	10,357,000
Total	296,031,000	530,850,000	866,856,000

Source: *Royal Commission on Indian Finance and Currency, Interim Report*, Appendix XXX, Cmd. 7070, HMSO, London 1913.

TABLE 14

WORLD GOLD STOCK

Years	Millions of Pounds	Millions of Dollars
1880	1,210	5,892
1881	1,230	5,990
1882	1,249	6,080
1883	1,267	6,166
1884	1,286	6,258
1885	1,304	6,348
1886	1,323	6,442
1887	1,342	6,535
1888	1,362	6,631
1889	1,383	6,734
1890	1,408	6,854
1891	1,432	6,971
1892	1,459	7,104
1893	1,489	7,247
1894	1,523	7,414
1895	1,560	7,595
1896	1,599	7,782
1897	1,644	8,003
1898	1,700	8,273
1899	1,759	8,564
1900	1,809	8,803
1901	1,858	9,044
1902	1,915	9,323
1903	1,979	9,632
1904	2,046	9,960
1905	2,122	10,330
1906	2,202	10,712
1907	2,281	11,103
1908	2,368	11,524
1909	2,456	11,956
1910	2,545	12,387

Source: 'Statistiches Jarbuch für Deutsches Reich', reproduced by G. Cassel in the *First Interim Report of the Gold Delegation to the League of Nations*, Geneva 1930.

TABLE 15

WORLD STOCK OF GOLD MONEY

Year	Millions of Sterling	Year	Millions of Sterling
1850	230	1883	657
1851	243	1884	662
1852	268	1885	670
1853	294	1886	681
1854	316	1887	689
1855	338	1888	701
1856	361	1889	711
1857	382	1890	720
1858	401	1891	733
1859	417	1892	753
1860	433	1893	774
1861	447	1894	802
1862	459	1895	827
1863	468	1896	852
1864	476	1897	882
1865	490	1898	921
1866	506	1899	958
1867	519	1900	989
1868	531	1901	1,022
1869	543	1902	1,056
1870	556	1903	1,093
1871	568	1904	1,132
1872	577	1905	1,188
1873	568	1906	1,231
1874	594	1907	1,278
1875	601	1908	1,346
1876	610	1909	1,400
1877	621	1910	1,446
1878	634	1911	1,489
1879	639	1912	1,528
1880	643	1913	1,579
1881	649	1914	1,647
1882	653		

Source: J. Kitchin: 'The Supply of Gold Compared with the Prices of Commodities', in *First Interim Report of the Gold Delegation, op. cit.*

TABLE 16

WORLD STOCK OF MONETARY GOLD (millions of dollars)

Year	1 World	2 United States	% 2/1	Year	1 World	2 United States	% 2/1
1860	2,108	214	10	1888	3,411	706	21
1861	2,170	270	12	1889	3,452	680	20
1862	2,232	283	13	1890	3,493	696	20
1863	2,274	260	11	1891	3,516	647	18
1864	2,315	203	9	1892	3,659	664	18
1865	2,377	189	8	1893	3,762	598	16
1866	2,460	167	7	1894	3,907	627	16
1867	2,522	186	7	1895	4,031	636	16
1868	2,584	160	6	1896	4,155	600	14
1869	2,646	173	7	1897	4,299	696	16
1870	2,708	190	7	1898	4,485	862	19
1871	2,770	164	6	1899	4,671	963	21
1872	2,811	148	5	1900	4,816	1,034	21
1873	2,852	135	5	1901	4,981	1,125	23
1874	2,894	147	5	1902	5,147	1,193	23
1875	2,914	121	4	1903	5,312	1,249	24
1876	2,976	130	4	1904	5,498	1,328	24
1877	3,018	168	6	1905	5,788	1,358	23
1878	3,080	213	7	1906	5,994	1,476	25
1879	3,101	246	8	1907	6,222	1,466	24
1880	3,121	352	11	1908	6,552	1,618	25
1881	3,163	478	15	1909	6,821	1,642	24
1882	3,183	507	16	1910	7,028	1,636	23
1883	3,204	543	17	1911	7,255	1,753	24
1884	3,225	546	17	1912	7,441	1,818	24
1885	3,266	589	18	1913	7,689	1,871	24
1886	3,307	591	18	1914	8,020	1,891	24
1887	3,349	655	20				

Source: G. F. Warren and F. A. Pearson, *Gold and Prices*, New York 1935.

INDEX